NANDINI SENGUPTA

Play and Performance

PLAY & CULTURE STUDIES, VOLUME 11

Edited by
Carrie Lobman and
Barbara E. O'Neill

UNIVERSITY PRESS OF AMERICA,® INC.
Lanham · Boulder · New York · Toronto · Plymouth, UK

4501 Forbes Boulevard
Suite 200
Lanham, Maryland 20706
UPA Acquisitions Department (301) 459-3366

Estover Road
Plymouth PL6 7PY
United Kingdom

Printed in the United States of America
British Library Cataloging in Publication Information Available

Library of Congress Control Number: 2011925332
ISBN: 978-0-7618-5531-6 (paperback : alk. paper)
eISBN: 978-0-7618-5532-3

™ The paper used in this publication meets the minimum requirements of American National Standard for Information Sciences—Permanence of Paper for Printed Library Materials, ANSI Z39.48-1992

Contents

Foreword

Again it is my privilege to write a brief foreword as series editor for *Play & Culture Studies,* a publication of *The Association for the Study of Play (TASP)*. The theme of this new volume, the 11th in the series, is exploring the relationships among play, performance, development and learning. *Play and Performance* is co-edited by Carrie Lobman of Rutgers University and Barbara O'Neill of Brooklyn College, CUNY; their work and dedication to this project rewards all of us with a splendid addition to the series. Organized in three major sections, the book covers across its 10 chapters a rich array of topics relating to developing performances of play and creativity (a) in teaching and teacher education, (b) for enhancing human development in individuals with and without special needs, and (c) with respect to new theorizing and understanding about play in individuals and groups.

TASP began in 1973 and is proud of its record of meeting every single year since its first meeting in Detroit in 1974. Originally called *The Anthropological Association for the Study of Play (TAASP)*, the organization is multidisciplinary and includes anthropology, psychology, sociology, education, recreation, history, folklore, dance, cultural studies, kinesiology, and musicology, among others. TASP is committed to research and scholarship concerned with play using physical, biological, and semiotic sciences, philosophy and the humanities. In addition to being multi-/trans-disciplinary, TASP promotes lifespan and across-and within-culture investigations of play and play-related phenomena—antecedents, processes, consequences, structures, transitions, and contexts. Further, TASP is concerned that play policies and practices are informed by research and theory, and are in the best interests of persons and social institutions. TASP's mission also is to support and cooperate with other organizations having similar purposes.

In the epilogue of *Play and Learning* (1979) edited by Brian Sutton-Smith, Brian provided his usual cogent and brilliant commentary covering all the chapters that were based on presentations and discussions at the third Johnson & Johnson Baby Products Company Round Table Conference (among the distinguished participants were Jerome and Dorothy Singer, Mihaly Csikzentmihayli, Michael Ellis, Catherine Garvey, Greta Fein, Corinne Hutt). The title he gave to the epilogue he wrote was "Epilogue: Play as Performance." In contrast to language use in situations, which are *monologues* or *dialogues*, play forms and all expressive behaviors or communications are *quadralogues*. *Quadralogues* entail four parties: (1) players/actors or co-players/co-actors; (2) the group or individual that stages the event; (3) the person or persons that direct the performance; and (4) the audience (real or imagined).

One important point that was made in this epilogue and book was that the capacity for finding flow possibilities throughout one's life likely hinges in important ways on learning to engage in play and other expressive performances early in life. Another important point was that play expression/communication is both framed and performed. Framing often occurs with the help of play experts in the service of play novices. The framing and performance process of different play forms yield reality transforming and reality enhancing experiences. These notions also whisper to us as we read the pages of *Play and performance*. Relish the drama in the intellectual play stimulated by the chapters. I hope you have multiple flow moments reading this work. The volume is well framed and performed and is certainly a credit to the series.

Sutton-Smith, B. (1979). *Play and Learning*. New York: Garner Press.

Jim Johnson, Series Editor, The Pennsylvania State University-University Park, PA

Introduction

Play, Performance, Learning, and Development: Exploring the Relationship

Carrie Lobman and Barbara E. O'Neill

> Lack of play…could be the next global warming—without ample opportunity for forms of play that foster innovation and creative thinking, America's children will be at a disadvantage in the global economy (Hirsh-Pasek as cited in Cray, 2008)

> Free, imaginative play is crucial for normal social, emotional and cognitive development. It makes us better adjusted, smarter and less stressed (Wenner, 2009)

> We all are beginning to see the negative impacts from the lack of play among our citizens, including...attention-deficit disorder and limited creativity, to name a few. (Hopkins, 2009)

Pick up a newspaper, peruse the academic journals, listen to medical professionals on television, or talk to teachers and parents, and you are likely to hear a report on how play is being pushed out of people's lives (Elkind, 2007; Henig, 2008; Singer & Singer, 2005). A recent study of 16 countries, including the United States, India, Vietnam and Pakistan, found that children had fewer opportunities for free play than previous generations (Singer, Singer, D'Agostino & Delong, 2009). This is not just a concern for children, as research also shows that adults are working more, playing less, and are plagued by the increased stress that comes with a bad economy, and ongoing environmental and international crisis (Goldman-Mello, Saxton, & Catalano, 2010; Luo, 2010; Marlar, 2010). The evidence is that play is declining, and that this is having a negative impact on children's development, adult productivity, and on the lives of human beings around the world.

While we are in agreement that the loss of play is of serious concern. We also believe there is cause for hope. In the past two years key play researchers were invited to present at the Technology, Education, and Design (TED) conference, one of the leading venues for influential innovators. Newspapers and magazines featured multiple articles on the importance of play, including a cover story in the Sunday New York Times Magazine (Henig, 2008), and a lead story on the popular National Public Radio program, Morning Edition (Spiegel, 2008). A program designed to bring recess back into school made national news (Hu, 2009), and even in the midst of massive budget cuts, three new state of the art playgrounds based on the latest in play research opened in New York City (Kligannon, 2010). Clearly, alongside the many articles that discuss the demise of play, there is also an increasing focus in both the academic and the popular press, on the importance of play for people of all ages. Even more importantly, many of these examples focus on people who defy the trend toward diminishing opportunities for play and find creative ways of bringing play into the lives of children and adults.

The chapters in this volume represent an important sub-section of this hopeful trend. There are an increasing number of practitioners and academics that recognize and make use of a particular type of play activity—performance. This group includes people from a diverse array of fields including education, mental health, youth and community development, and communication. Evidence for the use of performance across fields comes from the biannual *Performing the World Conference*. This conference brings together people from over 25 countries, all of who are tapping into the human ability to perform in order to support development, learning, and progressive change for adults and children (http://www.performingtheworld.org). A glance at the list of presenters from fall 2010 gives a sense of the playful nature of performance programs.

"Acting Crazy: Performing anxiety and depression"

"Rapping on the Zone of Proximal Development (ZPD): How hip-hop has helped youth grow in Juarez"

"Theater of War; Drama for Veterans"

"Spicy Theatrical Stew: Community Development, Education & A Dash of Playful Chaos"

Therefore, while play presently seems somewhat endangered, performance, one of the oldest forms of play (Huizinga, 1950; Nachmanovich, 1990), appears to be on the rise as an activity that increasing numbers of people are experiencing, not just as audience members, but as active participants. The performance activities described in this volume, as well as many of those presented at Performing the World, are not just meant to entertain, but are designed to support people to learn, develop, and create in new ways.

The purpose of this volume is to present researchers and practitioners whose daily work offer us further hope with regard to the current use of play and performance. The chapters report on people who are working with or studying programs that serve people from early childhood through adulthood, in a variety of educational and therapeutic settings, and from a range of theoretical and practical perspectives. Overall, the volume provides vivid examples of successful practices and discusses the significance of performance as a developmental play activity.

PLAY AND PERFORMANCE

Psychologists and educators have long promoted pretend or dramatic play as a key developmental activity for preschool age children (Berk, 2009; Piaget, 1962; Vygotsky, 1978; Winnicott, 1982). Pretend play with its overt focus on fantasy, "what if," social interaction, and imitation provides children with an environment where they can, as Vygotsky said, perform "a head taller" than they are (Vygotsky, 1978, p. 102). In play children are the active creators of their activity and this allows them to try out new roles, relationships, and skills in a low risk environment. Children are able to do many things in play prior to being able to do them in the rest of their lives. When children play at cooking for example, they do not have to demonstrate to anyone their knowledge of food preparation as a prerequisite to the play. In the process of creating the play they create their performance of being a cook. As Vygotsky (1978) points out, that lack of necessary pre-requisite knowledge makes play an optimal zone of proximal development where children can take risks and learn new things, because they can try out activities that they do not need to already know how to do.

Most contemporary theories of development, including those that rely on the work of Vygotsky (1978), recognize that pretend play begins to diminish as children leave early childhood and enter primary school (Berk, 2009; Crain, 2005). The skills children learn through play—by doing what they do not yet know how to do—are then put to use for academic learning, work, and games with rules in older childhood and adulthood. According to some theorists, the creativity that is outwardly expressed in pretend play turns inward in the form of imagination (Gajdamaschko, 2005; Marjanovic-Shane & Beljanski-Risti, 2008). Pretend play, from these perspectives, is part of a developmental stage; it serves a purpose and then fades away.

Recently, however, some scholars have turned their attention to the importance of pretend play throughout the lifespan (Caposella, 2000; Göncü, and Perone, 2005; Rognilli, 2008; Terr, 2008). In particular, activities that allow people to *socially* exercise their imagination have been highlighted as key for mental and emotional health, and supportive of creativity and productivity throughout the lifespan. One way that the pretend play of early childhood manifests itself later in life is in the realm of performance, including theatre, dance, improvisation, and music. Performance shares some important characteristics with children's pretend play. Both include social imagination and creativity and, because they are not closely tied to "reality," both play and performance provide opportunities for people to experiment with and create new ways of being, seeing and relating.

Newman and Holzman (1993; Newman, 1996; Holzman, 2009) argue that our human ability to perform is inextricably linked to the possibilities for lifelong development. They have expanded, in both practice and theory, on Vygotsky's (1978) insight that very young children perform a "head taller" in play. Babies and toddlers learn through the process of playing in ways that are beyond their present abilities, but that they will grow into (i.e. speakers of language, readers of books, sketchers of pictures). In other words, in their everyday lives, young children *perform* who they are becoming. Children perform as conversationalists by taking turns babbling and become speakers; they perform as readers by pretending to read, as they become readers.

According to Newman and Holzman (1993; Newman, 1996; Holzman, 2009) older children and adolescents can do the same, when given the opportunity. They can perform both on stage and off, and learn and develop in the process. Newman and Holzman argue that the ability to *perform* is a critical characteristic of being human. Human beings are, as far as we know, the only species capable of being both who we are, and also performing who we are not. It is possible to perform MacBeth while still remaining Lawrence Olivier. People can do this off the stage as well. For example, when someone first becomes a parent they are performing both as who they are, someone who does not know how to parent, and who they are not, or who they are becoming, a parent.

While all human beings have the ability to perform both on and off the stage, it is not always easy to exercise this ability. When early childhood and its socially sanctioned play activities end, often at around age six, children are sent the message that it is time to stop playing around (performing who you are not) and stick to discovering/being who you are. We tend to relate to older children and adults as being a particular kind of person or as only being able to do certain kinds of things. It is easy to get stuck in scripted roles and relate to ourselves, and each other, with very limited expectations. In school and in the workforce people are rewarded for who they are and what they know how to do, not for who they are becoming. For many people this means that they stop doing what they do not know how to do. In other words, they stop performing, and as a consequence learning and development suffer. Performance, which can re-engage people in the process of becoming, is too valuable of an activity to be left only to young children and professional actors. Everyone can make use of the human ability to be both who they are and who they are not. This enables people of all ages to do new things and go beyond themselves.

RESEARCH ON PERFORMATORY LEARNING ENVIRONMENTS

There is a growing body of evidence documenting the developmental and educational value to people participating in theatre and performing arts activities (e.g., Arts Education Partnership, 1999; Heath, 2000; Heath, Soep and Roach, 1998; Carnegie Council on Adolescent Development, 1992; Jones, 2007; Mahoney, Larson and Eccles, 2005; O'Neill, 2008). One way to characterize the value of performance-based programs documented in these studies is that people learn and develop in environments in which they can choose to perform creatively (Heath, 2000; Holzman, 1997, 2000; Sabo, 2003). For example, in a study of community based youth programs, Heath (2000) determined that the highest quality programs were those that gave young people opportunities to perform in new and different types of roles. Heath stressed that these performances took place not just on stage, but in multiple locations within the program, and that through all of these experiences young people came to see themselves as "capable of acting outside and beyond the expected" (p. 39).

Other researchers have found that programs that do not take place on the stage, but that use theatre language and activities to help people see themselves as performers in everyday life, are also valuable. For example, Sabo-Flores (Sabo, 2003; Sabo-Flores, 2007), an evaluation expert, reports on the use of performance language in a program that was not theater based, citing the ways that youth move beyond their socially determined roles and "… become leaders within the program, performing as directors, board members, funders, researchers, evaluators, planners, etc…" (Sabo, 2003, p. 17). Sabo (2003) recommends that:

> …evaluation environments should be created in which young people and adults relate to one another as performers. Together they can articulate scripts and improvise various evaluation roles. This self-conscious use of performance supports a kind of playfulness—a trying on and trying out (p. 17).

Similarly, in the field of education, research on the use of improvisational theatre training for teacher development has documented how the use of performance activities and language positively impacts practice. Two recent studies have found that when teachers came to see themselves and their students as performers, and their class as an ensemble, their teaching became less role-governed and more creative—allowing opportunities for growth and development even in traditional classrooms (Lobman, 2010, in press; Sawyer, in press).

Given the benefits of performance programs, the current loss of play, and the relationship between play and performance, we believe that shedding light on performance activities is valuable for play researchers, practitioners, and advocates. The chapters in this volume cover an array of practices that can be seen across the play to performance continuum. Some authors come from a theater background; yet clearly articulate their use of theater activities in terms of helping students to play. Others situate themselves as play researchers, yet the descriptions of their practices leave no question as to the theatricality of the work. Taken together, the myriad ways that play is performance and performance is play becomes clear, sometimes blurring the need for distinction, but always offering new ways of seeing and understanding.

ORGANIZATION OF THE BOOK

While we recognize that there are multiple ways of organizing the chapters in this volume, we have chosen to divide them based on what we see as their primary contribution to the emerging field of play and performance. We begin with five chapters that have strong implications for the field of education, at both the classroom and the teacher education level. The next three chapters, while located in different arenas, focus more broadly on the developmental value of performance. The volume concludes with two chapters that expand the current conceptualizations of play and performance and have specific implications for how to understand and study these activities.

Section 1. *Play and Performance in Teaching and Teacher Education,* offers case study reports on examples of performance being used as an educational tool in a range of settings. In the first of these chapters, *Playworlds—An Art of Development*, the authors report on five different international programs, all of which draw on the work of Lindqvist (1995) to create imaginary worlds where children and adults play and make art together. Their examples substantiate the authors' assertion that such play, co-created by children and adults, can produce rich learning environments. They urge readers to reconsider the role of the teacher in children's play as they call into question whose development is of interest, urging Playworlds as a model where children and adults can both develop.

In *Complicating the Role of Play in Building Classroom Community,* Wisneski also calls into question the role of the teacher in children's play. She challenges the assumption that children's play, free of adult intervention, automatically produces an inclusive classroom community. Her case study of a third grade classroom details how children's play often upholds exclusionary practices that replicate injustices in our larger society based on gender, ability and race differences. She makes the compelling argument that if we want to create inclusive classroom communities, then play must be considered only as a starting point, and teachers and children should be taught to reflect on the processes of play in the classroom and its impact on creating inclusive community. While this chapter does not explicitly reference performance, many of the most successful and inclusive play examples include a dramatic or performatory quality.

This first section also includes several chapters that detail the promise of performance activities as a tool for supporting teacher development. In *Play Intervention and Play Development,* Bredikyte and Hakkarainen report on a teacher education program in Finland, where students are taught creative drama and improvisation techniques to use when intervening in children's play. The authors begin by arguing that at a moment when children rarely have enough time to engage in the mature forms of play that are crucial to development, there is a need for dramatic and non-instrumental interventions on the part of teachers. Through examples of student-led play scenarios, the authors identify the differences between successful and unsuccessful play intervention and document the ways their students developed as practitioners through their participation in creative drama play intervention training.

Harman and French also report on their work as teacher educators in *Critical Performative Pedagogy in Urban Teacher Education: Voices From the Field.* In this chapter these teacher educators use real-life scenarios and Boalian[1] inspired theater techniques in their multicultural literature class. Through this process the teachers were supported to become aware of and respond differently to social injustices in their schools. Harman and French describe the benefits of these techniques and reflect on their own work as teacher educators.

Finally, in *Bringing out the Playful Side of Mathematics*, Schectman and Knudsen share the ways they have adapted improvisational theater games to train math teachers to lead middle school students in mathematical argumentation. They compellingly argue and document the ways that math is a form of play and add to the growing body of literature that demonstrates the power of improvisation as a tool educators can use to promote play and development, while still teaching content.

Section 2. *Promoting Human Development Using Performance* covers three examples of practice that rely on performance activities to create an environment where the participants can grow and develop—at times, in rather unexpected ways. In *Play As A Staging Ground for Performance and Life,* Bailey details how she teaches creative drama to college students, emphasizing the importance of building an environment where young adults can play together. Using student self-report she conveys the many ways that performing together in creative drama activities led to growth in students' personal and professional lives.

The next two chapters in this section share examples of performance based work with children with Asperger's Syndrome and other special needs. In his chapter, *Playing with Asperger's Syndrome: "We're not supposed to be able to do this, are we?"* Murray uses descriptions of his work as a theatermaker in a residential school for youth. He reflects on how his own, as well as his colleague's, assumptions were continually challenged by the developmental strides students made during his Devised Theater sessions.

Finally, in the chapter, *Social Therapy with Children with Special Needs and Their Families*, readers are introduced to the work of Christine LaCerva, a practitioner of social therapy, a postmodern Vygotskian play therapy that relates to all human activity as performance. This chapter takes the form of an interview where LaCerva describes several examples of her work with children and parents. She introduces readers to her pioneering work with multi-family groups where children, youth and their families break out of scripted ways of relating and develop through a process of collectively created play and playful conversation.

Section 3. *New Understandings of Play and Performance* introduces two chapters that reframe present understandings of play and performance. These authors offer new directions for both research and practice. In *Play as Deconstruction*, Henricks introduces uninitiated readers into the world of postmodern thought, going on to carefully examine the parallels between play and the postmodern activity of deconstructing. He urges play researchers to consider play within its wider social and cultural context, emphasizing the importance of studying the process by which groups of players assemble and dissemble meanings.

DeZutter, takes a socio-cultural perspective in *Performing Groups as Distributed Systems*, making the argument that the correct unit of study for understanding performance creativity is the group, rather than the individual. Her case study of a youth improv ensemble provides detailed examples of how groups are able to be creative.

Together the chapters in this book offer practical and theoretical inspiration for play researchers and practitioners. Taken as stories from practice, we can feel encouraged by the rich play experiences that people around the world—from early childhood to middle childhood to adulthood—are involved in. Understood in the context of connecting the activities of play and performance, the chapters offer hope to those lamenting the loss of play in the 21st Century, and can broaden our understanding of what is play. It is our aim that fellow play advocates, researchers and practitioners will draw on the wealth of ideas introduced in this volume and join us in expanding the use of performance as a tool for creating playful environments where children and adults can create and develop.

REFERENCES

Arts Education Partnership. (1999). *Champions of change: The impact of the arts on Learning.* Washington, DC: Author.

Berk, L. (2009). *Development throughout the lifespan* (5th ed.). New York: Allyn and Bacon.

Caposella, A. (2000). Are children really more creative than adults? An examination of Lev Vygotsky's theory. Claremont Reading Conference Yearbook, 48–57.

Carnegie Council on Adolescent Development (1992). A matter of time: Risk and opportunity in the nonschool hours. *Carnegie Council Monograph.* Retrieved from http://www.carnegie.org/ccadpubs.htm.

Crain, W. (2005) *Theories of development: Concepts and applications (5th Ed.).* New York: Prentice Hall.

Cray, D. (2008, November 18). Experts bemoan loss of kids' play time. *USA Today.* Retrieved from http://www.usatoday.com/news/education/2008–11–18–playtime_N.htm.

Elkind, D. (2007). *The power of play: Learning what comes naturally.* New York: De Capo Press.

Gajdamaschko, N. (2005). Vygotsky on imagination: Why an understanding of the imagination is an important issue for schoolteachers. *Teaching Education, 16*(1), 13–22.

Goldman-Mellor, S., Saxton, K. & Catallano, R. (2010). Economic contraction and mental health: A review of the evidence 1990–2009. *International Journal of Mental Health, 39*(2), 6–31.

Göncü, A., & Perone, A. (2005). Pretend play as a life-span activity. *Topoi, "Play, Games and Philosophy." [Special Issue] 24*(2), 137–147.

Heath, S. (2000). Making learning work. *Afterschool Matters, 1*(1), 33–45.

Heath, S. B., Soep, E. and Roach, A. (1998). Living the arts through language and learning: A report on community-based youth organizations. *Americans for the Arts Monographs 2*(7), 1–20.

Henig, R. (2008, February, 17). Taking play seriously. *The New York Times.* Retrieved from http://www.nytimes.com/2008/02/17/magazine/17play.html?_r=1&oref=slogin&pagewanted=all.

Holzman, L. (1997). *Schools for growth: Radical alternatives to current educational models.* Mahway, NJ: Erlbaum.

Holzman, L. (2000). Performative psychology: An untapped resource for educators. *Educational and Child Psychology, 17*(3), 86–103.

Holzman, L. (2009). *Vygotsky at work and play.* London: Routledge.

Hopkins, T. (2009). Summit aims to stress the importance of play in children's lives. *Clemson University Newsroom.* Retrieved from: http://www.clemson.edu/newsroom/articles/2009/june/Summit_on_Play.php5.

Hu, W. (2009, March 14). Forget goofing around, recess has a new boss. *The New York Times,* Retrieved from http://www.nytimes.com/2010/03/15/education/15recess.html.

Huizinga, J. (1950). *Homo ludens.* Boston: Beacon Press.

Jones, B. (2007). The unintended outcomes of high-stakes testing. *Journal of Applied School Psychology, 23*(2), 65 -86.

Kligannon, C. (2010, July 26) A new kind of playground arrives (check out the canals). *The New York Times.* Retrieved from http://www.nytimes.com/2008/02/17/magazine/17play.html.

Lindqvist, G. (1995). *The aesthetics of play: A didactic study of play and culture in preschool* (Vol. 62). Uppsala: Acta Universitatis Upsalensis.

Lobman, C. (2010). Creating developmental moments: Teaching and learning as creative activities. In C. Connery, John-Steiner, V. & Marjonovic-Shane, A. (Eds.), *Vygotsky and creativity: A cultural-historical approach to play, meaning making, and the arts* (pp.199–213). New York: Peter Lang.

Lobman, C. (in press). Improvising with(in) the system: Creating new teacher performances in inner city schools. In K. Sawyer (Ed.). *The teaching paradox: Creativity in the classroom.* Cambridge: Cambridge University Press.

Luo, M. (2010, August 2). Ninety-nine weeks later, jobless have only desperation. *The New York Times.* Retrieved from http://www.nytimes.com/2010/08/03/us/03unemployed.html.

Mahoney, J., Larson, R., & Eccles, J. (Eds.) (2005). Organized activities as contexts of development: Extracurricular activities, after school and community programs. Mahwah, NJ: Erlbaum.

Marjanovic-Shane, A. & Beljanski-Risti, L. From play to art—From experience to insight. *Mind, Culture, and Activity, 15*(2), 93–114.

Marlar, J. (2010, June 8). Worry, sadness, stress, increase with length of unemployment. *Gallup.* Retrieved from http://www.gallup.com/poll/139604/worry-sadness-stress-increase-length-unemployment.aspx.

Nachmanovich, S. (1991) *Free play: Improvisation in life and art.* New York: Penguin.

Newman, F. (1996). Performance of a lifetime: A practical critical guide to the joyous life. New York: Castillo International.

Newman, F. and Holzman, L. (1993). *Lev Vygotsky: Revolutionary scientist.* London: Routledge.

O'Neill, B. (2008). *Storytelling and creative drama: A dynamic approach to inclusive early childhood education.* Unpublished doctoral dissertation. Teachers College, Columbia University.

Piaget, J. (1962). *Play, dreams and imitation in childhood.* New York: W.W. Norton.

Technology, Entertainment, and Design. (Producer). (2006) *Ken Robinson says schools kill creativity.* Available from http://www.ted.com/talks/ken_robinson_says_schools_kill_creativity.html.

Rognli, E. (2008). We are the great pretenders: Larp is adult pretend play. In M. Montola & J. Stenros (Eds.), *Playground worlds: Creating and evaluating experiences of role-playing games.* Retrieved February 13, 2010, from http://www.solmukohta.org/pub/Playground_Worlds_2008.pdf#page=200.

Sabo, K. (2003). A Vygotskian perspective on youth participatory evaluation. Youth participatory evaluation: A field in the making. *Special Issue of New Directions for Evaluation, 98*, 13–24.

Sabo-Flores K. (2007). Youth participatory evaluation: Strategies for engaging young people (Research Methods for the Social Sciences). New York: Jossey-Bass.

Sawyer, K. (in press). *The teaching paradox: Creativity in the classroom.* Cambridge: Cambridge University Press.

Singer, D. & Singer, J. (2005). Imagination and Play in the Postmodern Age. Cambridge, MA: Harvard University Press.

Singer, D., Singer, J., D'Agostino, H., & DeLong, R. (2009). *American Journal of Play, 1*(3), 283–313.

Spiegel, (2008, February, 21). Old-fashioned play builds serious skills. *National Public Radio: Morning Edition.* Retrieved from http://www.npr.org/templates/story/story.php?storyId=19212514.

Terr, L. (1999). Beyond love and work: *Why adults need to play.* New York: Scribner.

Vygotsky, L. (1978). *Mind in Society.* Cambridge, MA: Harvard University Press.

Wenner, M. (2009). The serious need for play. *Scientific American Mind, 20*(1), 22–29.

Winnicott, D. (1982). *Playing and Reality.* London: Routledge.

Part I

PLAY AND PERFORMANCE IN TEACHING AND TEACHER EDUCATION

Chapter One

Playworlds—An Art of Development

Ana Marjanovic-Shane, Beth Ferholt, Kiyotaka Miyazaki, Monica Nilsson, Anna Pauliina Rainio, Pentti Hakkarainen, Mirjana Pešić, Ljubica Beljanski-Ristić

Every Friday four adult actors entered a K-1 classroom and performed another scene from Lewis's novel, The Lion, the Witch and the Wardrobe. Every Monday the students in this class found a few of the words from the book, words concerning the novel's imaginary world of Narnia, on the floor of their classroom—"trees," "cave," "beaver dam," "castle," "table," "sewing machine," "cage"—and created these set pieces or props out of cardboard and paint over the course of the week. As the weeks went by, the classroom became covered in the colorful, delicately-wrought trappings of the world of Narnia until, eventually, the teacher stopped moving the cardboard structures for his traditional classroom activities, and, instead, moved these activities into Narnia. He had found that the children appeared to be the most fluent readers when they were sitting in the wardrobe.

As the Friday sessions came and went, the back came off the wardrobe so that the actors and the class could move through this portal into the world of Narnia. The ice in Narnia was real ice chips, cold on bare feet. The eggs and tea that everyone ate and drank in the cave of the faun, Mr. Tumnus, was real food and drink, tasty and filling. And the children's often asked question, "Who is the White Witch?!" was answered when the children's teacher entered the play in a white fur coat and long white gloves.

The children soon followed the actors and their teacher into this other world. Once arrived, they designed and carried out a plot to save Mr. Tumnus from the evil White Witch, and to make the White Witch "good." The children then moved their playful relationship with their teacher out of Narnia and into their classroom meeting area, where they guided their teacher in the design and rehearsal of a wild play of their "playworld" for their families.

In this final play of the playworld, many of the characters were played by several children simultaneously, some dialogue was improvised and some was memorized, and set pieces and props were a mixture of originals from the "playworld" and replicas—the wooden wardrobe painstakingly reproduced in one half size with cardboard and duct tape, etc. The play for the families was very long and the audience, men and women in their fatigues and armed with video cameras, had no separate space nor seats. These families watched their children's performance while standing in Narnia themselves, sandwiched between the wooden and cardboard wardrobes, in the shadow of the White Witch's castle, and at the entrance to Mr. Tumnus's cave. (A description of a playworld in a public school on a U.S. military base.)

In this article we present a unique form of pedagogy that has developed over the last three decades in five different countries: Sweden, Serbia (former Yugoslavia), Japan, Finland and the United States. This educational practice consists of adults and children jointly creating, entering and exiting imaginary or figured worlds (Holland, Lachicotte Jr., Skinner, & Cain, 1998). Adults and children both participate in adult forms of creative imagining, which require extensive experience (disciplines of drama, arts and science), and also in children's forms of creative imagining, which require the embodiment of ideas in the material world (play). This educational practice was partially inspired by key concepts of the socio-cultural perspective, but is also the product of diverse educational traditions and theories of play and art, which originate in the five national cultures mentioned above. Through our collaborative studies of this educational practice we have settled on a common descriptive term for this practice: "Playworlds" (Lindqvist, 1995).

Although not identical across our cultures, playworlds include several common features: a) Playworlds utilize many potentials of children's imaginative play. However, they also foster development by providing an arena for artistic and academic learning; b) Playworlds make full use of adults' engagement in children's play. We believe that children's play can be enriched through adults' participation in the adult-child joint construction of this play. Furthermore, playworlds also provide an arena for adult learning and development; c) Playworlds facilitate not only the cognitive but also the emotional development of children and adults. "Perezhivanie"[1], or emotional-cognitive engagement, of both children and adults allows playworlds to exist; d) Finally, various forms of art (from fine art to drama), and creativity in the sciences, are central to Playworlds. In fact, in playworlds play and art/science are mutually constitutive activities. In other words, play can be inspired by participation in and/or observation of various arts (visual, plastic, literary, drama, music, etc.) and by exploration of nature and human activities (sciences). Simultaneously, the artistic and scientific activities can be based on and incorporate play.

Our interest in playworld educational practice is driven by our view that playworlds may satisfy what we regard as a pressing and international need in education today. We believe that there is the need for a radically different approach to education in the face of the increasingly severe problems confronting current educational practices in all five of our respective countries: lack of internal motivation in academic settings, various forms of violence in schools (including pedagogical violence and coercive disciplinary methods (Matusov, 2009), as well as violence and bullying between students), and growing numbers of "dropouts" (including both the students leaving before graduation and teachers leaving the profession), are just the tip of a much larger iceberg.

It appears that the problems mentioned above are only intensifying when addressed by initiatives to "tighten up" and streamline the existing educational system. These initiatives, based on principles of behavior modification and policies of zero tolerance (Urbina, 2009), introduce increasingly punitive disciplinary measures directed at schools, teachers (see Zezima, 2010, on closing Rhode Island High School) and students. Simultaneously, these initiatives foster competition between schools for scarce resources, through the enforcement of strict and culturally insensitive standards of academic achievement. Such competition, in turn, leads to the abandonment of complex, creative and critical thinking by narrowing the curriculum to fewer and fewer decontextualized basic skills and by degrading instructional methods to drilling for the test and to scripted remedial instruction.

We believe that these disciplinary methods and strict standards are exacerbating problems plaguing education practices in our countries, rather than solving them. We take this as an indication that we should rethink our understanding of a root of current educational practices: the quality of the relationships between adults and children in educational settings. The basic principles and premises of playworlds offer us the possibility to rethink the relationship between adult and child in a key set of activities: imaginative activities.

In this paper we first introduce the key concepts about play and art that form the theoretical basis for the educational practice of playworlds. Next, we discuss how playworlds were constructed in each of our five countries, and introduce the educational and developmental topics that each of these playworlds brings to the fore. We conclude by discussing larger issues and problems in contemporary education across the five countries in which playworlds are taking place, and by exploring how and why the educational principles developed through playworlds may be useful for a successful transformation of contemporary education in these countries.

THE THEORETICAL BASIS OF PLAYWORLDS: ADULT-CHILD PRETEND PLAY

Common to almost all cultures, pretend play is also paradoxical and controversial (Sutton-Smith, 1997). It is a non-utilitarian whirl of complex social interactions in which real and imagined reflect each other in an endless recursive pattern of mirror inside mirror inside mirror (Bateson, 1972). Scholars of play cannot even agree whether play is universal and/or necessary to development, or not. However, regardless of these and other differences, most of the contemporary play research and theory assume that pretend play (also called "fantasy", "symbolic" and "dramatic" play) is most characteristic of young children and that it disappears, "goes underground," or becomes a part of adult forms of creative and sometimes play-like activities associated with the arts (Elkonin, Zaporozhets, & Shybut, 1971; Vygotsky, 1933/1976).

In contrast to the prevailing assumption that play belongs only to childhood as a leading activity at that particular stage of development, our research takes an essentially different approach. We focus on a unique form of adult collaboration with children based on rarely discussed potentials of imaginative and/or pretend play. This collaboration has a potential to initiate aesthetic, intellectual, social and emotional transformations in both adults and children.

Full involvement of both adults and children in the playworld experience, especially the quality of the emotional-cognitive engagement (perezhivanie), is a very important aspect of playworlds. We believe that the dynamics of this full engagement is, in great part, the result of the fusion of adult and child participation in meaning making in playworlds. Furthermore, in playworlds children's play is enriched by cultural artifacts and adult participation while, simultaneously, adult participants in playworlds revitalize their ability to engage in symbolic play.[2]

We further believe that the appearance of the loss of "playfulness" in adults is a result of two factors: first, adults are often precluded from engagement in symbolic play by various cultural norms of acceptable conduct and behavior; and second, the adult forms of imagination often, although not always, make play less necessary for their development. However, most cultures do allow, or even require, adults to engage in some forms of symbolic play in particular circumstances including theater and other forms of dramatic arts, carnivals, etc. See Göncü and Perone (2009) for more on pretend play as a lifespan activity. Playworlds establish a special set of circumstances that allow the "child-like" imagination of adults to animate their behavior while allowing children to participate in forms of adult activity, and playworlds allow these two events to happen simultaneously through adult-child joint engagement.

CULTURAL-HISTORICAL VIEWS OF THE ROLE OF PLAY AND ART IN DEVELOPMENT

> "... In short, art represents its own process of coming into being and insofar, exemplifies and objectifies the distinctively human capacity of creation. It is in the self-recognition of this creative capacity that human beings come to know themselves as human..." (Wartofsky, 1979, p.357)

The concepts about play and art, which lie in the root of playworlds, originate mainly in Vygotsky's theory of play and imagination and his psychology of art (Vygotsky, 1925/1971, 1930/2004, 1933/1976, 1978). They are, however, complemented and further transformed by taking into account other important theoretical and philosophical sources such as: Wartofsky's philosophical writings on art and education (Wartofsky, 1979); Bakhtin's writing on dialogue as the basic form of human engagement with others (Bakhtin, 1984; Bakhtin & Holquist, 1981); Lindqvist's aesthetic theory of play and a the pedagogical practice she called "Playworlds," which is based on her radical reading of Vygotsky (Lindqvist, 1995); Marjanovic-Shane's study of metaphor in child development (Marjanovic-Shane, 1989a, 1989b); Hakkarainen's educational experiments in Narrative Learning in Finland (Hakkarainen, 2004, 2006, 2008); and Japanese pedagogue Saitou's notions of Kyouzai—Kaishaku[3] (Miyazaki, 2008, 2009a, 2009b, 2010).

As we move away from characterizing play as a frivolous, purposeless or solely childish pastime, it becomes important to understand Vygotsky's concept of the zone of proximal development (Vygotsky, 1933/1976, 1934/1986, 1978). Vygotsky defines the zone of proximal development as the "distance" between what a child can do on her own and what she can do in collaboration and with adult guidance (Vygotsky, 1934/1986, p. 187). This concept implies that all (higher) psychological functions first appear on the inter-personal plane, i.e. as joint activities among and between children and adults, and are then gradually internalized, moving into an individual's own intra-personal sphere (Vygotsky, 1978, p. 57). Thus, psychological functions, abilities and knowledge go through periods of "construction" during which the child is in "the zone of proximal development" together with an adult and/or other children. Therefore, we believe that to understand the nature of processes that take place in the zone of proximal development, one has to situate that development in interpersonal relationships and within an environment shaped by cultural and historical artifacts.

Vygotsky asserts that play is an activity which generates the zone of proximal development. His famous metaphor to describe a zone of proximal development generated by play is that "in play children perform a "head taller" than they currently are" (Vygotsky, 1978, p. 102). In his conception of the zone, play is the original form of imagination, a novel psychological process, which starts to emerge in early childhood. Imagination, "like all functions of consciousness, […] originally arises from action… we can say that imagination in adolescents and school children is play without action" (Vygotsky, 1978, p. 93).

According to Vygotsky (1978, p. 94), two main attributes of play are the creation of an imaginary situation and the construction of rules that define this situation. In Bakhtin's terms, any created imaginary situation can be understood in terms of a "chronotope"—that is, a distinct unity of time, space, values and rules (Bakhtin & Holquist, 1981). The very creation of an imaginary situation implies that the players (i.e. authors of the imaginary situation) are exploring the characters (heroes), their value systems and the rules governing these imaginary situations that give them their nuanced meanings. In order to better understand the role and the dynamics of play and/or arts, especially drama and literature, we draw on both Bakhtin's (Bakhtin & Holquist, 1981; Bakhtin, Holquist, & Liapunov, 1990) and Vygotsky's (1925/1971, 1930/2004) studies of the multilayered relationships between the playworld chronotopes. These are the play (imaginary) chronotope, the art chronotope, and the reality chronotope, i.e. the social, cultural and historical moments in the actual lives of the players.

Playworlds can lead to significant changes in almost all developmental domains:

1. Perception and attention: In play, the child's attention and perceptual processes become liberated from their dependency on "here and now." When creating an imaginary, "surreal" situation, the child focuses his/her attention on events, characters and relationships that are different from her/his immediate physical and social situation. "Thus, a condition is reached in which the child begins to act independently of what he sees" (Vygotsky, 1978, p. 97).
2. Cognition: Play involves considerable cognitive processing. The child transforms his/her own past experiences and knowledge of the world to create an imaginary situation with distinct characters, relationships be-

tween characters, and means of acting and reacting to dramatic situations of exploration, tension, conflict, victory and defeat. In this process children use objects and each other to stand for imaginary objects and characters. Vygotsky described this as the creation of "meaning" that dominates "objects" (1978, p. 100).

3. Will and self-direction: Play creates conditions in which the child develops self-direction and will. In play a child develops an ability to suspend immediate, impulsive and reactive behavior in reality, while developing and executing planned, purposeful and willful acting in an imaginary situation. The child is, thus, exploring rules of "behavior" in the constructed imaginary situation. Vygotsky described this as "meaning" starting to dominate "acting" (1978, p. 100).
4. Emotional development: Play also creates conditions for significant emotional transformation and growth. Novel emotional perspectives and "lived experiences" are created by the juxtaposition of two simultaneously existing, yet distinct emotional realities: the reality of the child-actor-creator in relation to the reality of the child-character within the imaginary situation. This emotional duality can lead to an experience of emotional transformation or "overcoming" (*perezhivanie*), in which the child gains a novel emotional perspective and a reflective empathy with other people's emotions.

Vygotsky saw this form of emotional transformation in play as akin to the emotional transformation that occurs in art. In the "Psychology of Art" (1925/1971) Vygotsky explored issues related to the dynamics of aesthetic emotional transformation. He saw art as a particular, social form of transformation of human emotion and cognition that, through "catharsis", generates the development of higher forms of insight and sensibility in the world, in the self and in relationships with others. It was Vygotsky's studies of play, imagination and art that inspired G. Lindqvist to create her aesthetic pedagogy, which she named "Playworld" (Lindqvist, 1995).

Lindqvist's approach (1995) to play emphasizes the relationship between play, art, and the process of children's cultural development. Lindqvist asserts that play is a dynamic meeting between the child's internal activity (emotions and thoughts) and his/her external activities. When a child is engaged in aesthetic activities (various arts), these activities may transform the child's inner world. Lindqvist's pedagogy of creative play is designed to investigate how aesthetic activities can influence children's play. Her "aesthetics of play" is an investigation focused on understanding and describing the nature of the connections between play and the aesthetic forms of drama and literature. According to Lindqvist, development needs to be described in terms of meaning making and consciousness rather than as a type of learning that is primarily cognitive.

Creative pedagogy of play is Lindqvist's "didactic method" in which children and adults create playworlds together. The projects, Lindqvist designed were based on themes that were implemented using play and various arts such as literature, drama, dance and theater. The projects were often intergenerational: the older children's capacity for acting in a theater play was combined with the younger children's pretend play and this combination would produce conscious dramatizations. Lindqvist saw a need for a comprehensive theory concerning the role of the aesthetic subjects in child development. In her view, influenced by Thomas Ziehe (1986), art and aesthetics should permeate all activities and subject domains in school.[4]

The role of the aesthetics in human development was also a topic of several essays by Wartofsky (1979). For Wartofsky art is, first of all, an activity. More than merely a product, artwork represents the very activity of its creation and appreciation. Art is a form of engagement in life that generates the distinctly human ability to become a "being which can come to know itself" (Wartofsky, 1979, p. 358). Therefore, according to Wartofsky, the "activity of art is (an) humanizing activity" and "repression and distortion of this activity… leads to dehumanization" (p. 358).

Wartofsky (1979) also argued that art is a tertiary artifact. The activity of constructing a tertiary artifact is "a free construction in the imagination of rules and operations different from those adopted for ordinary 'this—worldly' praxis" (p. 209). This activity is derived from our ordinary perception, "but transcends or violates the usual constraints" (p. 209). It is 'off-lined' or detached from the real world praxis, but provides a perceptual hypothesis concerning the real world. Thus, art activities and children's imaginative play, as it is characterized by Vygotsky (Vygotsky, 1930/2004), appear to have homogeneous structures.

We can, therefore, look at imaginative play as a meaning making activity that gives reality a new meaning. As Vygotsky (1930/2004) claimed: "A child's play is not simply a reproduction of what he has experienced, but a creative reworking of the impressions he has acquired" (1930/2004, p. 11). Imagination is an essential aspect of all thought: "It becomes the means by which a person's experience is broadened, because he can imagine what he has not seen, can conceptualize something from another's person's narration and description of what he himself has never directly experienced" (1930/2004, p. 17). Imagination is an important component of all aspects of cultural life, essential to the artist and the scientist alike. Quoting T. Ribot, Vygotsky claimed that all human-made objects, every one, can be called "crystallized imagination" (1930/2004, p. 5).

Moreover, the relationship between imagination and reality is circular. Experiences in the real world provide imagination with resources for new creations. Imagination and play become richer when based on rich real experiences. As Vygotsky argued: "the creative activity of the imagination depends directly on the richness and variety of a person's previous experience because this experience provides the material from which the products of fantasy are constructed" (1930/2004, p. 14–15). Both art and play are activities, which become richer through exploration in the real world and construction in the imaginative world. As experience of the real world becomes richer through exploration, imaginative worlds become richer. In turn, as imagination becomes richer through its construction, real world experience becomes richer.

Art and play are two activities that can stimulate and enrich each other: Fruitful imaginative play of children will motivate and provide resources for children's (and adult) art activities, and art activities also provide resources for children (and adults) to develop their imaginative play. Furthermore, in playworlds play is considered an early form of exploration similar to that in art and science. The heart of playworlds, therefore, is adult-child collaboration through joint play and art, or joint play and science.

Although they occur simultaneously, the nature of the engagement of the children and the nature of the engagement of the adults in playworlds are quite different. In fact, for many reasons engagement with children in play is not always easy for adults. The adults, even the experienced teachers, often have trouble taking children's play deeply enough to become fully and unconditionally emotionally engaged. However, the importance of the adults' emotional engagement in the preparation of resources is derived from the pedagogical tradition in Japan of Kyouzai-Kaishaku, or 'interpreting the teaching material' (Miyazaki, 2009b, 2010). The legendary practitioner Kihaku Saitou argued that the teacher's preparation should not be simply the accumulation of knowledge of the teaching material, but rather emotional engagement with the teaching material: the teacher should find something new and exciting for themselves in the teaching material. Without this step, according to the tradition of Kyouzai-Kaishaku, children will not, themselves, engage with the topic being taught.

Finally, complex relationships between teachers and students (or between the adults and the children) are transformed through the joint engagement in creating playworlds. Teachers and students become collaborators who work on the same artistic or discovery project. Teachers (adults) take a lead in the creation of the project, while taking different roles in the process. They can be actors, portraying characters within the play (Baumer, Ferholt, & Lecusay, 2005; Ferholt & Lecusay, 2010; Lindqvist, 1995); they can be directors, leading playworld workshops and directing performances while children participate both as actors and co-directors (Marjanovic-Shane & Beljanski-Ristić, 2008); they can be visual artists, architects or engineers, involving children in arranging environments for play through "installation" or visual art projects (Miyamoto, 2010); and they can be researchers (of life) leading children into new discoveries. The dynamics of the teacher-student relationship has a special quality in play, when according to Vygotsky (1933/1976), the participants "enter" a zone of proximal development (ZPD). According to Ferholt and Lecusay (2010), all of the forms of development described above (psychological, educational and social) are fostered in playworlds because playworlds require full involvement of all the participants—children and adults—in the topic of the playworld and in the play itself.

Although not identical in all of their observable characteristics, the playworlds that we will describe below are based on the above set of premises concerning play, imagination, and the arts, and concerning the special type of adult-child collaboration that playworlds embody. In the next section we will describe playworlds in our four countries.

PLAYWORLDS IN FOUR COUNTRIES

How does such joint engagement between adults and children occur? What does the process entail? What is required to build trust and collaboration across generations? In this section we will present "episodes" that showcase some of the exuberance, discovery and emotional and cognitive transformation that children and adults have experienced in playworlds.

A Serbian Playworld: Developing Collaboration between Children and Adults

From 1989–1991 the University of Belgrade, Serbia, and Drama Studio "Škozorište" organized an afterschool project called "Drama Workshops: The Real and the Fictive Planes in Guided Socio-Dramatic play." The purpose of this playworld was to explore the ways that play and art can create deep collaboration between children and adults: how to build a process in which both the adults and the children are the leaders; how to entice the adults to incorporate play dynamics and structures into their dramatic work; how to inspire children to incorporate dramatic structures into their play and be active, creative, critical and reflexive individuals; and, finally, how to create a performance in which the audience can join in and participate, in the same way in which children join in play.

In this project children and adults created a master performance weaving together stories from children's lives, their imaginative play, traditional children's games and Shakespeare's drama *Hamlet.* In the performance, traditional games were transformed and play acquired new meanings. As a scene from *Hamlet* and a traditional game became fused, our understanding of the game and our experience of Shakespeare's scene become infused with personal emotions, wonderings and reflections and a sense of hairs rising along the spine. Everyday, trivial routines suddenly become experienced as centuries-old forces flowing though all of us with the power to move us and transform our destiny.

This playworld project lasted two school years. The two-hour workshops took place twice a week. The participants in the project of the Drama Studio "Škozorište" were about 50 children from Belgrade elementary schools, all 7 to 14 years of age (1st to 8th graders), and six to seven adults including the workshop leaders, a cinematographer and a researcher. We present here a few key moments, "snapshots" of some of the events in the workshops, which lead to this final, cathartic performance, and which were, as well, a part of the performance itself.

At the beginning of the project, the children and the workshop leaders discussed how to jointly make plans about what to do in the workshops during the school year. Their starting points were themes and activities that were considered by the children to be the most important in the life of any child; and also works of dramatic art that were familiar to children. For this project the children and the adults chose to work on Shakespeare's Hamlet.

During each workshop the adults carefully listened to the children, letting them take the lead in exploring the key themes from their everyday life: immediate situations in their families, with their peers and with adults; their games, their play; and their dreams. For instance, these themes included such questions as: What is a secret and how does one keep a secret? How does it feel to be scolded by a parent or another adult? etc. The children also took the lead in exploring those lines and scenes from "Hamlet" that related to these themes. For instance: "What, has this thing appear'd again tonight?" or "It is not, nor it cannot come to good." or "Have you forgot me?"

Each theme from "Hamlet" was first introduced as a topic that would be of interest to the children because it related to their own lives. Children would then tell and dramatize stories from their own lives. In the following workshop, the same topic would be revealed in the text of the play "Hamlet," and children would explore how to create Shakespeare's scenes and connect them to their own stories.

One of the topics that was chosen for exploration was the need, the nature and the meaning of children's play, and specifically of the traditional games that these children played. Participants looked for the situations in these games that were similar or reminiscent to events described in some key scenes of "Hamlet." They explored how to play a game in such a way that it could be transformed into a "Hamlet"-game.

In one episode, which followed the above topic of exploration, seven children (six girls and one boy, all between 8 and 9 years of age) are seated on the floor in a circle together with the workshop leader, Mima:

> Mima: Why do children play? Why do you play?

Children offer their opinions and analyses of play:

> Maya: Children play, because it is a fun part of the day, and it makes them happy.
>
> Lily: You would be bored if you did not play. There is something beautiful… They do not merely sit with no purpose… Children mostly play together in groups.
>
> Sheila: If children only talked to each other they would become bored very soon.
>
> Stanley: Children play to acquire new knowledge and to develop thinking.
>
> Annie: I like to play better than I like to study. Once my mother went to take a nap and told me to study. But I could not live without my toys and I took them and played, and played! And did not do my homework.
>
> Maya: I'd like to add, that sometimes when you play, you think of something that may also happen to you in real life. For instance, sometimes when you play, a doll may get sick, and sometimes YOU can get sick in life, too…
>
> Lily: I would also like to add that children sometimes, when they cannot do something in life, they do it in play. They do it to their dolls. … The boys and the girls wish for something to happen, but that cannot happen immediately, so they play.
>
> (From the transcript of a video recording, January 16, 1991)

This is the first cycle of questions in this playworld regarding the topic of play and the first exploration of the possibility of correspondence between imaginary situations in some games and scenes from Hamlet. The next task for all the participants is to explore the question of whether or not they can find in their games a theme or an event that is the same or similar to a theme from Hamlet. For instance, the encounter between Hamlet and the Ghost is about the appearance of something or someone scary, refusal to believe in the veracity of such appearance, counting out the hours before the scary event, the flight of those who are scared, etc. In response to this task, small groups of children create their own "Hamlet-games." A group of four 7–year-old girls choose a variant of a traditional game called "The Witch Ain't out Tonight."

As they prepare their presentation, they run across the room, giggle and whisper in each other's ears. They chase each other; they fall with smiles on their faces, rise and start again.

Toward the end of the workshop, the groups present their "Hamlet-games" to each other as their own "resolutions" of the main task for the day. The presentation created by the 7–year-olds starts with two of them in roles of "children" kneeling in front of the third girl who plays their "mother."

> The mother sends children to the basement to bring something. They cross the room to the "basement," where the fourth girl, who plays the ghost, frightens them in a haunting voice: "Booo-a-ha-ha." Three times they run back to the mother and tell her that there is something scary in the basement. Each time the mother reassures them that what they saw was something trivial, like "Grandpa's old underwear" and sends them back. She addresses one of them as Hamlet. Finally, the mother tells children to wait while she herself goes to the basement where she talks with the ghost. The "mother" and the "ghost exchange a set of ritualized questions and answers. She runs back to the children; they form a little circle and start running around, skipping and singing a song "One hour passes—the ghost did not appear! Two hours pass—the ghost did not appear! Three hours pass—The ghost did not appear…" When they come to the fourth hour, the "ghost" appears and starts to chase them. They all fall to the ground one by one. (From a transcript of a video recording, January 16, 1991)

In the process of the playworld, the meaning of this particular game will be transformed, as it becomes a part of the artistic performance of "Hamlet" that was performed for a real audience.

During two years of the workshops in "Škozorište," the participants explored four parallel, yet interconnected "planes" or "chronotopes" (Bakhtin, 1994): "life," "dreams," "play" and "art." In each of these realms (chronotopes), they were building and exploring the same themes. For instance, their first exploration of "play" as a theme started in the chronotope of "life" with their reflections on the reasons they play and their own process of preparing to play. From that chronotope, they transitioned into the "play" chronotope in which they were playing about creating a children's play. They then created a small skit to perform for other groups. This was the chronotope of "making art," in which they began to sketch elements for their masterpiece performance.

In the opening of the master performance, these chronotopes are symbolically represented by three tight circles of children and a large, surrounding circle of the audience. One group of about eight children plays a scene using stylized movements and gestures. Their performance stays in the chronotope of imagination and dreams. They sit in the circle, dressed in black and take turns sending movements around the circle: they sway, waving their arms, whisper without sound or push away imaginary forces that seemingly engulf them.

Representing the chronotope of play, another circle of children is performing "Hamlet-games." At the start, while the audience is still entering and getting seated, this circle repeatedly chants "Zeemy, Zaamy, Zoom!" as they play a variant of the game "Paper, Rock Scissors." Against the background of the powerful music, they create a feeling of a trepidation and mystery, foreshadowing the encounter between Hamlet and the Ghost.

The third group of children, representing the chronotope of "dramatic arts," recites the lines of Shakespeare's text from the start of "Hamlet." While the audience is entering, they keep repeating, again and again in monotonous and stylized voices: "Who is there?" "Nay, answer me. Stand and unfold yourself." "It is so cold tonight." "Has this thing appear'd again to-night?" and "I have seen nothing."

When the audience is finally seated the performance starts. The circle of dramatic arts begins the scene of the appearance of the ghost using Shakespeare's text. However, the ghost actually "appears" in the circle of children who perform in the chronotope of "children's play." They play the "Hamlet-game" based on the traditional game "The Witch Ain't Out Tonight." In this transformed game a mother keeps sending children to bring "a sword," "armor," etc., but the children, frightened by a ghost in the cellar, keep running back to the mother, until she herself goes to the cellar and encounters a ghost.

Traditional games that seemed to be just common routines without particular depth, merely formulaic incantations, "crystallized" products of tradition brought to these children over centuries of transmission of children's lore (Duran, 1995), suddenly gain a fresh, actualized, live meaning in this playworld. The magic quality of the unpredictability of faith in the chant "Zeemy, Zaamy, Zoom" creates foreboding premonitions that something scary, terrible and awesome will happen and sets the tone for the first scene and the whole performance. A similar transformation happens to the game "The Witch Ain't Out Tonight." When played as a traditional children's game, it is merely a variation of tag—with lots of laughing. The "scary" is parodied, used as a tease. Running in the circle has elements of glee and vertigo (Huizinga, 1955), rather than the somber tone of the words that they sing. However, within the children's performance of "Hamlet," the fear of the unknown, the suspense, the desperate cries for help and the cold, detached, cruel mother, all burst out of the mold of a traditional game with almost a breathtaking force.

The Serbian playworld shows the power of the collaboration between the children and the adults not only to create a novel interpretation of Shakespeare's Hamlet, but also to redefine the educational practice into a transformative activity. Children's lives gained special meanings when their emotions in every day situations, their wishes, hopes, conflicts and memories, could be connected to situations in Shakespeare's drama. Their routine games became alive with new significance in the story of Hamlet. They learned by reading and performing Hamlet. Above all they experienced a change as they were treated as collaborators in creating an artistic theatrical performance, and as they found out that their thoughts, feelings, interests and opinions mattered dearly to the accomplished adults with whom they were working.

A JAPANESE PLAYWORLD: EXPLORING THE RELATIONSHIP BETWEEN PLAY AND ART

The Japanese playworlds, called 'Hakken to Boken' or the 'Discovery and Adventure' project, take place in a private kindergarten in a rural area in central Japan. For the practitioners at the kindergarten, children's play and art are central to the kindergarten curriculum, and the practitioners' view of play and art is shown best in the name of their project: Discovery and Adventure. This name shows their beliefs that play and art are the exploration of something new in the worlds of imagination and reality. Furthermore, the practitioners at the kindergarten believe that in both play and art, the activities in the two worlds of imagination and reality are connected closely and enrich each other. Their views, developed and elaborated in practice alone, are similar to Vygotsky's thought (1930/2004) on play and imagination, and Wartofsky's thought (1979) on art: Both play and art activities are used in the construction of an imaginative world, new and different from the reality, yet based in the rich experience of the reality. The structural homogeneity between play and art is the basis of the Japanese Playworlds. The purpose of which is to produce a fruitful relationship between children's play and art activities and to stimulate children's development.

The playworld projects are each implemented through a year-long educational curriculum. Though the influence on younger classes is not ignored in the project, the eldest children, who are 5–6 years olds, are the focus of the playworld studies. The kindergarten has three classes of 5–6 years olds, and there are nearly 30 children and one teacher in each of these three classes. Before the school year starts, which occurs in April, "the theme of the year" for the playworld is determined by the chairman of the board, who is in charge of the art education of the kindergarten, and by the principal, who is in charge of all aspects of education in the kindergarten. The theme of the year is the starting point for the various activities of the project for the year. The theme is always general and abstract, so that the children and teacher of each class can develop their activities in their own way, following their own interests.

In 2008–2009 the theme for the kindergarten's playworld was "Forest and Seas." In the "Tsuki" (Moon) classroom the activities focused on the rivers that connect the forest and the seas, and the fish living in these rivers. In May, the "Fish Lab" was built in the classroom with large blocks. This lab underwent many changes throughout the year and remained the center of the children's play. Sometimes children became "the lab researchers," other times they became "fish." Not only did they create imaginative play as "the lab researchers" and "fish," but they also learned about fish and rivers by reading books about fish and rivers.

Throughout the year, children engaged enthusiastically in the activities of the world of rivers and fish, lead by the teacher of the class. As noted in the theoretical section of this paper, Japanese practitioners believe that the joint activity of children and adults occurs not only when they actually play together, but also when adults prepare themes and resources for children's play. Japanese practitioners believe that, for children to engage emotionally in the theme and other resources for their play, it is necessary for the teachers to discover the theme and the resources with which they, themselves, can engage emotionally.

Again, it is not easy for teachers to create such "joint engagement" with children. For instance, for the teacher of the Moon class, who was new to conducting playworld projects at the time of this river and fish project, it was difficult at first to find resources related to this topic with which she could engage emotionally. Assisted by other veteran teachers, she eventually selected the fish as the class's theme, as fishing was her hobby. Through the ensuing successful playworld experience, in which the children engaged fully, emotionally and cognitively, with the topic of fish, she became more confident with her selection of resources and she expanded the topic from fish to the related topics of rivers, dams, and even environmental issues. As this teacher studied these topics on her own and presented them as the resources to the children, the children of the class enjoyed the topics and developed many play activities around them.

Below is a description of one episode in the earlier days of this playworld year, which helps us to see how imaginative play developed in the "Moon" classroom during this "Forest and Seas" playworld.

> In a corner of the classroom, there is the "Fish Lab" made with large wooden blocks. There are some boys around this lab. The teacher comes into the Fish Lab, and calls children with a "wireless" telephone, saying, "Can you hear me? The situation has become terrible! The river is polluted. Change the camera in the upper reaches of the river." One child, Taro, then turns the pages of a bundle of papers hung on the wall, and brings to the front of the papers a page with the words "Up Reach." This seems to be the monitor of the camera. Another child,

> Jiro, answers, saying, "It is clean." The teacher then says through the wireless, "It is not correct. The Masu-trout is having trouble. Watch the middle reaches." Taro turns the page again and displays "Middle reaches." Taro answers, "Yes, the middle reaches are polluted." The teacher said, "Oils are flowing into the area. The area is polluted." The play temporarily stops here, and boys and the teacher leave to other areas of the room.

As this episode shows, the teacher participated actively in the children's play and thus stimulated their play activities.

The play around the Fish Lab continued throughout the year. The Moon dam was constructed after the teacher brought news about real dams in the surrounding area into the class. Next a spa and the hotel were constructed, and fish dishes were served there! The children also kept reading about fish, drawing pictures of fish, studying environmental issues, and playing sometimes as lab researchers and sometimes as fish.

As noted earlier in the paper, one of the foci of the study of the Japanese playworlds is to produce fruitful relations between play activities and art activities for children. Although there are many opportunities for the children to engage in art activities at this kindergarten, most important among these opportunities is the art class for the eldest children, which is called "Hakken to Boken part 2" (Discovery and Adventure #2). This class, led by the chairman of the board, is comparable to the graduate thesis at a university: it is held in the eldest children's last 4 months in the kindergarten and no theme is set by the teacher: It is up to children to decide what they draw in their pictures.

Pictures of the Moon class children reflected many playworld activities. Experiences that the children had had in playworld activities became resources for their pictures. For instance, every child in the Moon class included a river and fish in their picture. Analysis of the titles of the pictures and motifs that appeared in the pictures showed that there were two paths through which children's imaginative play activities were reflected in their pictures.

One path was most direct. Here, children took the imaginative roles they played in their playworld activities and objects from their imaginative worlds into their pictures. The children drew "the Moon dam," "the fish lab researcher," "the fish lab," "water fairy," and "camphor tree fairy," all of which were from their playworld. (The camphor tree fairy was related to a camphor tree in the kindergarten's garden, which became an object of the observation and was named "the tree of the class.") This camphor tree was put into the imaginative world of children: children played the role of the camphor tree fairy and showed that this fairy was the guardian of the water. Some of the children's pictures had titles such as "fairy of water guarding the river," "fish and water fairy on the waves," "friends of the Moon river living in the fish lab," and "discharging the water from the Moon dam," and these titles suggested that the worlds that children developed in their pictures were direct extensions of their imaginative play in their playworld.

The other path that was less direct, in the sense that children did not use their experiences of the imaginative play activities themselves in their pictures, but instead used the experience they had in the real world though play-related activities. Children's imaginative play led them to pursue various kinds of learning activities related to topics of their play, such as reading books, seeing picture books and listening to their teacher's discussion of newspaper articles concerning fish, rivers and environmental issues. The knowledge accrued in this learning about the real world was used in the children's pictures. There was, for example, a picture titled "Ibi River, Kiso River and Nagara River." These three are the big rivers running nearby, and the teacher often referred to these rivers in the daily activities. Or there were pictures titled "fish in the upper reach," and "a conger and its group." The children had studied fish in their picture books and were now experts on fish! In fact, many types of fish, drawn with realistic body shapes, appeared in children's pictures. Other motifs popular in the children's pictures included "the name board of Ibi River," "a dredging ship" and "a nearby real dam with its name board." Children had seen the former two when they went to the nearby estuary of the Ibi River on their school trip.

It should be noted that the children's interest in the books, newspapers, dams and the real rivers were motivated by their imaginative play activities about fish and rivers, and that these resources were not only used in the art products but also in the children's further imaginative play activities. Imaginative play activities were generated by the children's motivation to explore the real world. Real world experience, then, were used as the resources in the play activities and art activities. The relation between play and art is not unidirectional but circular: Each can enrich and motivate the other.

FINNISH PLAYWORLDS: CREATING A PEDAGOGICAL MODEL TO DEVELOP CHILDREN'S AGENCY

Thanks to the work of Pentti Hakkarainen, playworld activities in Finland are more widespread than in the other four of our five countries. For this reason, we will briefly describe these activities as a whole before focusing on a specific Finnish playworld.

Playworld activities in Finland (see Hakkarainen, 1999, 2004, 2006, 2008; Rainio, 2007, 2008a, 2008b, 2009, 2010) have three roots: mixed age teaching groups designed for the development of children's school readiness; the model of The Fifth Dimension (Cole, 2006); and the model of play pedagogy developed by Lindqvist (1995). Different types of playworlds have been designed and studied in Finland during the past ten years. The first type aimed to enhance children's play activity and simultaneously offered a possibility for pre-service teachers to develop their professional competence in guiding children's joint play. The second type of playworlds has been carried out in math, literacy and technical creativity. In these playworlds, problems are embedded in storylines and aim at the development of general abilities (Hakkarainen, Peppanen, Safarov, & Vuorinen, 2009). The third type of playworld sought to construct transitional activity systems in multi-age classrooms (4–8 years). The activity in the multi-age classroom is grounded in a play-based curriculum, which develops children's creativity, imagination, learning motivation and school readiness. Hakkarainen, together with the teachers of the mixed-age teaching groups, applied Lindqvist's playworld pedagogy to develop an early education model in which the developmental potential of play could be systematically used to support a successful transition from preschool to school (Vygotsky, 1978). The understanding guiding these playworlds is that the results of developed pretend play may have long standing consequences on learning motivation and potential, and on creativity, in later life.

All of the Finnish playworlds' approaches combine education and play through adult-child joint engagement. The idea is that sense and motivation for learning are constructed through narrative elements. Narratives and stories are used to build up problem-solving situations that the children face (compare Bruner, 1986; Egan, 1986). These narratives contain "sense-making tasks" needed to orient child's motivation and personal engagement. Such narrative forms of learning, in which there is a problem or a contradictory situation that cannot be overcome in ordinary, familiar ways, are powerful means of creating an emotional stance towards learning and the desire to solve a contradictory situation. This learning process is directed first and foremost to the child and to the child's own actions in relation to others (Hakkarainen, 2004; Rainio, 2008a).

Rainio (2010) argues in her study that playworlds can be seen as a pedagogical practice that can transform the involvement of students from passive to more active. Through aiming to break up the "traditional" composition of classroom order, the playworld activity has a potential to encourage student ownership, agency and involvement (Rainio, 2008b). In one of the playworlds conducted in Finland in 2004 using the famous children's book by Astrid Lindgren, "The Brothers Lionheart," the teachers' objectives were to enhance collaboration, to motivate students, and to encourage them to take active roles in the classroom (Rainio, 2008a, p. 121). According to Rainio, the objective of narrative learning and play pedagogy for the teachers was to use play and drama to make classroom learning more personal and meaningful to the participants. Interestingly, it also had a potential to lessen the need for teacher control and teacher-imposed order, which are usually typical in classrooms (Rainio, 2008b). Below is a description of an episode within the Brothers Lionheart Playworld:

> Suddenly, that morning, a teacher acting as one of the villagers from Cherry Valley and a pupil acting as Sofia, a leading figure in the story, arrive in the classroom: Sofia has found one of her homing pigeons. The pigeon has something strapped around its ankle. It turns out to be a "trust certificate," which Jossi (a character played by a teacher) had signed with a mark of his thumb. In it, Jossi has sworn an oath that he will abide by Tengil's will, even if it means betraying his own people, the Cherry Valleyans. The children were on the mountains (the school's attic) at the time of the event and they are aware that Jossi is a traitor and cannot be trusted. Jossi, however, does not know that they know this. (Hofmann & Rainio, 2007, p. 315)

In this episode, a teacher and a pupil acting as characters from the story find an important note that proves that their fellow friend, Jossi from the Golden Cockerel Inn, a controversial figure played by another teacher, cannot be trusted any longer. From this finding follows a long and complicated discussion between the children and the adults about Jossi's character, why he has betrayed his people, and whether he can be forgiven and trusted again. Finally, the children and the two other teachers decide to forgive Jossi and take him with them, as they are heading to their adventure to Wild Rose Valley to save its people from the hands of Tengil.

Later in this adventure, Jossi and the Cherry Valleyans find a sense of togetherness in the playworld:

> Jossi: Well, then we'll be heading for the last battle towards the end of the journey. We cannot make such a long journey several times. How many of you will join me in this journey? (Hands are rising and the children climb onto the tables, shouting: Me, me, me!)
>
> Jossi: Good. Three cheers for the brave people of Cherry Valley.
>
> Everyone: (shouting) Hurrah, hurrah, hurrah!
>
> Jossi: Be prepared to leave in exactly one week. And thank you once more.
>
> Some children: You're welcome! (Hofmann & Rainio, 2007, p. 313)

In this playworld a sense of what we call shared agency was constructed between the students and the teachers in the Brothers Lionheart playworld activity. This shared agency was constructed as the children gained agency in relation to Jossi as they subjected him to their judgment, making him admit and justify his betrayal. The children and Jossi reached a common agreement that was connected to the shared mission of saving the people of Wild Rose Valley. Only the children and the teachers as a group could accomplish what needed to be accomplished. In this way the children's initiatives led the narrative forward.

A U.S. Playworld: Understanding Emotional-Cognitive Transformations (Perezhivanie)

Hakkarainen and Lindqvist's playworlds were the models for the original U.S. playworlds. However, the first U.S. playworld was created together with the representatives from all of the other nation's playworlds and U.S. playworlds have been a place for international scholars of playworlds to collaborate. Thus U.S. playworlds are built upon theory and practices of playworlds in all of the other four countries, as well as being heavily influenced by their home at the Laboratory of Comparative Human Cognition, and thus inspired by Cole's (2006) Fifth Dimension work and also the play pedagogy of Vivian Paley (Paley, 1984, 1998).

The U.S. playworlds have also been inspired by work in ethnographic film (Rouch, 1974, 1978), phenomenology of film (Sobchack, 1992, 2004) and performance studies (Schechner, 1985). Due to this influence, U.S. playworld research has offered insight into playworlds as a method ("film-play") that can allow for study of phenomenon that involve intense emotional involvement (See Ferholt, 2010).

In Lindqvist's creative pedagogy of play adults and children work together "to bring (a piece of) literature to life" (1995) through drama. Together adults and children transform a classroom into a world inspired by a book and, in the process, the book into a world inspired by a classroom. This paper began with a brief description of the first U.S. playworld in which, over the course of an entire school year, 20 kindergartners and first graders and their teacher moved the world of C.S. Lewis's The Lion, the Witch and the Wardrobe into their classroom on a military base and the world of this classroom into Lewis's novel.[5] This is the playworld we will describe below, with an emphasis on the workings and ramifications of perezhivanie in playworlds.

This playworld began when, on the first day of school, the children found a locked wardrobe in their classroom, whose origin no one appeared to know. A few months later their teacher, Mr. Michael, was not able to read the next chapter of The Lion, the Witch and the Wardrobe aloud because, as he told the children, "The words in the book have disappeared!" To the sound of rain, the researchers came into the classroom playing the child heroes of the book: Susan, Peter, Edwina and Lucas.[6]

When the children's teacher entered the play in a white fur coat and long white gloves, the children became visible to the adult actors and entered the story as story designers. This was a turning point in the playworld, as the children began to stay in from recess and after school to sit in the White Witch's castle and recount the dreams they had had the night before about Narnia and their classroom; or to draw pictures in which they saved members of their family who had died, or were deployed in Iraq, from the White Witch; or simply to spend a few extra minutes sitting on the floor of the wardrobe amongst the soft fur coats. Another turning point in this playworld was when Mr. Tumnus was saved from the White Witch, breathed on until he turned from stone back to living faun, and the children's boisterous chanting: "Party! Party! Party!" filled the room for several long minutes: none of the adults could quiet the chanting. After this the children joined the inhabitants of Narnia for a giant feast, and then it was time for everyone to leave Narnia through the wardrobe, closing the back of the wardrobe, the portal to another world, for good. When the researchers said their goodbyes (the acting by adults was finished as the plot inside Narnia had finished), it was, oddly not only the children who were crying. Instead it was many of the adults.

When this "playworld proper" was completed, the children decided that they needed to represent the playworld to their families in such a way that they would be able to take these school experiences home with them for the summer. Like the researchers in the project, returning to the laboratory at the university, the children were faced with the task of representing the playworld both to themselves and to outsiders. All participants, adults and children, needed to contain their experience of the playworld for transport, to carry these experiences to a new time and place, and then to revive these experiences in such a way that they would be comprehensible to a new audience, and, also, despite the passage of time and process of translation from medium to medium, still recognizable to themselves.

In order to make their experiences of the playworld comprehensible to their families, and hence to their future selves, the children came up with the wonderful plan of staging a play about the playworld for their families. In an effort to stay true to their memories, not to reenter the playworld but to revive its form with a temporary "breath of life," the children designed, after much debate, a production that was avant-garde and unexpected, and that succeeded in maintaining and conveying the creative integrity of the playworld. In the children's play about the playworld a wooden wardrobe was reproduced in cardboard, and this replica was erected next to its wooden counterpart for use in the play. As described at the start of this paper, some of the carefully and lovingly created costumes from the playworld were replaced by paper symbols of these costumes, while others were used as costumes in the play. Some of the lines in the play were taken from the playworld, while others were new creations. Some of the children played themselves, and others played characters that had been played, in the playworld, by adults. Some of the children stayed in one character for the whole play, and others played a new character every scene—meaning that in most scenes there were multiple actors playing each of the characters.

At one point in the creation of this innovative and impressive production, when a disagreement concerning the design of the play arose, it appeared that an impasse had been reached. At this point the child and adult participants saw what could be accomplished when the adults and children worked together, in a discussion, as they had worked together in their adult-child joint play (see Ferholt & Lecusay, 2010):

> A group of children sits on one side of the room insisting that the play be designed one way, while another group of children sits on the other side of the room and insists that the play be designed another way. Every child refuses to be persuaded by the opposing camp to change his or her view, or even to compromise. Finally the children's teacher, Michael, says that the dilemma is unsolvable and that the only way to proceed is to split the class in two, so that each person can create the type of play they desire.
>
> The discussion has been difficult and very long. The floor is littered with the bodies of the younger children, heads in arms, picking at noses and shoelaces. But one child, Pearl, sits on a table and speaks with great eloquence. She tells us: "Everyone (in this class) is my best friend."
>
> As if they have been physically lifted by Pearl's words, several of the children on the other side of the room, children who have not budged all afternoon, simply stand up and walk over to Pearl's side of the room. The most outspoken advocate for the opposing camp, Nancy, crosses the room and sits down right next to Pearl, and then rests her head on Pearl's knee. Another child from the opposite side of the room, Alice, suggests that the whole class perform the play two times, one time according to each of the two designs, and her unexpected solution is greeted by children on both sides of the room with huge smiles and exclamations of "Oh!"
>
> In celebration, Michael takes the class outside for a run in the field. One child, Rachel, says as she runs, "I feel like I'm flying." Pearl looks up at the sky as she runs and says, "I look up and I go faster." Andrea, Pearl's younger sister, runs backwards and asks, "Why am I walking backwards?" She answers herself, "I don't have to look. I know where I am I'm going." Michael and the researchers still look at each other in amazement when they watch the film of this event together. Andrea was able to describe, at this point, a certain quality of the experience of the playworld, and of the power of Pearl's words—a quality of perezhivanie—that the adults would only understand, through their research of this playworld, three years later. (Excerpted from Ferholt, 2009, 2010).

Researchers involved in analysis of this U.S. playworld are working to show that, as with the Serbian playworld, the power of the collaboration between the children and the adults created educational practice as a transformative activity for children and adults (Ferholt, 2009). This work draws most heavily from Fyodor Vasilyuk's (1988) definition of perezhivanie. Vasilyuk (1988) adapts Vygotsky's use of the term to describe a form of inter-subjectivity in which we insert ourselves into the stories of others in order to gain the foresight that allows us to proceed: an internal and subjective labor of "entering into" which is not done by the mind alone, but rather involves the whole of life or a state of consciousness.

On playworld days, children resisted going home when they were sick, or even missing school for family vacations; and adults regularly worked on props and costumes late into the night despite their many other obligations. Participants of all ages were involved in this playworld with their "whole" selves, and experienced changes in many domains of their lives through the process of creating this playworld. As this playworld's teacher, Michael, said: "And in hindsight it's one of the coolest things—I mean not just at school, obviously at school—but it's one of the coolest things I've ever been around and done."

CONCLUDING REMARKS

In playworlds, play and art are not "free" periods, interspersed relief from the otherwise drudging "labor of learning," but are instead practices whose intrinsic characteristics are inseparable from genuine learning and teaching. Play and art should, therefore, be at the core of educational design. We agree with Wartofsky that the study of science and technology becomes dehumanized when it is separated from "free" activity, while, at the same time, in such a separation the notions of "art" and "creativity" are "degenerated into some notion of the "production" of instant art, or "objects" requiring neither skill nor the delicious deliberation required for the difficult work of coordinating hand, eye, and heart" (Wartofsky, 1979, p. 344).

The social cultural conception of educational practice that playworlds manifest, exposes the falsity of dichotomies created in the modern Western understanding of human development, and in related concepts of childhood, learning and teaching practices. These dichotomies include: childhood vs. adulthood; play vs. work; emotion vs cognition; art vs. technology; aesthetic vs. truth; imagination (fantasy) vs. realistic thinking; and knowledge understood as an abstract, decontextualized, predefined and absolute "body" of facts and concepts vs. knowledge as lived experience of constructing ways to relate to the world, to create relationships with other people, and to create opinions, sensibilities, insights, values and responsibilities. Furthermore, playworlds are not a utopian solution, but have already been shown to be a vital and, thus far, sustainable, alternative to currently dominant educational practices.

The ideal of modern western childhood emphasizes the innocence and malleability of children (Ariès, 1962; Fass, 2007). This historically relatively new separation of childhood and adulthood leads to two seemingly contrary, yet related, approaches to children's play. Adults promote and often direct children's play towards adult-determined developmental goals by arranging spaces for play, supplying toys for use in play, and providing books and movies that are specially directed to develop children's fantasy and imagination. Or, adults encapsulate children's play and protect it from adult participation by understanding and promoting children's play as a "free," "spontaneous" and "innocent" activity that must not be contaminated by adult involvement.

In playworlds, evolving from a cultural-historical approach to development, childhood is not seen as a timeless and sharply delineated "stage of development," separate from the lives of the rest of the community and subverted to the "protection" and/or authoritative control of the adults. It is "not the result of purely top-down forces of ideological and institutional control, nor ... the free space of individual expression," (Jenkins, 1998, p. 3). On the contrary, bestowing upon the child an image of a full-fledged, albeit young human being creates conditions for genuine collaboration between adults and children. It gives children legitimate rights to participate in and question adult practices (Lave & Wenger, 1991), and to learn by engaging in complex and meaningful projects. At the same time, this conception supports adults in active engagement in the fantasy play of young children, as a means of promoting the development and quality of life both for the children and for themselves (Ferholt, 2009).

Playworlds can be organized at all levels of education, from kindergarten to higher education, by using culturally appropriate and age-related activities. We have studied and described playworlds organized in kindergartens and as transitional activities from kindergarten to the first grade, and playworlds as powerful activities for children living in difficult social conditions (i.e., refugees and children of soldiers who are away at war). We have also studied playworlds with older children (up to 14 years of age) as after school activities of choice. It has become clear to us that such deep engagement in joint activities leads to lasting transformations and development of all participants, including adult participants, although to understand why this is so, much more playworlds research is needed.

Playworlds research is also relevant for teacher education and training, and could incorporate drama, improvisation and training in other creative domains such as visual art, dance and music. Playworlds have the potential to develop teachers' abilities to create strong and safe communities of learners, and to develop teachers' abilities to design curriculum and instruction in collaboration with and based in the interests of the students. Playworlds may also serve to motivate teachers' interest in the content of their lessons, and to improve their ability to learn from their students, thus improving both their effectiveness as teachers, and their lives.

Finally, there is currently a worldwide tendency to emphasize the cognitive side of learning and to start academic schooling earlier. Aspects of learning and development related to the development of self and social relations, so visible in playworlds, currently are, at best, neglected, and are very often intentionally suppressed. Playworlds could become a promising and a potent model, or at least provide a set of principles for high quality early and later education in many different cultures.

As we have discussed above, playworlds may also prove radically important outside of current educational practice. Ferholt and Lecusay (2010) state:

> (Playworlds) raise the question of just what sorts of development we would like to foster in schools: only development which will allow children to succeed in formal educational settings, and possibly development toward adult stages of knowledge, wisdom or skill, or, also, creative development, development toward an unknown future which is significant to adults and children alike, in their roles both in and out of schools. (p. 82)

In playworlds, both children and adults continue to discover something new—not only about the surrounding worlds, but also about themselves in relation to this world and in relation to others in this world, through experimentation in the imaginative activities of play and arts. Playworlds provide both children and adults, to use the term of the philosopher of dialogue, Bakhtin (1984), with the arena for "unfinalizable" learning which does not aim at any particular end, but, instead, aims at the processes of discovering the unexpected.

REFERENCES

Ariès, P. (1962). *Centuries of childhood : A social history of family life.* New York: Vintage Books.

Bakhtin, M. M. (1984). *Problems of Dostoevsky's poetics.* Minneapolis: University of Minnesota Press.

Bakhtin, M. M., & Holquist, M. (1981). *The dialogic imagination : four essays.* Austin: University of Texas Press.

Bakhtin, M. M., Holquist, M., & Liapunov, V. (1990). *Art and answerability: Early philosophical essays* (1st ed.). Austin: University of Texas Press.

Bateson, G. (1972). *Steps to an ecology of mind; collected essays in anthropology, psychiatry, evolution, and epistemology*. San Francisco,: Chandler Pub. Co.

Baumer, S., Ferholt, B., & Lecusay, R. (2005). Promoting narrative competence through adult-child joint pretense: Lessons from the Scandinavian educational practice of playworld. *Cognitive Development, 20*, 576–590.

Bruner, J. S. (1986). *Actual minds, possible worlds*. Cambridge, Mass.: Harvard University Press.

Cole, M. (2006). *The fifth dimension: An after-school program built on diversity*. New York: Russell Sage.

Duran, M. (1995). Dijete i igra. [Child and play] Jastrebarsko: Naklada Slap.

Egan, K. (1986). *Teaching as story telling*. Chicago: The University of Chicago Press.

Elkonin, D. B., Zaporozhets, A. V., & Shybut, J. (1971). *The psychology of preschool children*. Cambridge, MA: M.I.T. Press.

Fass, P. (2007). *Children of a new world*. New York: New York University Press.

Ferholt, B. (2009). *The development of cognition, emotion, imagination and creativity as made visible through adult-child joint play: Perezhivanie through playworlds*. University of California San Diego: San Diego.

Ferholt, B. (2010). A synthetic-analytic method for the study of perezhivanie: The application of vygotsky's method of literary analysis to playworlds. In C. Connery, V. John-Steiner & A. Marjanovic-Shane (Eds.), *Vygotsky & Creativity: A cultural-historical approach to meaning-making, play, and the arts*. New York: Peter Lang.

Ferholt, B., & Lecusay, R. (2010). Adult and child development in the zone of proximal development: Socratic dialogue in a Playworld. *Mind Culture and Activity, 17*(1), 59–83.

Göncü, A., & Perone, A. (2009). Pretend play as a life-span activity. *Topoi, 24*, 137–147.

Hakkarainen, P. (1999). Play and motivation. In Y. Engestöm, R. Miettinen & R.-L. Punamäki (Eds.), *Perspectives on activity theory* (pp. 231–249). New York: Cambridge University Press.

Hakkarainen, P. (2004). *Narrative learning in the Kajaani fifth dimension*. Paper presented at the American Educational Research Association 2004 Annual Meeting, San Diego.

Hakkarainen, P. (2006). Learning and development in play. In J. Einarsdottir & J. T. Wagner (Eds.), *Nordic childhoods and early education* (pp. 183–222). Greenwich, Connecticut: Information Age Publishing, Inc.

Hakkarainen, P. (2008). The challenges and possibilities of narrative learning approach in the Finnish early childhood education system. *International Journal of Educational Research, 47*(5), 292–300.

Hakkarainen, P., Peppanen, T., Safarov, I., & Vuorinen, M.-L. (2009). Professional development through narrative teaching and learning. *Submitted to ISATT*.

Hofmann, R., & Rainio, A. P. (2007). "It doesn't matter what part you play, it just matters that you're there." Towards shared agency in narrative play activity in school. In R. Alanen & S. Pöyhönen (Eds.), *Language in action. Vygotsky and Leontievian legacy today* (pp. 308–328). Newcastle-upon-Tyne: Cambridge Scholars Publishing.

Holland, D. C., Lachicotte Jr., W., Skinner, D., & Cain, C. (1998). *Identity and agency in cultural worlds*. Cambridge, Mass.: Harvard University Press.

Huizinga, J. (1955). Homo ludens: A study of the play-element in culture. Boston: Beacon Press.

Jenkins, H. (1998). *The children's culture reader*. New York: New York University Press.

Lave, J., & Wenger, E. (1991). *Situated learnin: Legitimate peripheral participation*. Cambridge: Cambridge University Press.

Lindqvist, G. (1995). *The aesthetics of play: A didactic study of play and culture in preschool* (Vol. 62). Uppsala: Acta Universitatis Upsalensis.

Marjanovic-Shane, A. (1989a). *Metaphor beyond play: Development of metaphor in children*. Unpublished Ph.D. Thesis, University of Pennsylvania, Philadelphia.

Marjanovic-Shane, A. (1989b). "You are a pig": For real or just pretend?—Different orientations in play and metaphor. *Play & Culture, 2*(3), 225–234.

Marjanovic-Shane, A., & Beljanski-Ristić, L. (2008). From play to art—From experience to insight. *Mind, Culture, and Activity, 15*(2), 93–114.

Matusov, E. (2009). *Journey into dialogic pedagogy*. New York: NOVA SCIENCE.

Miyamoto, M. (2010). *Milkway: Workshop in IBI-Youchien 2009*. Ibi, Japan: Ibi Youchien and Mie Miyamoto.

Miyazaki, K. (2008). *Imagination as collaborative exploration: Art education in Saitou pedagogy*. Paper presented at the 3nd Annual Research Symposium on Imagination and Education.

Miyazaki, K. (2009a). *Kodomo no manabi kyoushi no manabi: Saitou Kihaku to Vygotsky—ha kyouikugaku. [Children learn, teachers learn: Kihaku Saitou and Vygotskian pedagogy]*. Tokyo: Ikkei Shobou.

Miyazaki, K. (2009b). *Teacher as the author of polyphonic novel: Bakhtinian analysis of a Japanese view on dialogic education*. Paper presented at the 2nd International Interdisciplinary Conference on Perspectives and Limits of Dialogism in Mikhail Bakhtin.

Miyazaki, K. (2010). Teacher as the imaginative learner: Egan, Saitou and Bakhtin. In K. Eagan & K. Mdej (Eds.), *Engaging imagination and developing creativity in education*. Newcastle upon Tyne: Cambridge Scholars Publishing.

Paley, V. G. (1984). *Boys & girls: Superheros in the doll corner*. Chicago: University of Chicago Press.

Paley, V. G. (1998). *The girl with the brown crayon*. Harvard: Harvard University Press.

Rainio, A. P. (2007). Ghosts, bodyguards and fighting fillies: Manifestations of pupil agency in play pedagogy. *ACTIO: International Journal for Human Activity Theory, 1*, 149–160.

Rainio, A. P. (2008a). Developing the classroom as a figured world. *Journal of Educational Change, 9*(4), 357–364.

Rainio, A. P. (2008b). From resistance to involvement: Examining agency and control in a playworld activity. *Mind, Culture and Activity, 15*(2), 115–140.

Rainio, A. P. (2009). Horses, girls, and agency. Gender in play pedagogy. *Outlines—Critical Practice Studie, 1*, 27–44.

Rainio, A. P. (2010). *Lionhearts of the Playworld: An Ethnographic Case Study of the Development of Agency in Play Pedagogy.* University of Helsinki, Finland, Helsinki.

Rouch, J. (1974). The camera and man. *Studies in the Anthropology of Visual Communication, 1*(1), 37–44.

Rouch, J. (1978). On the vicissitudes of the self: The possession dancer, the magician, the sorcerer, the filmmaker, and the ethnographer. *Studies in the Anthropology of Visual Communication, 5*(1), 2–8.

Schechner, R. (1985). *Between theater and anthropology.* Philadelphia: University of Pennsylvania Press.

Sobchack, V. C. (1992). *The address of the eye: A phenomenology of film experience.* Princeton, NJ: Princeton University Press.

Sobchack, V. C. (2004). *Carnal thoughts.* Berkeley: University of California Press.

Sutton-Smith, B. (1997). *The ambiguity of play.* Cambridge, Mass.: Harvard University Press.

Urbina, I. (2009, 10/12/2009). It's a fork, It's a spoon, It's a ... weapon? *The New York Times.*

Vasilyk, F. (1988). *The psychology of experiencing.* Moscow: Progress Publishers.

Vygotsky, L. S. (1925/1971). *The psychology of art.* Cambridge, Mass.: M.I.T. Press.

Vygotsky, L. S. (1930/2004). Imagination and creativity in childhood. *Journal of Russian and Eastern European Psychology, 42*(1), 7–97.

Vygotsky, L. S. (1933/1976). Play and its role in the mental development of the child. In J. S. Bruner, A. Jolly & K. Sylva (Eds.), *Play—Its Role in development and evolution* (pp. 537–554). New York: Penguin Books, Ltd.

Vygotsky, L. S. (1934/1986). *Thought and language* (A. Kozulin, Trans. rev. ed.). Cambridge, Mass.: MIT Press.

Vygotsky, L. S. (1978). *Mind in society: The development of higher psychological processes.* Cambridge: Harvard University Press.

Wartofsky, M. W. (1979). *Models: Representations and the scientific understanding.* Dortrecht: Reidl.

Zezima, K. (2010, 2/24/2010). A Vote to Fire All Teachers at a Failing High School. *The New York Times.*

Ziehe, T. (1986). Ny ungdom. Om ovanliga lärprocesser (Plädoyer für ungewöhnliches Lernen). Stockholm: Norstedts.

NOTES

1. The term *perezhivanie* comes from Russian with the specific meaning of a lived through and emotionally experienced event (or memory of such an event). We use it here in this sense, a sense that is somewhat different from the overall meaning of the English "experience," which includes less stress on emotion and points more to accumulated knowledge and expertise than to the fact that someone actually, personally lived through an event.

2. Cultural artifacts include among others: stories, art works, music, dance and improvisational and traditional children's games.

3. In Japanese this term means: "interpreting the teaching material"—i.e. successful teaching, in Saitou's view, depends on the teacher's reinterpretation of and renewed personal engagement with the curriculum. (See more about this concept further in the article).

4. Due to a severe illness Lindqvist no longer conducts research or writes.

5. This took place before the 2005 movie of this book was released and during the first years of the 21st century U.S. war on Iraq.

6. For those of you who are familiar with the story, to suit our actors' inclinations we changed the genders, and so the names, of two of the heroes.

Chapter Two

Complicating the Role of Play in Building Classroom Community

Debora Wisneski

Dewey stated that school is a "form of community life" (Dewey, 1897, p. 18) and described play as a vital form of community participation for young children. Thus, drawing on the ideals of an inclusive, democratic, and caring community, early childhood educators have promoted the need to build community in classroom settings through play activities (Bredekamp & Copple, 1997; Copple & Bredekamp, 2009). This chapter presents data from a case study of a third grade U.S. public school classroom in which children's play becomes a powerful avenue for children and their teacher to understand and experience aspects of community, particularly inclusion. However, children's play episodes become sites for bonding *and* for upholding prejudices and discrimination, thereby fostering exclusion. The strong attraction of normalization for the children, along with the adult view that children's play is "natural" (therefore, so are the exclusionary practices involved in play), contradicts and complicates the educational view of the positive power of play in building community. By highlighting the tensions in play and exploring our understanding of community through play, new understandings regarding the potential and limitations of building classroom community through play are possible.

PLAY AND THE CLASSROOM COMMUNITY

Within the field of early childhood education in the United States (traditionally covering childhood from the age of infancy to 8 years old), progressive values of community, democracy, and inclusion have been the foundation for developing shared and engaging experiences for young children. Currently, the National Association for the Education of Young Children (NAEYC) maintains that the first goal in implementing developmentally appropriate practices in early childhood settings is to develop and maintain a classroom community (Bredekamp & Copple, 1997; Copple & Bredekamp, 2009).

What do early educators mean when they refer to classroom community? Prevailing definitions of community in early childhood education emphasize the relationships of the children and teacher or caregiver in a particular classroom setting. Community in the classroom is defined as developing a sense of belonging to a group, sharing and helping others within the group, and finding emotional and physical safety within this group (Epstein, 2009; Howes & Ritchie, 2002; Peterson 1992). Mara Sapon-Shevin (1995) outlined the traits of community in the classroom as the following: communities provide opportunities to show ourselves fully, provide opportunities to know others well, and opportunities to reach out, to connect and help others. Based upon the importance of classroom community in early childhood education, much attention has been given to how educators should establish and maintain classroom community. Teachers are encouraged to have children work together on projects, spend time having class meetings, and establishing routines in order to establish a classroom community (Balaban, 2003; Charney, 1992; Perlmutter & Burrell, 2001; Pohan, 2003). Shared experiences or activities are the keystone to creating classroom communities.

The importance of shared experiences, communication, and social relationships in building classroom communities is predominantly drawn from the educational philosophy of John Dewey. In his Pedagogical Creed, Dewey (1897) stated that school is a "form of community life." More importantly, Dewey (1900/1990) associated the process of developing community through common bonds with the social experiences essential in play. He stated:

> A society is a number of people held together because they are working along common lines, in a common spirit, and with reference to common aims. The common needs and aims demand a growing interchange of thought and growing unity of sympathetic feeling. The radical reason the present school cannot organize itself as a natural unit is because just this element of common and productive activity is absent. Upon the playground, in game and sport, social organization takes place spontaneously and inevitably. There is something to do, some activity to be carried on, requiring divisions of labor, selection of leaders and followers, mutual co-operation and emulation. (pp. 14–15)

Thus, when early childhood educators plan for shared experiences in order to build classroom community, play activities are considered to be vital. Play provides the context for children to learn about the importance and functioning of community life. The fundamental social interactions that are involved in play, such as sharing of materials, negotiating roles and rules, and including others within play experiences are perceived as a positive avenue for socialization, development of social skills, and learning about relationships (Bruner, 1991; Epstein, 2009).

In the document "Developmentally Appropriate Practice in Early Childhood Programs" Copple and Bredekamp (2009) note "creating a caring community of learners" as the first guideline for implementing developmentally appropriate practice. Practitioners are instructed that:

> Relationships are an important context through which children develop and learn. Children construct their understanding of the world around them through interactions with other members of the community (both adults and peers.) Opportunities to *play together* (emphasis the author's), collaborate on investigations and projects, and talk with peers and adults enhance children's development and learning. (p. 16)

There are myriad forms of play in the classroom setting that have been identified as part of building classroom community throughout early childhood literature. The following are a few examples of how these different types of play have been related to building a sense of community, from adult directed games with children to free play on playgrounds with little to no adult intervention.

Games, organized and chosen by adults, are one way play is used as a tool for developing classroom community as presented in the text "Because We Can Change the World: A Practical Guide to Building Cooperative, Inclusive Classroom Communities" (1999). The author Sapon-Shevin acknowledges that while games like "Keep Away" or "Musical Chairs" are traditional forms of play, they are structured in a way that encourages exclusion or teasing. Instead, educators can choose to organize cooperative games where there is no competition, but rather games that require children get to know one another and learn to help one another. These types of games are designed to explicitly teach a lesson regarding the goals of community like sharing, inclusion, and working together, which focus on the relationships between children and adults.

In Devries and Zan's (1994) "Moral Classroom, Moral Children," the authors give a description of a "Community Classroom" as one in which children played in activities such as, singing songs, enacting children's stories, using Play-Doh to make sculptures, playing board games, pretending to play "house" or "restaurant," and building with blocks. Outdoor play activities were also included in the "Community Classroom." Some of these play activities were planned by the teacher; others were designed or freely chosen by the children. In the "Community Classroom" the children are allowed to interact with one another through these play experiences and the teacher is viewed as a mentor who helps children resolve arguments that arise in play and who organizes materials and play activities. Children are described as being self-regulating by choosing their play activities, thus participating in community.

Socio-dramatic and constructive play that occurs in interest centers where children can choose the theme of their play and the materials are also types of play that lead to community building. Cuffaro (1995) describes this type of play with a group of kindergarten children over a two-week period in which the children create a city of buildings and vehicles using wooden blocks in a block center. Besides negotiating what structures to build, including a police station, restaurant, and homes, the children also create rules. Some children pretend to be police officers handing out tickets to other children who drive their toy cars too fast. The teachers were present to help guide the discussions surrounding the play, but allowed the children to make the decisions about how to play. Cuffaro (1995) describes the play in the following manner,

> The children achieved a sense of groupness through the community they created out of the common interests and work they shared in the block area. This sense of community carried over to other areas and activities. In varying degrees, each child experienced being a significant part of the group. (p. 51)

Cuffaro's interpretation of socio-dramatic and constructive play highlights the cooperative nature of play when children are guided by an adult but shared common goals and themes in play.

Finally, another form of play that has been identified as the context for children to negotiate friendships and inclusion and exclusion within classroom communities is through recess play on playgrounds (Wohlwend, 2004). Generally, teachers are observed as being less involved in recess play; nonetheless, the play experiences at recess, such as, chasing games or using playground equipment are experiences that provide a rich social dynamic believed to be necessary for building relationships. This freedom within play provides another potential opportunity for children to communicate and share experiences and common goals, much like Dewey described.

A few studies have begun to systematically document and raise questions regarding the experiences of classroom community in early childhood settings (Vasconcelos and Walsh, 2001; Lash, 2008). These studies have employed a social constructivist lens to show what the children and teacher experience in the process (such as rituals and negotiations), how children have agency in creating community, and how sometimes school policies may interfere with the children's activities and attempts to build relationships. These studies begin to shed light on the struggles and frustrations in the process of children becoming a community and learning about community in the process.

Perhaps a more popular rendering of the process of making meaning about community through play is seen in classroom accounts of play as documented by kindergarten teacher Vivian Paley. In the book *You Can't Say You Can't Play* Paley (1993) describes how she and her kindergarten students struggled with exclusion when she recognized that some children would not allow other children to play during playtime. When Paley instituted a class rule that no child could tell another child that he or she could not play, a great debate erupted on whether this was a fair rule or not. When considering the patterns of this group of children's rejection in a classroom, Paley noted that "it is the *habit* of exclusion that grows strong; the identity of those being excluded is not a major obstacle" (p. 117). She explains that the children who are excluded are not different than the others. Rather, "what makes them outsiders is simply that they are *treated* as outsiders" (p. 68).) In her most recent account of play in *The Boy on the Beach: Building Community through Play*, Paley (2010) concludes that is important for all children to find their special role in play dramas in order to be included in the classroom community. Through these stories we see that there is a complicated process of understanding community through the play experiences.

This chapter examines data from a case study of a third grade classroom (Wisneski, 2005) in the southwest U.S. in order to illuminate how a teacher and children in a public school setting understand aspects of community and how they interpret their own play experiences in relation to community life. I contend that the lived experiences in the process of understanding classroom community for teachers and children are often more complex and complicated than the early childhood education literature suggests. Furthermore, while in theory play may be seen as the answer to creating classroom community, the data in this study reveal that giving children opportunities to play does not automatically create an inclusive community. By using a social constructionist lens, I explore play and community building in a classroom in a manner that takes into account local and societal contexts in order to provide complexity to the interpretation of the lived experiences of play and community. The following section explains how a social constructionist lens can help highlight the context of play experiences and how children and their teacher come to make meaning of community.

PLAY AND CLASSROOM COMMUNITY AS CONTEXTUALIZED LIFE EXPERIENCE

In this study the philosophy of social constructionism was used as a guide for examining community through play. The general principles of social constructionism view knowledge as being created through a collective process requiring an interpretation and re-interpretation of our lived experiences, which are bounded by the historical and cultural contexts in which we live (Crotty, 1998). Thus, the concept of community was interpreted and re-interpreted throughout the study by the participants' reflection on the lived experiences of play and classroom events while the context of school and society provided a backdrop to that understanding.

Graue and Walsh (1995, 1998) have warned that research has lacked close attention to the contexts in which children live and call for an interpretive research to focus on the details of context. They suggest that context should be considered in interpretive research through "a culturally and historically situated time and place, a specific here and now" (p. 9). The "specific here and now" includes local specific contexts *and* the larger societal contexts in which children and teachers live. In this study context was considered by documenting the children's social interactions and experiences that intertwined with the school culture similar to the peer culture perspective used in early childhood ethnographic research that suggests that there are two overlapping cultures within educational settings—the children's peer culture and the classroom culture that focuses on the academic needs (Fernie, Kantor, & Whaley, 1995).

Another component of context is the socially constructed positionings of the teacher and children that shape children's and adult's relations with others often based on gender, race, or class. How we relate to one another based on our underlying biases towards another's positionings is not always apparent or explicit in our interactions. Karen Gallas' (1998) statement regarding positionings in her research with young children expresses this sentiment:

> Over time, however, it became clear that the children I taught did not naturally separate their understandings of gender from those of race or class. They did not categorize their social actions according to a particular kind of stratification, much as I and other adults might. Their interactions were much more holistic-that is, they were rooted in the contexts of their particular historical moment in school, and it became clear to me that much of what I saw had to do with issues of power and social control (p. 3).

While it may be true that young children may not explicitly categorize their understanding of social interactions according to labels such as gender, race, or class, children are aware of certain social power dynamics and interact with one another based on these power dynamics. Just because children may not use the labels that adults use in describing the stratification of these power dynamics, it does not mean that issues around gender, race, class, and other differences do not influence the social power dynamics in classroom communities. Much research has demonstrated that children during the early childhood years are developing biases regarding race and class, developing limited concepts of gender, and developing prejudices against people with disabilities (Copple, 2003; Derman-Sparks & Edwards, 2010).

Young children's learning about community through play does not happen in a vacuum, nor does community learning in a classroom occur only in play experiences. Children's learning of community is influenced by the school culture, larger societal norms, and interpersonal relationships developed within a multitude of school activities. Cosaro (2003) states, "We can develop a better appreciation of the complexity of kids' cultures by remembering that they arise out of the highly diverse and complex adult cultures and societies in which they are embedded" (p.194). As some play folklorists have recognized, "play and games are not separate from life but are interwoven within it in multiple ways" (Sutton-Smith, Mechling, & Johnson, 1995, p. 70); therefore, attempts to explore the context of play are critical to our understanding of play. Thus, this study takes into consideration aspects of context to make sense of what happens when children and their teacher attempting to build community through play.

A CASE STUDY METHODOLOGY

The School Context: Carter Elementary School

The selection of the site, Carter Elementary School, and participants, Jill Roth and her class of third graders (the school name, the teacher's name and all children's names are pseudonyms), was based upon typical case sampling (Mertens, 1998). The teacher and class were chosen based on the teacher's and principal's interest in the research topic and the demographics of the classroom and teacher, so as to be representative of a typical South West Independent School District classroom. The racial make-up of the school was approximately 47% Caucasian, 44% Hispanic, 8% African American as documented by the school district. There was a small part of the population that is East Indian and from various Asian cultures including the Vietnamese, Chinese, Korean, and Taiwanese. The school was located in a working class/lower middle class neighborhood. Furthermore, the choice of exploring community in a third grade class was inspired by the works of Vivian Paley and William Corsaro. Each author has explored aspects of children's play primarily in the preschool or kindergarten age ranges. Yet, each recognized that as children become older they begin to be more reflective on their play experiences. For example, in *You Can't Say You Can't Play* (Paley, 1993) turned to the older children in her school to help her understand the exclusionary play of the younger children. Also, Corsaro (2003) has noted that in his research on friendship the older children displayed a "more reflective awareness and talk about friends and friendship" (p.72). The third graders of Room 321 were often reflective and willing to discuss their feeling and ideas about classroom experiences.

From the school building's appearance, caring, citizenship, and community were displayed as important values to the staff, parents and children. The school mascot was the "Caring Cougar" and an oversized poster of the smiling creature greets you upon entering the front doors of the school. Outside the gym doors was posted on large yellow butcher paper promoting 5 ways to enjoy P.E. class: "Be RESPECTFUL to others. Be FRIENDLY. Be CO-OPERATIVE. Be ENCOURAGING. Wear gym shoes." The enlarged words were the officially designated school values that permeated the school experience through signs, the school song and pledge, and school assemblies using the values as the themes for the assemblies. The school's mission was: "To work as a community to encourage independent thinking, foster a lifelong love of learning, and create responsible citizens."

Participants: Jill, the Teacher, and the Third Grade Class of Room 321

Jill was a white middle-class female in her late twenties. During the time of the study she was completing her third year of teaching in the Southwest Independent School District in the third grade. Jill had received a baccalaureate degree in Psychology with a minor in Educational Psychology from the local State University. She received her teaching certificate through an alternative program before coming to Carter Elementary School. In a pre-study interview, Jill shared that she believed teaching and learning is an adventure. She believed that the classroom environment should be one that is organized, nurturing, and caring. Jill was chosen for this study because her teaching beliefs and practices matched much of the language supporting building classroom community in the field.

This third grade classroom, referred to as the children of Room 321 in this study, could be considered "illustrative not definitive" (Patton 1990, p. 173) of the school in various ways. The children in Jill's class generally reflected the ethnicity of the whole school population. According to the school records, one child was identified as African- American, six were Hispanic, and thirteen were Caucasian. According to their school records, the children were eight or nine years old. There were 10 girls and 10 boys. The only language spoken by the children throughout the whole study was English. English was spoken in all the homes of the children, as well. Four children were officially identified as having special needs, including, autism, general reading disability, and dyslexia. Each of these children received services from special education teachers outside the regular classroom at different times during the day. The social studies textbook was even titled "Communities" and the children studied different types of communities throughout history and around the world. Most of the children in the class reported that they had been classmates since kindergarten at Carter Elementary.

Methods and Analysis

In this case, I used an instrumental case study approach as defined by Stake (1998) in which a particular case is "being examined to provide insight into an issue or refinement of a theory" (p. 88) using ethnographic methods of collecting (Glesne, 1999; Spindler & Spindler, 2000).Throughout the spring semester from January through June (in the year 2003) I was a part of the classroom experiences of Room 321. For the first six weeks of the study, I attended the classroom for the full school day. At first my role was only that of an observer. I also observed during informal teacher and children interactions, such as on the playground at recess or during visits to the school library. I used this time to familiarize myself with the routines and procedures of the class, and to begin to get to know the children through their friendships and interests. Eventually, I began to take a more active role in the class. I became the after lunch reader of the chapter book "The Wheel on the School" (De Jong, 1972). During group project work, I became a resource for the children and helped them as they worked in groups. I also helped the teacher and children organize a community charity event in which the class collected donations for a local homeless shelter.

Along with being a participant of the classroom, at the very beginning of the study I also held group discussions with the children about their understanding of community and private interviews with the teacher about her ideas of community. These conversations guided my participant observations of daily classroom functions. After initial analysis of the data I would choose critical events (Patton, 1990) in relation to classroom community to discuss further with the teacher and children. Then I would schedule time to conduct in- class whole group discussions, small group interviews with children, and individual interviews with the teacher in an attempt to make sense of the shared experiences with the participants. After the interviews and discussions on a critical event, I continued to observe and participate in the classroom in order to continue to investigate the topics that arose through the interviews and discussions.

Analysis of data began early and was continuous throughout the data-gathering process. This process begins with assembling raw data to construct a case record. Records were framed around children in the classroom, the teacher, and critical events as defined by myself but confirmed later by the teacher and children (Patton, 1990). I generally followed the interpretive model of analysis of these case records which, according to Hatch (2002) requires a reading of the data for a "sense of the whole," reviewing impressions, studying memos, rereading data and coding places where interpretation is supported or challenged, and sharing interpretations with the participant. In this case, during the process of collecting data, my impressions were shared with the children and teacher. Finally, the case study was written in a format providing narratives of critical classroom events and themes arising from the study. The narratives were organized based on the themes and important events of the school year. Towards the end of the school year, I began spending less time during the day with the class conducting direct classroom observations, but kept contact with the class and teacher everyday through interviewing, spending lunches with the children, and attending special occasions such as, school assemblies and the last day of school.

INCLUSION AND EXCLUSION WITHIN PLAY AND CLASSROOM COMMUNITY

The following themes regarding what is community were identified by the children and teacher: 1) everyone feels safe and comfortable, 2) everyone is included and not left out, 3) everyone works together and tries to help others, and 4) everyone tries to be a good citizen. However, through the course of the study for each of these identified qualities of classroom community, the teacher and children found there were struggles around maintaining these aspects of community. For example, while it was agreed upon by both the teacher and the children that to be in a community, one must work with others and try to help, many children often refused to help one another or refused help from others when they worked on homework for fear of getting the wrong answers. The context of the situation often changed the children's and teacher's view of their concept of community.

This chapter explores just one of the themes of community—everyone is included and not left out—through three play events. In the following sections, first a description of how the teacher and children explained community is presented. Next, I provide three critical play experiences that demonstrate how different children in the class were included and excluded in the play. Analysis of each play event through the context of classroom culture and through the social positionings of the children illustrates that play did not guarantee inclusion. Furthermore, when play events did offer the opportunity to have children included, this did not always translate into inclusion within other class experiences. Finally, I present excerpts from the interviews with the teacher and children to highlight their perspectives on inclusion and exclusion, in order to demonstrate how larger societal forces shaped their understanding of inclusion in community. These excerpts also highlight ways in which play events provided the opportunity to discuss the exclusion that occurred in the classroom community.

Community Is……. Never Being Left Out

Throughout the study the children stated their ideas about what they thought community means in school. They were often reflective about what was important to them in a classroom community and shared their thoughts in formal interviews and during class meetings or in the course of an activity. The following description of the community was collected from field notes that captured a whole group class discussion, children's essays, and an interview with the teacher.

> One day during read aloud time Alexandra announced to no one in particular, "*Just because people look different than you, that doesn't mean you should leave them out.*" Her proclamation was received with quiet nods from the other children sitting in the circle. (Researcher Field notes, February 18, 2003) Alexandra's statement and the children's responses led me to revisit artwork and essays that the children created when asked to draw or write about "what community means to me" at the beginning of the school semester. Alexandra's statement seemed to confirm what many of the children had expressed early on. According to these artifacts, feeling close to the group and having friends in class was part of being a classroom community. For example, Tanya wrote that friends helped you feel "safe" and "excited" to be in school and friends help make things "easier." Charlotte wrote that not having friends in the classroom was "sad and lonely". Kylee wrote in an essay: "It feels good to be friends when you have problems, when you play games it makes new friends." (Class artifacts, January 8, 2003)
>
> The teacher, Jill, described her efforts to build community in a private, formal interview: "In the beginning of the year we talked about showing respect, played getting-to-know-you games, talked with partners about yourself, talked about how it feels when you are left out. How no one likes it so we don't do it in our class. I had goals at the beginning of the year. My goals for the kids were for them to work with each other, work on academics together, and set up a class that is predictable so they are comfortable." (Interview Transcript, December, 2002).

Corsaro (2003) has indicated, when children ask during play, "We're friends, right?" they are making a "simple request for community" (p. 217).

This sentiment seems to be similar to the explanation of community for the children in Room 321. According to the data, play was a part of the process for making friends and not being left out. Kylee's statement that friends are made when you play games together illustrates this connection. While children did not use the term community to explain their relationships, they did refer to friends and not being left out when asked about the idea of community. The teacher also saw a connection between play and community building by using games as a tool to help the children learn to not let anyone be left out. Having friends in school meant you were included, and not having friends meant being left out. Interestingly, despite the class's desire to be an inclusive community, Alexandra's statement of concern for people being left out if they look "different" acknowledges that exclusion did take place in the classroom. The "simple request for community" was not always answered with friendship or inclusion. Viewing the following play events sheds light on how the request for community or friendship was answered in the context of the classroom.

Critical Play Experiences: Moments of Inclusion and Exclusion

As the children of Room 321 expressed in their writings, friendship was important in their school experience and play was an avenue they used to become friends. Participation in playgroups at recess, at lunch, and any other free times then became a marker of inclusion in the class. The children were constantly observant of who played with whom and what games were played. Shared play experiences were usually sanctioned during recess times on the playground (composed of a playscape, swing set, track and field, and basketball courts behind the school building), in the classroom during rainy days, or in the school cafeteria before school and at lunch. During these times the children would break away into small groups, negotiating who would participate, what would be the play theme, and how to engage in the play. Even while children from other classes inhabited the same outdoor or indoor spaces, the children of Room 321 exclusively played with each other in small groups.

Rather than presenting the play events in isolation, each play event is presented with descriptions of the context of other class experiences including the children's positioning and interactions in other class experiences to demonstrate different ways in which some children were left out, or excluded, in the classroom and through play and how some were given prominent roles in play. The rituals of the play offer a glimpse into how the children negotiated their play activities around the school culture and their positionalities.

Nachos and Cheese Dance Troupe: Shifting Contexts/Shifting Roles

In the classroom, Derrick was observed being in the middle of arguments with many of the other children and he was often rejected when he was assigned to work in small groups. Derrick was the only African-American boy in the class, the tallest, and very outspoken. In the work groups he was observed arguing with his teammates over how to answer math problems. He also would try to lead small groups on how to manage an assignment, but was often met with protestations and someone different would be chosen by the group to be a leader. Jill, the teacher, also would find herself in arguments with Derrick when he would question her directions to the class or ask questions that seemed off topic. Jill related to me that the semester before I entered the classroom, one of Derrick's arguments with another boy in class, Jerrold, led to Jerrold yelling a racial slur at Derrick that the whole class observed. Derrick responded by hitting Jerrold. Jill mentioned that while she could not condone hitting, she understood Derrick's response and did not pursue any punishment for the transgression.

At lunchtime, the girls generally sat at one end of the classroom table in the cafeteria, while the boys sat at the other. However, Jerrold and Derrick are the only two boys who sat with the girls. The other boys did not "save" them seats, nor did they ask Jerrold or Derrick to sit by them. The girls generally did not talk with these two boys. In both cases these were two class members who were excluded in class activities and during free time like lunch or recess. So it was unusual when Derrick became a leader in play at recess time directly after lunchtime. The following describes the play event that Derrick led:

> For two weeks Alexandra, Mary, Derrick, Rosa, and Angela have been working on making up songs, choreographing dances to go with the songs, and creating signs as invitations to their "show". Yet, Derrick was allowed to play a lead role in the dance troupe play performance.
>
> The dancing and singing began during lunchtime one day while the children were eating in the cafeteria at their designated class table. Derrick was spending his lunchtime asking anyone sitting by him if they can give him any of their food. Usually his appeals for food were rejected, until one day he began to part-sing and part-rap his request. Derrick called out: "Gimme some nachos and cheese, please. I am so hungry. Put it in my mouth!" The girls laughed and Derrick's request was answered by a donation of food from the girls. Variations of this song and food game continue for several days until one day Mary, one of the girls in the class, took it upon herself to write down the words to the songs on a clipboard:

Give me sweets, give
Me food, you do not
Know. How hungry I am.
So put some food right in my mouth. Unless I
Will do it myself. I M
Hungry!
Nachos are hard
Cheese is so soft.
They are my favorite
Thing in the world.
So why don't you
Just go in our special
Club, if you like nachos and cheese.

After lunchtime one day, the group of girls who were sitting by Derrick proceeded outside for recess on the playground. Here they danced, sang, and jumped to Derrick's orders and the lyrics to his song. One of the girls decided that they should be a club and put on their show for the school. As the days progressed and this lunchtime and recess routine of dancing and following Derrick's songs continued, the club designated roles for its members, writing the following on a little scrap of paper:

Drums—Isabel
Chicken—Mary, Charlotte, Alexandra, Angela
Cheese—Tanya
Singer—Derrick, Charlotte, Isabel

At recess time the club's "rehearsals" of their performance began to draw an audience of other children in their class. The others were told that the club was "full" and if they were interested in the performance they should come to see them at their upcoming event. At this time, Mary, as self-appointed club secretary, developed the following announcement on another scrap of paper:

"Come see some of Ms. Roth's class on February 21 on Friday

It starts at 6:53 pm. Be five minutes early to get a good seat. Meet us at Carter's playground." (January 29, 2003– February 19, 2003, Researcher field notes and artifacts)

The events surrounding the Nacho and Cheese Club, as the group called themselves, were somewhat of a triumphant moment for Derrick and the girls of Room 321. During work and play in the classroom, up to this point of the school year and as seen during lunchtime, Derrick had been "left out," or excluded, by the other boys and girls. However, for a small moment during the recess times in the context of play, Derrick became a vital part of a "club." He belonged to the group and was accepted by a group of girls. Also, others began to see Derrick's contributions as attractive and wanted to join the club. To the children, these play experiences were the beginning of a new relationship with Derrick. The girls involved chose to be more accepting of Derrick, as opposed to rejecting his overtures to guide a dance club. For a while, play time allowed a chance for classroom relationships to be re-organized.

However, Derrick's new-found friendships through the dance club did not translate to acceptance within the classroom learning context. Acceptance and friendships during play did not transfer to acceptance and inclusion in the classroom, even with the same group of girls. The arguments between the other children and Derrick continued during work group time. Eventually, Derrick was moved to another third grade classroom at Jill's request due to his arguments in the classroom, his loudness, and "bossiness" when giving orders, according to Jill. This behavior was not appreciated by the teacher or other children in the classroom but this behavior was valued during the playtime. The dance club play was an opportunity for building friendships and community that was not extended beyond the play event itself.

Yu-Gi-Oh Card Games: Girls on the Sidelines

Tanya joined the class in January. As a new student she was friendly and asked to join in play and work groups. She was not shy to talk in large group discussions and seemed to be well-accepted in the class quickly. The following play event was one time in which she was not accepted.

> Due to damp and chilly weather, some days the children of Room 321 stay inside the classroom for recess. As the children filtered in from the cafeteria in a single-filed march they fanned out across the room and broke into small groups. The teacher mingled about the room watching the children play and talked with them about their play. Isabel and Angela each grabbed a piece of chalk and began drawing portraits on the blackboard. Alexandra and Rosa found crayons and paper and began drawing. Ethan and Jose pulled out large stacks of Yu-Gi-Oh cards from inside their desks. As they began a game, Juan, Tomas, David, Matthew, Tanya, Jerrold, and a few others huddled around the boys with the cards. Tanya was the only girl in the group.
>
> Yu-Gi-Oh card games include special cards with pictures of magical characters. Two players play a "match" and "duel" one another with the cards. Collecting "powerful" cards is also part of the game. As Ethan and Jose played the game, Juan and Tomas asked questions and the four boys argued over the rules and "powers" of certain cards. I stood outside the circle next to Tanya. I explained that I did not know the game well. I asked if she knew how to play. Gazing over the boys' shoulders, Tanya replied that she would like to play but

> she doesn't own any cards and the boys wouldn't explain the game to her. She had asked to play but no one responded. Still, she did not join any other group and continued to watch from the sidelines until the end of recess. (Researcher field notes January 10, 2003)

What is interesting about the Yu-Gi-Oh game is that Tanya's request to play was ignored by the players yet there was not strong protesting by Tanya or the teacher who was present. Even though there was the understanding that no one should be left out, Tanya was left out. What is also interesting is that during the recess times the children generally segregated themselves in play-groups according to gender. Girls very rarely tried to enter the boys' play and vice versa. My assumption while observing Yu-Gi-Oh games was that it was a "boy" game. Tanya was perhaps crossing the gender divide in play and was left out. Tanya's exclusion based on gender parallels segregation in other play experiences between the boys and girls (Thorne, 1997; Corsaro, 2003). Some play events provide a context that is exclusive and hinders building friendship and thus community.

Dolphin Chase Game: Adult Intervention

Recess games on the playground or in the classroom for the children of Room 321 generally were sophisticated encounters as seen in the card games and the Nacho Cheese Dance Club performances. However, Karen, a child with special needs who often left the classroom for special education, played a simpler game, usually alone. Karen calls her game "Dolphin Chase." In the classroom Karen is known to draw pictures of dolphins and make dolphin squeaks at every free moment. She is crazy about dolphins. Kylee is one of the only classmates who had been observed choosing to spend time talking with Karen. The "Dolphin Chase" game involves Karen pretending to be a dolphin who is hurt swimming in the sea. As the hurt dolphin, she squeaks and runs around the open field next to the playground. She invites other children to be the underwater veterinarian who must give the dolphin medicine. The veterinarian is supposed to chase the dolphin around the field trying to catch her. All the other children know about Karen's game even though they do not play. They have watched her play and have been invited by Karen to play, but all children decline. Karen is often left pretending that she is being chased.

One particular day as some of the children and I were standing together on the playground, Karen invited me to play the "Dolphin Chase" game. She wanted me to be the veterinarian. I accepted her offer and began chasing her about the field and playground. A few of the other children watched us from a distance. Not wearing running shoes, nor being an athlete of any sort, I had difficulty catching up with Karen, the hurt dolphin. As Karen runs past the group of her classmates and I come galloping behind her slowly, Matthew asks me what I am doing. I tell him that I am the veterinarian but I am having a hard time catching up with the dolphin. I keep on trotting along and Matthew begins to follow me. He intimates that he could do a better job than I at catching the hurt dolphin and in a brief moment Matthew is outrunning me and chasing Karen. Karen squeals with delight and runs away faster with Matthew close behind. We continue the chasing until the end of the recess period. When Matthew, Karen, and I line up with the other children to prepare to return to the classroom, Alexandra asks me why I played with Karen today. I respond, "Because she asked me." Alexandra seems to consider this and we no longer discuss our play as we begin our passage to the classroom for afternoon school work. (Researcher field notes, March 3, 2003)

In this play event, adult participation shifted play to negotiate inclusivity. My participation in "Dolphin Chase" caught the attention of the other children in the class. The idea of playing with Karen became a possibility for a moment when up until this time no children showed interest in playing with her. Karen's play was not seen as desirable to the other children until I began to play. In this case, my intervention into play allowed the typically developing peers to be included in Karen's play. The data illustrate that playtime that traditionally excludes some children like Karen can become more inclusive when adult intervention is provided to encourage more inclusive play.

Viewing each of these play episodes through a social constructionist lens shows how play could become an inclusive act that builds community or an exclusive act that upholds certain social barriers. Children's play events were sites for bonding *and* for rejection. Furthermore, in the context of the whole school day, play events were not the only sites for inclusion or exclusion in the school day. Play was part of the larger fabric of the classroom community experience and not a guarantee for helping build an inclusive community.

In the context of this third grade classroom of Carter elementary, inclusion and friendship was valued by the children and the teacher, yet despite the desire for no one to feel left out in school, there were moments and even patterns of exclusion of some children that seemed to be upheld by the members of this class. This contradiction between the participants' understanding of community in the reality of the lived community experiences in Room 321, provided an opportunity to discuss reasons for exclusion with the teacher and children. The following excerpts from interviews that followed these play events were an effort to examine more closely how exclusion was understood and explained by the teacher and children in the context of classroom community.

REFLECTIONS AND INTERPRETATIONS OF EXCLUSION IN CLASSROOM COMMUNITY

Following the critical play events, I held formal interviews with the teacher and the children regarding the issues of the exclusion that was taking place in the classroom and the playground. The starting points for the discussions were the play events. The play events provided the teacher and children a specific example of inclusion or exclusion in their class community and how inclusion and exclusion functioned in the classroom. In these discussions, play experiences in the classroom shifted the understanding from general ideas of community to specific and real issues of community. The play events were often linked to other play events and other classroom experiences such as gym class or math lessons. Through these discussions, the members of this class explained how exclusion was influenced by the participants' positionalities (or differences) and the strong draw of societal norms. The following are a few examples of the teacher and children's explanations of exclusion in their community.

Teacher's Perspective: Accepting Natural Exclusion

While Jill had stated early in the study that she used play to help build community, she seemed to be less involved in the children's play during recess times, even though she was present in the classroom and on the playground. Her lack of involvement in the play and ultimate acceptance of the exclusion of others in play was explored in an interview with Jill.

In this interview I share with Jill that I cannot help but be concerned with the children who are left out at recess, lunch, during the playtimes, and even during the group work times in class. I use the example of the Yu-Gi-Oh card games and how the children often exclude each other based on gender or by ownership. Jill replies:

> "So I guess I understand why some people might be left out by that. And I guess we need a conversation about it. But I'm not gonna step in and be like: "You can't do that." Now if somebody is saying something or their actions are really disrespectful then I would. I would say, "In our classroom we aren't like that." But to me that's almost natural exclusion. You know what I mean? It's like—we all like something. We all like to... You know, like, John [her husband] and his friends. I'm excluded from their game group. But that's natural exclusion. It doesn't bother me because for one thing, I'm not a guy and I don't want to play the game. You know? But that feels like natural exclusion to me. So when they talk about these things (referring to John's games), I don't know what's going on, but I have a choice. I can find out about the stuff or I can deal with it. And that is kinda natural. Now if they were over there like "Stay away from us. Go away." To me it's like it is exclusion. That's why I don't allow that kinda of stuff. But to me, the natural exclusion stuff- that's gonna happen. That's life." (Interview Transcript January 29, 2003)

A social constructionist perspective calls into question the idea that behaviors or ideas are "natural." Rather, social constructionism asks how this idea of "natural exclusion" has been constructed and interpreted. Jill's explanation of "natural exclusion" implies that subtly leaving someone out based on differences in personality or interests is natural and to be excepted because "that's life." Actually, Jill is acknowledging exclusion observed in the larger context of society and accepts it to a degree. Yet, Jill's stance seemed to contradict her statements that community is about being included and that games can help build inclusion.

A closer look at the patterns of exclusion and acts of exclusion in this third grade classroom show similarities in the larger societal patterns of exclusion based on positionality. For example, in the case of the Yu-Gi-Oh game exclusion was condoned based on assumptions or stereotypes of gender play. Jill interpreted Yu-Gi-Oh card games as only being interesting to boys and thus it was understandable that Tanya would be excluded. She believed there was some choice in the matter for Tanya and assumed that if Tanya wanted to play she could have. Gender segregated play was not perceived as harmful exclusion that could hurt Tanya's feelings and so it was not perceived as a form of being "left out" but of typical behavior. Jill believes that since some exclusion is just "natural", she did not need to intervene during the play in an attempt to help the children develop community. However, she does not consider that exclusion based on gender in play might perpetuate narrow views of gender roles and that this seems "natural" because discrimination based on gender is part of our larger society.

While not presented here, discussions with Jill were also held focusing on how exclusion was based on other differences among children such as, Derrick as the only African American child and Karen as the only child in the class with special needs. Jill held similar interpretations regarding the observed exclusion of these children by others which implied that personality or interests were the reasons for exclusion and therefore, "natural." The rejection of these students in and out of play events were not seen as being part of a larger societal context that discriminates against people based on race or ability.

Yet, research has shown that African-American young males in American schools are often excluded from the classroom and disciplined based on their teachers' misinterpretations or harsh interpretations of their behaviors (Ladson-Billings, 2009; Indiana Education Policy Center, 2000). In Derrick's experience, his behaviors of directing other's behavior and being boisterous were interpreted as positive in the play context but in the classroom context were interpreted by the teacher and other children as bossy, disruptive, and negative. The harsher interpretations of Derrick's behavior in the classroom resulted in Derrick's ultimate exclusion from the classroom. Derrick's experience seems to be an example of what the research has suggested happens to African- American young males in schools. While Derrick's race may not have been overtly mentioned by the teacher or children as the reason for his exclusion, it is possible that they may have harshly interpreted his behaviors based on certain racial prejudices. However, because race was not overtly mentioned, nor was there any critical reflection on how the teacher or children's actions may possibly be related to racial discrimination, his rejection may have seemed "natural."

In the case of children with special needs, evidence has suggested that negative views of people with disabilities is often developed early in children's lives and leads to rejection and prejudice of others with disabilities later in life (Stoneman, 1993). Yet, these attitudes can be positive if adults intervene and help children understand and appreciate their differences (Diamond & Stacey, 2003). For Karen, little intervention was taken to include her in the play or classroom, thus the children often kept their distance from her. However, from the "natural exclusion" perspective these would be natural and acceptable because the children had different interests in play. As we shall see from interviews with some of the children in the class, the strong draw to be "normal", "cool", or "popular" interfered with inclusion in their community.

Children's Perspectives: "Our class is normal."

In order to gain insight from the children, I interviewed small groups of children at different times throughout the school day stretched across a series of weeks. One child could choose a friend or two to join him or her with me off to the side of the classroom. Eventually all the children were interviewed in this manner except for Derrick who had been expelled from the classroom. Each interview began with me asking the children if they remembered a certain play event. If they did remember, I would ask them to explain to me what happened and how they felt about the experience. This storytelling usually led to the children explaining their actions or the actions of others. The children formed the interview groups, generally in two types of combinations: only children who were often excluded and only children who were seldom excluded. This was not planned, due to the fact the children were allowed to choose with whom they were interviewed in order for them to feel comfortable. Small group interviews were understood to be private unless the children agreed to share with the larger group at another time such as class meetings. When children who were often excluded were in an interview, the conversation revolved around their sad feelings of being excluded and their interpretations of why they might be left out. For example, Eliza believed she was excluded because others remembered that she wet her pants in kindergarten. These interviews confirmed that the children who were excluded were aware they were intentionally excluded. The following are excerpts from recorded conversations with two small groups of children. These interviews were chosen based on the social positioning of the children. These children were seldom rejected and were involved in play and class events with all the children in the class at some point. They were often those in the middle of the "action." Furthermore, these children seemed to control some of the power over who was excluded and included. These interview excerpts are presented here to represent how these children understood and accepted exclusion in their classroom community.

Being Popular

While the children did not use positioning labels based on categories such as race or gender, the children did categorize one another with labels of desirability. Charlotte advocates for inclusion of everyone but in doing so points out that some children are more undesirable than others:

> At the beginning of the year, everyone made fun of Karen because she talks funny. But then they got to know her and they stopped. I think they thought, 'What if they got picked on?' and I think they changed. But we don't get along right now. I don't think the clubs and groups are fair. I think we all should start getting along. Not just some people, but all. I don't care if they're not popular. It's not like that in our class. (Transcript February 28, 2003)

Charlotte was able to recognize the power and allure of the popular identity, but resists the notion that being popular in the class should mean excluding others who are not.

Being Normal and Cool People

However, Matthew does not share the sentiment that there is a choice in the matter of inclusion. He is quick to point out the undesirable features of Derrick and Jerrold and condones excluding them with the same phrase as the teacher, "That's life."

> Matthew complains about Derrick and Jerrold, two of the boys who are left out from playing, "Like Derrick. Yeah. 'Cause he is always making things up. He lies. And in P.E. today he was bossin' us around, tellin' us what to do in the tug- of- war and he pulled me away! That's why we leave people out." I ask, "You don't think you guys could work it out?" Matthew replies, "No. Like with Jerrold. He copies and we don't want him around us. He acts like his older brother. That's just the way it is."
>
> "It seems to me that sometimes you belong and sometimes you don't," I say, trying to clarify what Matthew means. He replies, "Yeah. That's life. It's not fair, but....," Matthew sighs and shrugs his shoulders. (Transcript and field notes March 7, 2003)

While it seemed that Matthew was satisfied with this notion that sometimes a person might not be accepted for good reasons, later he showed signs of being troubled by this, particularly when he declared acceptance was based on being "normal" and he realized he did not always fit the role of being normal.

> Matthew explains as Ethan listens, "Being normal is like wanting to be perfect. Like you probably think of doing bad things but you don't do it. That makes me feel bad because it is normal to mess up." "Who do you think is normal in your class?" I ask. "David is normal," Matthew states. (David is one of the taller boys in the class. He is quiet during schoolwork, but cracks jokes when the teacher isn't present. The teacher considers him one of the better students academically. Matthew and other boys laugh at his jokes and prefer to play with him.) Ethan interjects, "I have something to tell. Our class *is* normal. We like it the way it is because we got cool people in it." (Transcript and field notes March 7, 2003)

As Paley (1993) noted "it is the *habit* of exclusion that grows strong; the identity of those being excluded is not a major obstacle" (p. 117). As the data suggest, by third grade the habits of exclusion in play and classroom life are growing strong and potentially mirroring the patterns of discrimination in a larger society. Moreover, exclusion based on differences was interpreted as part of life and natural by the teacher, so acts of exclusion that might perpetuate patterns of exclusion based on identity were not considered or confronted. Overcoming these habits in order to become more inclusive was difficult for some children who desired to be "popular," "cool" or "normal." Like Gallas (1998) has observed, certain ways of being hold more power than others and affect how we treat one another.

What is the role of play in light of these interpretations of exclusion? The data illustrates that while play may not always be a site for inclusive practices, there is potential in becoming inclusive through play events. First, adult intervention by participating in play can encourage inclusive play. Secondly, play events provided opportunities for the teacher and children to ask difficult questions and discuss how exclusion occurs in their classroom, to re-consider exclusive habits and make new choices. These possibilities open up a new way of thinking about play in building classroom community.

RETHINKING PLAY IN BUILDING CLASSROOM COMMUNITY

Early childhood educators are perennial advocates for the use of play for learning. The benefits of play in the classroom are numerous. Play in educational settings has been promoted as the panacea for many curricular issues and classroom social ills, such as the case for using play as a means to build classroom community. A social constructionist lens requires that we look more critically at children's play in the classroom and in the context of other classroom practices, through the positionings of the teacher and children, and larger societal issues. Using such a lens in this case study, highlights how play does not automatically assure that children will become inclusive and build community even when the children and teacher agree this is their goal and desire. Play can be a site for inclusion but also a site for conflict and play can perpetuate patterns of exclusion. Play events can highlight the conflicts the children have when negotiating inclusion and provide an opportunity to examine more closely through reflection and discussion the meaning behind these struggles. Play and community in a classroom do not transcend the constructions of exclusion in the larger societal community. However, play does provide a context in which to learn how to negotiate the challenges and issues involved in building community.

For instance, while it became evident that not all children were included in play or considered part of the community, this did not become explicit until the teacher and children were given space to consider and re-consider the meaning of the play events in relation to their beliefs about classroom community and other classroom activities. Also, as the teacher and children were able to discuss their interpretations of the play events, patterns of exclusion and reasoning for exclusion were revealed highlighting the potential for learning about societal norms that exclude others based on differences. By bringing this to light, the potential for learning more complex ways of being a community and the opportunity to change exclusionary practices can be made possible.

CONSIDERATIONS FOR EDUCATORS STRIVING TO BUILD CLASSROOM COMMUNITY THROUGH PLAY

Early childhood teachers often heed the call for building classroom community in order to achieve goals of inclusion and equity. Viewing play as an activity that will result in creating an inclusive community without exploring the multitudinous variations of how play can promote or disrupt community building, limits our discussion. We need also to consider the potential and possibilities of play and the complexities of how we play and what sense we make of play. If play is not viewed in this manner we limit our understanding of what community can be.

The following are possible implications this classroom community study may offer for educators who desire to build community through play, but who recognize our living and learning about classroom community through play is a complex and complicated endeavor. First, educators must critically consider multiple contexts such as, the school culture, positionalities of the children, and the larger societal norms that may be influencing children's interactions and understandings of community. Second, educators will want to plan time for discussions with the children about their interpretations of play activities in relation to being a community. Finally, educators can look to conflict and exclusionary play practices as a potential opportunity for learning about community and to critique our interpretations of community, rather than an indication that classroom community has broken down.

Play is not the "answer" to building community; rather play is a way of learning about life and how communities function. Through reflection on how we play with one another, opportunities are available for the teacher and children to re-consider exclusionary behavior and make new choices. These possibilities open up a new way of thinking about play. What if we began to imagine play as the starting point for exploring our ideals of community such as democracy, care, and inclusion, rather than the destination? What if we began to treat play experiences as opportunities to make choices to change our exclusive social behavior? What if play was not viewed as only a strategy for building community, but rather as one part of the fabric of our community lives to reflect upon and study so we may learn more about ourselves?

REFERENCES

Balaban, N. (2003). Creating a caring, democratic classroom community for and with young children. In *Putting the children first.* NY: Teachers College Press.

Bredekamp, S., & Copple, C. (Eds.) (1997). *Developmentally appropriate practice in early childhood programs.* Washington, D.C.: National Association for the Education of Young Children.

Bruner, J. (1991). The nature and uses of immaturity. In M.Woodhead, R. Carr, & P. Light (Eds.). *Becoming a person.* London: Routledge.

Charney, R. S. (1992). *Teaching children to care: Management in the responsive classroom.* Greenfield, MA: Northeast Foundation for Children.

Copple, C., & Bredekamp, S. (Eds.). (2009). *Developmentally appropriate practice in early childhood programs.* Washington, D.C.: National Association for the Education of Young Children.

Copple, C. (Ed.). (2003). *A world of difference: Readings on teaching young children in a diverse society.* Washington, D.C.: National Association for the Education of Young Children.

Corsaro, W. (2003). *We're friends, right? Inside kids' culture.* Washington, D.C.: Joseph Henry Press.

Crotty, M. (1998). *The foundations of social research.* Thousand Oaks, CA: Sage.

Cuffaro, H. (1995). *Experimenting with the world: John Dewey and the early childhood classroom.* NY: Teachers College Press.

DeJong, M. (1972). *The wheel on the school.* NY: HarperCollins Publishers.

Derman-Sparks, L., & Edwards, J. (2010). *Anti-bias education for young children and ourselves.* Washington, D.C.: National Association for the Education of Young Children.

Devries, R., & Zan, B. (1994). *Moral classrooms, moral children: Creating a constructivist atmosphere in early education.* NY: Teachers College Press.

Dewey, J. (1900/1990). *The school and society and the child and the curriculum.* Chicago, IL: The University of Chicago Press.

Dewey, J. (1897). *My Pedagogical Creed.* Washington, DC.

Diamond, K. & S. Stacey. (2003). The other children at preschool: Experiences of typically developing children in inclusive programs. In Copple, C. (Ed.). *A world of difference: Readings on teaching young children in a diverse society.* (pp.135–139.) Washington, D.C.: National Association for the Education of Young Children.

Epstein, A.S. (2009). *Me, you, us: Social-emotional learning in preschool.* Ypsilanti, MI: HighScope Press/National Association for the Education of Young Children.

Fernie, D.E., Kantor, R., & Whaley, K.L. (1995). Learning from classroom ethnographies: Same places, different times. In J.A. Hatch Ed., *Qualitative research in early childhood settings.* (pp. 156–172). Westport, CT: Praeger.

Gallas, K. (1998). *"Sometimes I can be anything": Power, gender, and identity in a primary classroom.* NY: Teachers College Press.

Glesne, C. (1999). Becoming qualitative researchers. Upper Saddle River, NJ: Allyn & Bacon.

Graue, E., & Walsh, D. (1995). Children in context: Interpreting the here and now of children's lives. In J.A. Hatch (Ed.), *Qualitative Research in early childhood settings.* (pp. 135– 154). Westport, CT: Praeger.

Graue, E. & Walsh, D. (1998). *Studying children in context: Theories, methods and ethics.* Thousand Oaks, CA: Sage.

Hatch, J. A. (2002). *Doing qualitative research in education settings.* Albany, NY: State University of New York Press.

Howes, C., & Ritchie, S. (2002). *A matter of trust: Connecting teachers and learners in the early childhood classroom.* NY: Teachers College Press.

Indiana Education Policy Center. (2000). *The color of discipline: sources of racial and gender disproportionality in school punishment.* Bloomington, Indiana: Skiba, R., Michael, R, Nardo, A., & Peterson R.

Ladson-Billings, G. (2009). *Dream keepers: Successful teachers of African American children.*Thousand Oaks, CA: Jossey-Bass.

Lash, M. (2008). Classroom community and peer culture in kindergarten. *Early Childhood Education Journal,* 36, 33–38.

Mertens, D. (1998). *Research methods in education and psychology.* Thousand Oaks, CA: Sage Publications.

Paley, V. (1993). *You can't say you can't play.* Cambridge, MA: Harvard University Press.

Paley, V. (2010). *The boy on the beach: Building community through play.* Chicago, IL: The Chicago University Press.

Patton, M. (1990). *Qualitative evaluation and research methods.* Newbury Park, CA: Sage.

Perlmutter, J., & Burrell, L. (2001). *The first weeks of school: Laying a quality foundation.* Portsmouth, NH: Heineman.

Peterson, R. (1992). *Life in a crowded place: Making a learning community.* Portsmouth, NH: Heineman.

Pohan, C. (2003). Creating caring and democratic communities in our classrooms and schools. *Childhood Education*, 79(6), 369–373.

Sapon-Shevin, M. (1995). Building a safe community for learning. In William Ayers (Ed.), *To become a teacher: Making a difference in children's lives.* (pp. 99–112). NY: Teachers College Press.

Sapon-Shevin, M. (1999). *Because we can change the world.* Boston, MA: Allyn & Bacon.

Spindler, G., & Spindler, L. (2000). *Fifty years of anthropology and education 1950–2000: A Spindler Anthology.* Philadelphia, PA: Lawrence Erlbaum.

Stake, R. (1998). Case studies. In Denzin, N. & Lincoln, Y. (Eds.), *Strategies of qualitative inquiry.* Thousand Oaks, CA: Sage.

Stoneman, Z. (1993). Attitudes toward young children with disabilities: Cognition, affect and behavioral intent. In C. Peck, S. Odom, & D. Bricker (Eds.), *Integrating young children with disabilities in community programs: From research to implementation* (pp. 223–2481. Baltimore, MD: Brookes.

Sutton-Smith, B., Mechling, J., & Johnson, T.W. (1995). *Children's Folklore.* London: Taylor & Francis.

Thorne, B. (1997). *Gender Play.* New Brunswick, NJ: Rutgers University Press.

Vasconcelos, T., & Walsh, D. (2001). Conversations around the large table: Building community in a Portuguese public kindergarten. *Early Education and development,* 12(4), 499–522.

Wisneski, D.W. (2005). Complicating classroom community in early childhood. Unpublished doctoral dissertation, University of Texas- Austin.

Wohlwend, K. (2004/5). Chasing friendship: Acceptance, rejection, and recess play. *Childhood Education.* 81(2), 77–86.

Chapter Three

Play Intervention and Play Development[1]

Milda Bredikyte and Pentti Hakkarainen

The paper aims to present creative drama interventions in children's play performed by students participating in a university's course on play and child development. The main goal of these interventions is to support the development of more mature forms of play in a group of mixed age children attending a creative play club. Creative drama interventions were followed during one term (3 months). The most successful and the least successful play sessions are compared with the aim of defining the criteria for successful adult intervention in children's play. The impact of creative drama interventions on the student's professional growth is also discussed.

A recent interview study in sixteen countries (Singer, Singer, D'Agostino & DeLong, 2008) revealed that imaginative play is disappearing from children's lives. Only 27% of parents reported that their children are engaging in imaginative play activities. Yet, over 90% of these parents believe that play has a central role in promoting children's learning and development. This trend towards the disappearance of imaginative play was observed in both western, developed countries and non-western, developing ones. Moreover, the pressure for early academic learning and a fascination with early training of technological skills all over the world is radically changing the focus of pedagogical work and affecting the time allocated for play in early childhood institutions.

Our play observations in Finnish day care centers reveal a general tendency of play regression. The following data is from a play session of 25 children (4–6 years) in a day care center of a small city.

> Anu[2] (5:2) and Kati (5: 7) start their play session by lifting a plastic basket filled with animal figures onto a table. They pour the contents on the table, and each girl starts to group a few figures on her own side. Anu selects wild animals

> (a lion, a tiger) and Kati chooses domestic animals (cats, horses, cows). No joint play is initiated; each girl manipulates her own animal figures on her own side of the table. The whole classroom is divided into play pairs or individual players. Only two groups, of three children each, have started joint play. In the first group, three girls play "House". Each girl has a pretend role and interacts with the others as if she were in that role. The second group consists of three boys playing "Squirrels". They lie on benches; nothing else happens during the session.

We argue that play promotes child development only if the child moves from elementary to mature forms of joint play. We propose that advanced forms of play have a unique impact on the cultural development of the child (Hakkarainen & Bredikyte, 2008, 4).

Western play research has mainly concentrated on the effects of play on cognitive, social, and academic development, which Sutton-Smith (1997) concluded to be the wrong emphasis. In the cultural-historical tradition, play is considered to be a source of development of general learning potential and abilities. El'konin (1978, 2005) listed the following effects of mature forms of imaginative play: (1) development of motivation; (2) understanding of the other person's perspective; (3) developing the imagination; (4) developing volition and self-regulation. Several researchers have found that an increasing number of children do not develop mature forms of play before school age (Mikhailenko & Korotkova, 2001, Bodrova & Leong, 2007).

This study is a part of experimental work that has been carried out at the Research Center for Developmental Teaching and Learning at Kajaani University Consortium, University of Oulu, Finland. This chapter describes a project that trains teacher education students how to intervene effectively in children's play in order to support the development of more mature forms of play. We analyze the effects of interventions on both the children and the students.

THE DEVELOPMENT OF PLAY AND THE IMPORTANCE OF MATURE FORMS OF PLAY

According to Vygotsky play in the early childhood years (from 2–7) includes two crisis periods (at three and seven years). We suppose that it can be divided into three qualitatively different periods using initiative as the criterion for division. At the beginning of that period (2–3 years), adult initiative is very important. The continuity of role actions and understanding of the conventionality of play has to be supported by the adults. After this early period, the children's own initiative is crucial. Adult presence may be a necessary condition for play, but adult initiative may disrupt the play process. After five years there is a need for adult help in enriching the moral challenge and symbolism of play (Hakkarainen & Bredikyte, 2008, p. 7).

We argue that play is not only a developmental contributor and the main age-appropriate form of learning (Vygotsky, 1977), but also the primary form of children's thinking in the early childhood years. Play actions could be understood as the materialized thoughts (needs, wishes, ideas) of which a child is not completely conscious. Play actions are a form of expression for children's ideas and can substitute for language at a very young child. According to Vygotsky (1977), "a child's symbolic play may be understood as a very complex system of speech aided by gestures" (p. 135). Vygotsky (1977) saw the role of play in the development of the human mind as a movement from concrete operations to abstract thinking; as a movement from thinking in gestures to thinking in words.

We understand the development of play as the development of children's thought and their ability to express their thinking—first in gestures and actions through play and other symbolic media, and then gradually through oral narratives. Children use play as a medium to create narratives about themselves and about the world. Narrative can be understood as "a universal mode of thought" and "a form of thinking" (Bruner, 1996, Donald, 1991, Nelson, 1996). Narrative is a necessary basis for formal, theoretical thinking, and is also a central factor for many art forms, especially those that depend on oral or written language. We view the development of narrative thought in children as a necessary step towards formal thinking and theoretical comprehension of life.

The defining feature of mature narrative (sjuzhetnaia igra) play is the ability of the players to develop shared ideas and to construct a plot (storyline) together. We call this form of play narrative role-play and use the following criteria to define it. Such play is:

- Social/collective in character (several participants)
- Imaginative (based on productive imagination)
- Creative (not stereotypical and repetitive)
- Developed over time, lasting as much as several months or longer (developed by individual, children, a group of children or adults)
- Challenging (demands action at the highest level of play skills)
- Based on a narrative structure (a storyline is constructed during play)

This type of play constitutes a motivating storyline, and through the storyline's enactment provides exciting experiences, or 'perezhivanie' (a term more common in theatrical terminology, but which also has the same meaning in play). Perezhivanie results in a new and deeper understanding of phenomena, and is one of the results of mature narrative role-play. Vygotsky claimed that, "the activity of the actor is itself a unique, creative work of psycho-physiological states" (1984, p. 321), and the same is true for creative play. Involvement in creative play provides the opportunity to 'experiment' with different psychological states, social roles, and relationships.

In Vygotsky's (1977) opinion, the essential feature of play is the imaginary situation that could be defined as the space between the real (optical/visual) and the sense (imaginary) field. This means that proper play starts only when a player (child or adult) is able to see self and the situation from an internal and external point of view simultaneously. Kravtsova (2007) called it double subjectivity and claimed that this ability is necessary in order to comprehend the psychological essence of play. Moreover, Kravtsova states that this double point of view is absolutely necessary for those who analyze play activity.

In play analysis, it is important to keep in mind the fact that mature forms of play activity proceed on two planes, as Vygotsky (1977) has indicated. He asserts that during play a child is operating with an "alienated meaning in a real situation". To put it in other words, the child is acting in an imaginary situation (based on some idea), operating/manipulating objects with substituted meanings while simultaneously acting in a very concrete and realistic way.

For the researcher who is analyzing children's play, it is crucial to look not just at the child's outside actions but to try to find out the real meaning (the child's initial idea) that is behind the outside form. It is often only possible to 'open' this deeper meaning by either observing children's play for a longer period of time or stepping into the play and 'provoking' the child to respond by performing further actions, thus revealing his or her basic idea.

Observations in day care institutions and survey studies indicate that mature forms of play are becoming infrequent. The necessary adult guidance of children's joint play and the enrichment of moral challenge and symbolism of play is often minimal. Scandinavian "free" play nowadays consists of short replays of the high points from TV-series, computer games and other virtual media. Teacher education does not train teachers in the necessary play competencies (Hakkarainen, 2010). Therefore there is a need for approaches to early childhood teaching that include helping children to develop more mature forms of play, for example, by having adults intervene in children's play.

PLAY INTERVENTION

There are a number of different approaches and intervention methods for promoting children's play. In Anglo-American settings, play intervention tends to focus on its pragmatic effects as seen in a recent review of the literature by Mages (2008). In this review creative drama intervention is defined as "an improvisational, non-exhibitional, process-centered form of drama in which participants are guided by a leader to imagine, enact, and reflect upon human experience" (David and Behm, as cited in Mages, 2008, p. 127). However, when one examines the criteria for successful drama intervention in this review the focus is on the concrete impact of creative drama experiences on children's language use and skills (language development). The review ends with a recommendation for future research proposing the development of a strong research paradigm that allows the systematic manipulation of cross-study variables in order to reveal mechanisms within creative drama. This same goal of revealing the mechanisms of play in the form of measurable variables and controlled gains is also expressed in a comparative study of play therapies (Reddy, Files-Hall & Schaefer, 2005). We think that this aim and the definition of creative drama are fundamentally at odds with each other. By definition, creative drama and play should be open to unexpected results.

For us, the impact of play on the development of a child's general learning potential must be the primary focus of any play intervention, as well as any study of such intervention. Play is a process of creating something new, such as an idea, a sense, or a meaning. Participation in this creative process develops new psychological traits and gradually leads to a new level of functioning. The child can acquire certain academic skills more easily during play, but such learning should not be the main goal of creative drama interventions and play activity, nor the main criteria of evaluating the effectiveness of the intervention.

In our play interventions, joint creativity and improvisation is the central focus, rather than academic learning. We aim for the transition from simple to more mature forms of play, and believe that the best ways to acquire and develop play skills are: modeling of higher forms of play (that of elder children or students), providing the possibility to join play activities, and providing all necessary support for successful play participation. Our goal is that the child moves to more mature forms of play and takes responsibility for organizing and developing the play activity together with other children.

Participation of adults (students) is an appropriate method for the co-construction of joint "playworlds," a term introduced by Gunilla Lindqvist (1995). According to Lindqvist, a playworld is a conscious effort to create a "shared culture" or imaginary world, which "children and adults come to share when they interpret and dramatize the theme in the classroom" (p. 70). By taking different roles and enacting dramatic events of a story, the participants become involved into the perezhivanie of a common phenomenon.

It moves students 'inside' the play activity and puts them in a more equal position with the children. From a developmental point of view, this is a very challenging situation that requires genuine involvement and a high level of sensitivity and creativity from the participants.

In a similar vein, Sawyer (1997) defined children's play as an improvisational activity and compared it with the activity of improvisational actors as well as jazz musicians and other artists. Lobman & Lundquist (2007) introduced a practical method enhancing educators' improvisational facility.

Research findings from our Play Lab revealed that flow experiences (Csikszentmihalyi, 1990) are a part of most successful students' play interventions. For this reason, we also consider the level of emotional involvement of the participants when evaluating play as successful or unsuccessful. Many teachers resist becoming emotionally involved with children in the classroom. Some professional teachers told us that emotional involvement means a lack of professionalism. In their opinion, a teacher should always be neutral, in their words, "objective," an observer whose main task is to organize, guide, and control the situation.

The most challenging task for teachers is to be spontaneous; to improvise, to have the courage to make mistakes, and to be creative and inventive. Often teachers are not used to collaborating with children and taking children's ideas into account rather than imposing their own. They are afraid to "make mistakes" or "lose control" of the children in their charge and in fact are avoiding, even resisting, spontaneity and creativity in their work. These are the main reasons why creative drama methods are used to develop the play skills of both children and adults.

We plan our creative drama interventions to promote the development of mature forms of creative play among children in our Play Lab. The general aim of our research is to find out if play interventions affect the play skills of the participants. The first step in our intervention is to present a very short (7–10 minutes) puppet show to the children during our morning meeting. Usually we start with a traditional animal folk tale and develop it further, adding new events and adventures that "borrow" some of the themes and ideas from the children's play during the previous session. Often children make comments, and students also directly ask the children to give some advice to the characters in a critical situation. Sometimes our puppet presentations have a direct impact and the children develop these adventures further in their play. More often the children take only some of the ideas and then use them quite creatively in their play.

In this study we are not analyzing the connections between the students' puppet presentations and children's creative play. The goals of this particular study are: to define the criteria of successful creative drama interventions by adults, and to discuss how participation in creative drama interventions affects the students.

RESEARCH METHODOLOGY

Description of the Project and Participants

The present study is part of a larger research project that has been carried out in the Play Lab[3] at the Kajaani campus of Oulu University in Finland since 2002. The two main goals of the project are: (1) to study children's play and its effects on child development, and (2) to involve university students in this process as a part of their studies and research activities.

Creative club activities for children are a part of the mandatory university courses for the students studying early childhood and primary education (future kindergarten and elementary school teachers). Three courses; Pedagogy of Under 3–Year-Olds[4], Pedagogy of Play[5], and Guiding Learning in Early Childhood[6], organize their studies around Play Lab activities. Each course is organized so that every second week students have a theoretical lecture for 2 hours, and every week they have 4 hours of seminar and 4 hours of practical work with children in the Play Lab. In addition, students might spend 1–2 hours for planning and preparing the upcoming activities. Most of the students attending the course study together for 3–5 years, but there are always 2–8 students from classroom teacher education programs attending the courses as well.

Creative drama methods are studied as a part of the play pedagogy course. Students are introduced to several creative drama methods and the main principles of improvisational theatre, and have to apply them to working with children. We call it learning by practicing. The creative drama methods most broadly applied are playworlds (Lindqvist, 1995) (book and video available in Finnish), dialogical drama with puppets (Bredikyte, 2000), teacher in role (Toye & Prendville, 2000), 'mantle of the helper' (Heathcote & Bolton, 1995), and story dramatizations (Paley, 1992, 1997, 2001).

Our main goal is to find the most appropriate and effective ways to support the development of children's joint play. Creative drama is our main tool. In their everyday practice with children, students use the dialogical drama with puppets method as a part of a morning circle, preparing a short puppet presentation or dramatization. Later the same students, in roles or with puppets, might join children's play activities and help to develop a joint playworld. We use all of the methods in a rather free manner. Many students apply creative drama methods later when practicing in day care and primary schools, building various playworlds in their classrooms while implementing narrative learning projects.

The Setting of Mature Narrative Roleplay

The experimental development of play has taken place at Oulu University campus in Kajaani, Finland since 2002. Our site is a club of children's creative play. Approximately 62 children (0–6 years) from 30 families have attended the laboratory for creative play over the past six years. The club's activities form part of the university courses in early childhood education.

Once a week a group of 15–20 children (between the ages of 3 months and 5 years) attend the club for creative play and participate in specific activities with the university students. Children come with their parents and stay for 4 hours. During each session a music teacher and a university teacher/ researcher are also present.

The setting of the play environment is a small, cozy house on campus. There are seven rooms, including a kitchen and a space in the basement that can be used for creative activities. Eight main areas are available for children's activities: (1) blocks and building play area, (2) home play area, (3) story reading, telling and music area, (4) an area for board games, (5) meeting & art area, (6) handicraft area, (7) creative drama area, and (8) a kitchen. All the areas are "open" to the children, and students are available to provide necessary support.

Organization of the Activities

At our site, researchers and students discuss and plan the curriculum and schedule all activities in detail; later the students are responsible for the practical implementation of the planned activities with the children. After each play session, the activities are discussed in a seminar. Students and the researcher watch the video material (important and interesting episodes), reflect upon field notes, share their ideas, and plan the activities for the next session.

The activities can be divided into three major types: (1) guided activities for all children, (2) "free" supported activities in small groups or individually, and (3) independent play activities in small groups or individually. Only group activities and some projects are planned in detail, other activities are improvised.

At the beginning of our work (in the autumn), time is divided equally between the above activities, but our goal is one hour of adult initiated activities and two hours of child initiated activities. In principle, we try to keep this balance and provide enough space and time for the children's independent play activities. The general rule is that the children's participation is voluntary; they can come and leave whenever they wish regardless of the plans and time schedule. Consequently, the only way to attract children is to build an interesting and motivating activity.

At the Play Lab, three to four students are assigned to support children's play in the centre, one student is responsible for video recording, and one to two students write field notes. All these students, except the person filming, may become involved in joint play. Often students stop writing and join in the play if they suddenly come up with a good idea. We have decided that creative play is the most important activity, so the other activities of the adults are subordinated to it.

The students are assigned to promote joint narrative play among the group of children remaining in the creative drama centre after the puppet presentation. They are instructed to take an active role in children's play and to apply the most suitable elements of the creative drama methods. Students are encouraged to use the whole building and to connect narrative play activities with other creative activities. In practice, this means that the players might be using all rooms in the house to create such environments as a "castle", "forest", "robber's hiding place", "jail", "far away land" etc. Activities such as making different props and costumes, drawing a map, painting a castle, or constructing a ship or a house are also a part of the play.

Methods of Data Collection and Analysis

We gathered qualitative data from twelve-play sessions during one term focusing on narrative role-play activities in the creative drama centre (occupying two rooms on the ground floor) after the students' puppet story presentation. All activities in the site were recorded on video with several cameras, and the recordings were later analyzed in planning seminars with the students. During the six years of the study, video recording and field notes have become a natural part of the environment.

We obtained four types of data from each play session:

1. A joint report by the group responsible for the activities in the centre, which is compiled after the session.
2. A report by the person filming, usually student or researcher, compiled after the session.
3. A report by the researcher based on his/her field notes and video observation, compiled after the session.
4. Student observations (1–2 persons) about the activities. The observations are made during the session; they are edited later and reflective observations are added.

The reports are written independently by each group and later compared and discussed during joint seminars with all participants (students). All reports include reflection at the end. Student's reflections are used as an important resource for analyzing play sessions and interpreting the data. Their experiences of direct participation in play enable us to capture the inner state of an adult player in addition to the changes in children's participation.

The analysis of play sessions and student interventions starts with writing explicit narratives of each session. Data from the four different types of reports are included in the written narratives. In addition, each play session is characterized taking into account the following aspects: student's and children's involvement (i.e., children stay in the centre during the whole session, very concentrated, refusing to eat or leave); eagerness and enthusiasm (i.e., children demand students to play with them, ask to continue the theme/play, invite other children, etc.); joyfulness and playfulness (i.e., shining eyes of the participants, excited voices, laughter, jokes, etc.). These three aspects of involvement, eagerness, and playfulness are used in grouping play sessions into 'successful' and 'unsuccessful'. Ten play sessions were defined as successful and two sessions as unsuccessful adult interventions.

The following questions were used in a general evaluation of play interventions:

1. Was the play social?
2. Was the play imaginative and creative? (Vygotskian definition of reproductive and productive imagination is used)
3. Was it persistent?
4. Was the play challenging? (Requiring work at the edge of one's abilities)
5. Were participants in roles?
6. Was some story line (sjuzhet) constructed?

The next set of questions describe more precisely the process of play interventions:

1. How was the activity constructed:
   a. Spontaneously improvised, co-constructed.
   b. Partly planned, partly improvised.
   c. Initially planned and creatively implemented, or imposed and guided.
   d. Shared, parallel or separate simultaneous activities in the same area.
   e. Spontaneous and chaotic, not guided.
2. Was the main theme (fabula) shared by participants?
3. How was dramatic tension created?
4. Were participants emotionally involved?
   a. What was the level of involvement (flow experience) of the participants?
   b. What was the level of performance? (Classification of Morgan and Saxton, 1987 is used).

5. Were the dialogues creatively improvised? What kinds of dialogues prevail?
   a. In role
   d. Out of role (metacommunication)
   c. Out of play conversations

By answering these questions, the specific aspects of each play session and the character of adult intervention, including the phases of preparation, implementation, and reflection, were revealed. Explicit play narratives were followed by short characteristics of each play session.

FINDINGS

In the following paragraphs we describe our findings after analyzing all 12–play sessions. First we give short descriptions of successful and unsuccessful play sessions and describe their main characteristics. Then we describe in detail the main features of successful adult intervention and discuss their impact on the student teacher's professional development.

Successful Play Intervention

The play session named "Castle play" was the most successful play activity during the autumn term. The activity lasted about 90 minutes, 8 children of various ages (from 3.8 to 10–years-old) and 4 students participated. Here is the short story line of the play:

> Three brave knights (three boys in knight's costumes) started fighting and chasing a dragon. At the same time, two girls decided to build a castle. After the castle was built, two robbers attacked the castle and stole two crowns. Everyone went searching for the robbers and missing crowns. A King from a distant kingdom made a visit to the castle. After his visit, a letter from the robbers demanding money in exchange for the crown was received. Knights decided to arrange a "trap" for the robber and to catch him. The plan succeeded and one robber was caught and taken to the jail. At that time, another robber captured the King and kept him in an unknown hiding place. Brave knights went to search for him, and soon they found the robber, rescued the King, and brought the robber to the jail. The King was brought to the castle and a party was arranged. (6 episodes)

Analysis of Key Characteristics of Successful Play Intervention

The theme of play came from the children and was shared by all participants. Three boys started the play. Immediately after the puppet story presentation, they put on helmets and started running around the building, fencing with swords, and proclaiming that they were searching for the dragon. Students and children were familiar with this "historical" play theme that had been going on for six years in our play lab. Brave knights fighting evil was the leading play theme among our children since the first year of play lab activities.

Students took the children's idea as a starting point for joint play. They proposed building a castle and at once two girls joined the activity. One student took the role of the princess and through that role could "guide" children in some complicated situations. Other students changed their roles depending on the emerging script of play.

When the castle was ready, one knight discovered a message in a castle post box that said, "Be aware of the robbers!" Everyone became very excited, and the knights were ready to defend the castle. Just a few minutes later the two robbers (students in roles) attacked the castle and managed to grab two golden crowns in spite of the fact that knights were fighting fiercely.

After the attack, the children became interested in who the robbers were and where they went when they disappeared. They started running around and searching for any possible traces of evidence about the robbers and their hiding place. One girl proposed putting two guards at the entrance to the castle in case the robbers returned. Two students, the same ones who played the robbers, took the roles.

After the first attack more children joined the activity, and it became clear that the student's participation was a success. Soon a new message was found in the post box. Each new event was introduced/constructed quite spontaneously depending on the situation and children's behavior. The student who was filming wrote in her report, "The storyline had not been planned exactly; the events in play activity were evolving naturally." (Anne's field notes, 10.18.07).

The students were constantly having a dialogue with the children and decided on their next steps in response to the children's actions. For example, when children were building a castle, the students decided to have a post box near the gates because one boy was very eager to be a postman bringing newspapers to the castle. After that, the students decided to put the robber's message in the postbox, prepare a robbery episode, and evaluate the children's reaction. The excitement and shining faces of the children was a sign for the "robbers" to proceed.

There were not many explicit negotiations between students and children; mainly it was the student in the role of princess who was participating in the children's discussions. She was the one who was passing children's ideas to other students. For that reason, each new event was to a certain degree unexpected by the children, but the next step was made only after children reacted to the previous one. For example, if children showed no interest in some idea or event, the students would make a new proposal and move in another direction. In this way, the students managed to keep the children's interest and involvement during the whole activity.

This principle of "turn taking" in constructing play events is crucial. Such dialogic interactions can be described as "creative improvisations" (Sawyer, 1997, 2001) that are typical for children's pretend play. The concept of "co-regulated communication" by Fogel (1993) may also be relevant here. The character of the interactions reveals that the activity is co-constructed and co-regulated between students and children.

Students reported in their reflections that it was very challenging to decide what are the right moves and how to enact them. On the other hand, seeing how involved and excited the children were was a huge satisfaction. "It was both fun and tense because we became more and more involved with play activity and we did not want to spoil it. If we think now about what happened we were really playing, and it was fun and challenging at the same time" (Henna's field notes, 11.18.07).

An outstanding attribute of the activity was the deep emotional involvement of the participants. Both students and children were immersed in the activity. This might be connected with the student's decision to take roles and enter into the children's play. The students were always encouraged to take roles in the creative drama center, but not all the students were eager to do so. On this occasion, though, they felt it was the only way to involve children of such different ages in joint play. As a result, all of the students were in roles as well as most of the children.

The students managed to create quite a complicated plot right from the beginning. Some events were planned, such as the robbery and the "trap" for the robber, but some just arose from the situation. For example, when students needed more characters they had to play several different roles in different episodes. The tricky thing was that two guards protecting the castle from the robbers had to play the robbers as well. When the robbers first appeared, their faces were covered and children did not identify them. But the older girls became suspicious about the guards and led the rest of the children to find the truth.

Some children were very smart players and demanded that the events should be planned and performed "truthfully". This posed a challenge to the students. The participation of older children "forced" the students to be inventive and creative in telling lies, changing costumes, and finding hiding places in order to keep the secret as long as possible. Without older children, such exciting and long play activity probably would not have occurred. Their participation raised the play to the construction of a complicated plot-play narrative. The improvisational character of student intervention introduced a qualitatively new level of challenge and developmental impact. It is important to note at this point that creative improvisation of this nature can only be learned through practicing (Lobman & Lundquist, 2007, Sawyer, 2001).

We can conclude that the activity was spontaneous, improvisational and creative. Students were constructing a coherent storyline through dialogic interactions with children. A dramatic tension was created with robber's roles, dangerous events, and deep 'in role' involvement. Activity was spontaneously improvised and co-constructed in a dialogic form; the students took into account the children's ideas all the time. All of the students and most of the children were in roles and emotionally involved; "flow" elements were evident in most of the play episodes. Most dialogues were in roles and creatively improvised. The activity was very challenging and motivating. Emotional involvement of the participants is an essential character of successful play intervention.

Unsuccessful Play Intervention

The play session "Ship play" was one of the two unsuccessful play interventions during the autumn term. It lasted about 40 minutes; 3 children (from 3.4 to 5–years-old) and 4 students participated. One child "escaped" in the middle of the play and returned only for the last episode. Another young boy was constantly leaving "boring" episodes and coming back when more exciting events happened.

Two children, a girl and a boy, started building and furnishing a ship, and the students supported them. After the ship was ready, children went shopping, prepared food, and went to sleep. There were two princesses in the ship, while the other participants were just travelers. At a certain moment robbers attacked the ship and stole the crown. Everyone left to chase the robbers and search for the crown, but the search was unsuccessful. Then the travelers received a message with a map showing where the stolen crown was hidden. They started a new search but couldn't find the crown. Back in the ship, the travelers ate, slept, and searched again. Two robbers attacked the ship and tried to kidnap the princess. One robber was caught and the other one disappeared with the princess. The children searched for the princess, rescued her and finally found the crown in a dark Goblin's cave. (5 episodes)

Analysis of Key Characteristics of Unsuccessful Play Intervention

In their reports, the students wrote that they were not satisfied with the activity. They described the activity as "boring" for both them and the children.

The students were surprised that the children were not emotionally involved in the episodes with the robbers. They thought it would be the most exciting event and create dramatic tension. Instead, long episodes of fishing, making food, and sleeping in the ship were more attractive for both the children and the students.

Careful observation and analysis of video material revealed that the robbery episodes were poorly organized and performed. When two robbers (students in roles) attacked the ship it didn't look like an attack. Two persons with masks unexpectedly entered the room, took two crowns and simply left. The princess (student in role) made a "surprised" face and was looking at the children as if waiting for some reaction from them, but the children looked at her and were not sure how to react. "The robbers have stolen our crowns, we should go to search for them," said princess in a calm voice. Without enthusiasm several children (2 boys and a girl) followed her.

The search episode was rather long (about 7 min.). Children were going around the building without finding any clues or signs, nothing unexpected happened, and they were observing other children's play more than searching for the robbers.

When the searchers returned back to the ship, the students proposed going fishing, then eating and sleeping. This episode was again long (10 min.), but children and students enjoyed it and were more involved than in the robbery and search episodes.

In the morning, the message with a plan showing the robber's hiding place was found in the ship. Children and students went to search for it but did not find anything. After they returned to the ship, two robbers (students in roles) attacked the ship. One robber was captured and imprisoned by children; the other disappeared with a princess (student in role). Children went to look for the princess. Two children soon returned back to the ship. One boy, in the role of a knight, and two students finally found the princess, and then an interesting situation occurred. "When we finally found the kidnapped princess, Erno (3.4 years-old boy in role) the knight did not want to save her and said that we (students) should save her. We burst into laughter. Somehow I was unable to take the play seriously. We were pretending that we were playing and could not hide our smiles in most important episodes. Children definitely noticed this and were not seriously involved as well." (Anne's field notes, 11.22.07). The comment reveals that students did not take the activity seriously.

After the princess was rescued, students initiated two more search operations because the crowns were still missing. One of the operations was a disaster; two boys left for other play activities and the girl stayed to make food in the ship. Then a new message came hinting that the crowns were hidden in goblin's cave. The cave was set up in a dark cellar room. This "dangerous" and exciting task mobilized and brought together all three children, and even two younger girls joined them.

Discussions with the students revealed that they planned the play events beforehand and tried to follow the plan during play session. The students implemented pre-planned activity, formally taking roles and guided children to follow their plan. The last most successful episode in Goblin's cave was not pre-planned; it came as a spontaneous idea to one student when she saw that children were not interested in playing together anymore. This episode saved the whole activity; both the students and children clearly enjoyed it.

It is important to prepare for the intervention. In fact all of the students were asked to make some plan and to discuss possible ideas to be elaborated during the play session with the children. This "bank" of alternative ideas is a part of the preparation. The success of the intervention depends heavily on the implementation of the plan. At this stage, the emotional involvement, the 'perezhivanie' of the evolving situation, which should result in emotional sensitivity to the situation and the people involved, becomes very important. One has to be "open" to children's proposals and ideas and be ready to incorporate them. Sensitivity helps the students to make the right choices, and all pre-planned ideas provide the basis for spontaneous improvisation.

Such sensitivity was missing during most of the episodes in this intervention. Students did not leave the space for the children's ideas to be incorporated into their plan and were not ready to improvise together. The character of the implementation stage is best described in the report by the student who was filming: "No spontaneity, no creative improvisations, no dramatic tension, and the whole activity is 'not alive' for the students" (from the summary of play session, 11.22.07).

This might explain the reason it was so difficult to find the theme for joint play. "It was rather difficult to start the play, although children were waiting for us to start playing with them right after the puppet presentation. I couldn't find out what the kids were interested in. In addition, Roosa (4.6) and Urho (5) seemed to have no interest in playing together." (Niina's field notes, 11.22.07). Instead of proposing several ideas for joint play, students were 'pushing' their plan, which resulted in individual children constructing their 'own' play themes inside the main play.

The whole activity was not coherent; the episodes were all very different from each other. The episodes connected with the robbery were less successful than episodes in the ship. During home-type play episodes in the ship students were more involved, more relaxed, and even spontaneous. There was an impression that students were somehow resistant to playing the robbers story. Why, then, did they try to introduce robbers into their play? Probably because they knew that this was the favorite play theme for many participating children, or maybe they were afraid to change their plan.

Joint discussions revealed that the students were not trying to construct a plot that would be interesting and exciting for them. That's why they were not motivated to participate and really play with children. Their roles and interactions with the children were formal; the students were not emotionally involved in the activity. A lack of student emotional involvement is one of the explanations for unsuccessful play intervention.

We can summarize that the activity was planned beforehand and later implemented following the initial plan. It felt more like a stereotypical home play (i.e. long episodes of preparing food, eating, sleeping), with episodes from stereotypical robbers play mixed in, which was quite boring for both the students and the children. The storyline was a schematic repetition of previous play sessions except for the last episode in the Goblin's cave. Although the story line seemed coherent, the play activity itself was more like a collection of separate episodes. No dramatic tension was present in spite of the fact that some students and children were in roles (not in all episodes) and pirates were attacking the ship. Children did not want to search for the princess when the pirate captured her. There were very few in-role dialogues, and those that occurred developed mostly out of play conversations.

We were happy that only two intervention sessions were 'unsuccessful'. On the other hand, analysis of these two sessions with students became a very important learning opportunity. By analyzing the student's reflections, watching the videotaped episodes, and comparing these unsuccessful episodes with successful ones, we managed to grasp the factors necessary for a successful intervention.

PLAY INTERVENTION AS A TOOL FOR PLAY DEVELOPMENT

As a result of the analysis of 12 play sessions, the following characteristics of the students actions that led to successful adult intervention were singled out: (1) motivating shared theme; (2) active 'in role' participation of students; (3) emotional involvement of students; (4) dialogic character of interactions; (5) dramatic tension in play script; (6) coherent and fascinating script; (7) elaboration of the 'critical' turns in play. In the following sections we will examine each of these characteristics in order to understand the necessary criteria for successful adult play intervention.

The Motivating Theme

The theme of danger was the main theme of all the play sessions during the autumn. This was a theme of serious debate amongst the adults involved. The theme had already been dominant among 4 to 5–year-old boys for the previous four years. New children came but the theme continued to live despite the students' resistance. Some kind of resistance was raised every time when a new group of students started the course in Play Lab. Some of the students claimed that the theme of danger, and all kinds of fighting, is "violent" play, which should not be supported, in educational institutions. After long discussions between researchers, students and parents, the students agreed to build play activities 'exploring' the theme of danger. This decision did not eliminate other possible play themes if they were to arise during the course of activities.

Really exciting play started only when a mysterious and dangerous event happened or a character created a dramatic tension. Often the idea came from the children. The importance of the theme of danger is revealed in children's active participation in creating tension. From the third play session on, children started 'helping' students in creating tension in joint play. In addition to the robber's character, the girl Roosa (4.6) introduced a troll's figure. A young boy, Erno (3.4), introduced robbers (session 5), during the next play session (No 6). He actively searched for and arrested the robbers, but in a few minutes, when appointed to guard the prison, he set them free (4 times during one play session). During the following session (No 10), a girl, Lotta (4.10), took the leading role and created tension by introducing a pirate captain and a robber who had stolen Santa Claus, his compass, and a Christmas tree just three weeks before Christmas! During the next play session (No 11), a boy, Jyrki (4.6), introduced dangerous Snowmen, living on a far away, northern island. During the last play session (No 12), after a student had read a message announcing the King's arrival, the children unanimously decided that the mysterious King must be dangerous and that they had to be ready to protect their castle.

In role participation and emotional involvement. The most critical step of student participation was a decision to take a role and enter into the children's play. The 'in role' position forced the participants to follow the rules imposed by the role and to think both as a chosen character and as themselves simultaneously. This was the critical moment for many students, when they realized that at the same time as they act, they should carefully follow the children's reactions to the character's behavior. "I suddenly realized that I could guide children's reactions and behavior through the behavior of my character!" (Viljami's field notes, 11.01.07).

This is the moment when students become emotionally involved in the relationship both with their own character and with the participating children. They become sensitive to the evolving situation and the situation starts motivating their further steps. At this point, the student may start a dialogue between his character and the children that helps him to clarify an interesting theme or topic for their joint interaction.

In all twelve sessions, students applied the same intervention strategy; they took roles and made attempts to enter into the children's play. Ten attempts were successful and two failed. The explanation can be found in the fact that in both unsuccessful cases the students only announced their roles without being deeply involved in the activity. A student reflected in her report: "We were pretending that we were playing." (Anne's field notes, 11.20.07). The experiences from successful play sessions are quite different: "It was exciting for them [the children] to see that adults were completely immersed in play. For me it was funny to see my peer students' involvement in roles, and it helped me to carry out my own role as the Captain." (Anna's field notes, 10.04.07). Deep involvement results in flow experiences (Csikszentmihalyi, 1990) and a high level of performance. This is evident from both the video observations and the students' written reflections.

The students emphasized that their involvement was closely related to the children's involvement. "The children were very enthusiastic and involved and I noticed myself that I was totally involved and absorbed by the play activity." (Henna's field notes, 11.01.07). It seems that involvement in the emotional 'perezhyvanie' is one of the most important characteristics of a successful play intervention. Some students indicated that role position helped them to understand what the imaginary situation really meant. "For the first time I realized the meaning of the imaginary world. This is the world which you can create as you wish because you create the rules of this world. It gives you a feeling of freedom, and the only limit is your own imagination. At the same time, it is a "tricky" freedom, because you can destroy the imaginary world as soon as you break the rules you have created…" (Niina's reflections, 1.15.2008).

The Character of the Interactions

An important aspect of a successful intervention is the character of the interactions between children and students. In successful sessions, these interactions are spontaneous and dialogic; students listen to and hear the children's ideas and use them as a starting point of joint activity. The students reflected on such moments, "We tried to bring new elements into play … but at the same time it is important to keenly observe children and pick up hints from them about the direction of a fruitful play activity. … Such play requires rather heavy thinking in a situation where nobody knows what to do next. But the intensive observation of children helps a lot." (Anna's field notes, 10.04.07).

Students involved in all of the successful sessions sought to cooperate with the children as the only way to construct an exciting play activity. Sawyer (1997) pointed out that one of the most improvisational activities of 3–to 5–year-old children is social pretend play. It is no wonder that the two most successful activities were spontaneous improvisations with no initial plan, just a very general idea. In such cases, genuine interaction is the only productive way to move forward. A set of guidelines that improvisational actors have developed for their work were very useful to the students, especially "no denial", "don't write script in your head", and "listen to the group mind" (Sawyer, 2001). All of the participating students in successful sessions reported on the improvisational character of play activities. They also described two aspects of such improvisational activities: challenge and enjoyment. "It was fun and challenging at the same time". (Henna's field notes, 11.18.07).

Motivating Aspects of Adult Participation

A coherent and fascinating plot was extremely important for motivating student involvement. Students were talking about the feeling of satisfaction and excitement they had when they managed to co-construct an exciting storyline that captured the attention of all of the participants.

There were additional important aspects in successful activities that made those activities exciting and motivating for the students. Often the same students played several roles, constantly changing costumes, which is usual in children's play. Some students played both a castle guard and a robber, or a policeman and a robber, during the same session. Sometimes they helped the children (as policeman or guard) to search for themselves (as robbers). Some children did not realize that the students had dual roles, but older children suspected it without being able to identify the real persons behind the role. Suspicions created additional tension and students wanted to keep the secret as long as possible.

Students wrote about humor and having fun together. "We had a lot of fun playing together. Every time as someone would propose some 'crazy' idea, we supported it and were eager to implement it immediately!" (Niina's field notes, 10.04.07). Besides playing with the children, the students were also playing among themselves so there were several levels of play going on at once. When the students experienced the state of deep emotional involvement with the children, they realized that unexpected turns in a story line were crucial for their own involvement and participation, so they started improvising and being more spontaneous. For example, as time went on they created unexpected, funny or provocative situations more often. One student (Henna's field notes, 11.01.07) explained that it was a great satisfaction to see a look of surprise or excitement on other students' faces. "Such situations just inspired me and gave feeling of satisfaction!" she admitted. Even though the main story line was planned together, there was always space for improvisation in successful play interventions.

It seems that this multi-layered play is a necessary condition of real adult involvement and creativity. Playing together has to be fun for adult participants as well. This multi-layered aspect of play was not present in the unsuccessful play interventions. That might also be the reason why some students described in their reflections that it was difficult to participate. We presume that participation for the students was difficult because the children were not exited and sometimes even not interested (they would leave the play activity or were coming and leaving constantly). We think that the level of children's involvement is connected with the level of adult involvement; children are very sensitive and have a perfect intuition to detect who is really playing and who is just pretending.

Critical turning points in play activity. Properly handling the critical 'turning points' is a significant factor characterizing successful adult play intervention. At such moments, play activity slows down, becomes repetitive and boring, and moves towards a dead end. Adult help is crucial at these turns. In all successful sessions, the students managed to provide appropriate help. Participation in successful play sessions demonstrated how students could anticipate when the play was becoming boring before the children explicitly expressed it. In those situations, the students have to do something (introduce a new character, turn of events, etc.) before the dead end. On the other hand, students admitted that interesting play activity can not last forever (our play sessions lasted from 45–90 minutes), so it is important to plan a logical ending which provokes children to develop the same theme next time.

All these listed criteria are very closely intertwined, all are necessary steps in a successful adult intervention, and all bring about certain changes not only in the children but in the students as well.

DISCUSSION

Play Intervention is carried out for the sake of improvement, help, or "provocation", which in turn will move the activity and the children's level of performance forward. Our goal in intervention is to initiate the construction of joint play activities, or playworlds, (Lindqvist, 1995), lasting for a period of time.

Construction of a playworld can be seen as an activity that supports the development of new skills and competencies (including the whole variety of cultural/symbolic tools) in the participants. We also want to see the deeper, psychological level. For us a creative process that transforms human experiences is essential. In a playworld, all of the participants become involved in experiencing, or 'perezyvanie', a common phenomenon. This process requires participants to "step out" of their own understanding and to "meet" the understanding of 'another'. Often it is a dramatic clash of two, three or more different understandings based on different experiences.

The playworld creates the opportunity to acquire shared experiences and, as a result, new understanding. Shared experiences foster change in people and move them to a new level of functioning (including new skills) because of the deeper relationship and deeper understanding of both the phenomenon and each other. The process is dynamic and dialogic; participants constantly "force" each other to move forward exploring new ideas and new possibilities. We think this is the mechanism of how the Zone of Proximal Development in play and in interactions is created.

Students described in their reports and discussions some of the changes. Our play interventions were planned with the aims of supporting the development of children's play and providing opportunities for the university students to develop their competence in guiding children's play. We have to admit that the impact on the students was beyond our expectations. The experiences of the students participating in successful play sessions became a significant step in their professional growth as teachers. Here are some conclusions from students' discussions and final reports.

1. It is not simple to play with children, participation in play requires:
   a. Learning the 'language' of play
   b. Real involvement—"once accepted you really have to play, not just 'pretend' that you are playing…"
2. Play with children is a challenge but also a pleasure.
3. Playing requires creative thinking, improvisational skills and the courage to explore new possibilities.
4. Children like adults who play with them; they view them as friends.
5. Playing with children helps to understand their ideas and their thinking better.
6. It is amazing how easily an adult in role can influence a child's behavior!
7. If children are deeply involved in play, they are able to concentrate well for a long time.
8. If play is motivating, children can learn many things that are necessary for the activity.
9. The ability required of the teacher is to learn to be involved in play and to be able to observe the whole situation as if from the outside at the same time.

In teacher education, play intervention may seem a waste of time when the immediate benefits are not visible. Sawyer (2001) points to the potential of play in his emphasis on the improvisational character of play: "By creatively improvising their play drama, children are learning the creative skills that are essential for everyday social life." (p. 109).

The actual process is quite slow, and changes in an individual child's behavior are easier to notice than group level changes. It takes a long and 'hard' play before children become skilful players with the ability to construct a play story together. The same could be said about adults; it takes a long time of practicing before adults become competent players.

CONCLUSIONS AND IMPLICATIONS

Analysis of student's participation in play interventions provides us with some significant insights into teacher education. Participation in play interventions (in-role participation) appeared to be a difficult task for most students. It took some time (2–4 weeks) before they became involved in joint play activities with children.

More careful analysis of the sessions and comparison of both successful and unsuccessful sessions enabled us to define the most significant aspects of successful adult interventions: (1) motivating shared theme; (2) active 'in role' participation of students; (3) emotional involvement of students; (4) dialogic character of interactions; (5) dramatic tension in play script; (6) coherent and fascinating script; (7) elaboration of the 'critical' turns in play. The most critical aspect is emotional involvement, which is closely connected to the character of implementation (improvisational, spontaneous, creative) and students' ability to construct a multi-layered play.

Collaborative co-construction of joint activity (play, learning) promotes development of all participants, both children and adults (professional growth). Analysis of the students' reflections and final reports revealed the growth of their professional knowledge and understanding obtained from the participation in play interventions. Their increasing ability to function on more professional levels could be observed from session to session as well. A necessary skill of a professional teacher, the ability to capture adults' and child's point of view simultaneously, is best developed in shared play activity with children.

The analysis of play interventions during one term enabled us to capture the changes in individual children's behavior and their ability to participate in joint play with different age children and adults. It did not reveal qualitative changes in children's ability to construct an exciting narrative play activity collaboratively as the time scale is too short to capture such developmental processes. We can observe children transition from simple to more complex forms of play when we analyze longer episodes of play development in our Play Lab. This strengthens our belief that child development could be best supported through the construction of shared activity.

REFERENCES

Bodrova, E. & Leong, D. (2007). *Tools of the Mind: The Vygotskian Approach to Early Childhood Education* (2nd ed.). Columbus, OH: Merill/Prentice Hall.

Bredikyte, M. (2000). *Vaidybinis dialogas su lelemis (VDL)—vaiku verbalines kurybos aktyvinimo metodas* [Dialogical drama with puppets (DDP) as a method of fostering children's verbal creativity] (Unpublished doctoral dissertation in Lithuanian), Vilnius Pedagogical University, Vilnius, Lithuania.

Bruner, J. (1996). *The Culture of Education.* Cambridge, MA: Harvard University Press.

Csikszentmihalyi, M. (1990). *Flow.* New York: Harper Perennial.

Davis, J. H., & Behm, T. (1987). Terminology of drama/theatre with and for children: A redefinition. In J. H. Davis & M. J. Evans (Eds.), *Theatre, children and youth* (pp. 265–269). New Orleans, LA: Anchorage.

Donald, M. (1991). *Origins of the Modern Mind.* Cambridge, MA: Harvard University Press.

El'konin, D.B. (1978). *Psikhologiia igry* [Psychology of play]. Moscow: Pedagogika.

El'konin, D.B. (2005). Psychology of play (I-II). *Journal of Russian and East European Psychology*, *43* (1), (2).

Hakkarainen, P. & Bredikyte, M. (2008). The zone of proximal development in play and learning. *Cultural-historical Psychology*, *4* (4), 2–11.

Hakkarainen, P. (2010). The challenge of teacher competences in Finnish educational system. Kyoto: Kyoto University Press. (In print, in Japanese).

Heathcote, D. & Bolton, G. (1995). *Drama for Learning: Dorothy Heathcote's Mantle of the Expert Approach to Education.* Portsmouth, NH: Heinemann.

Fogel, A. (1993). *Developing through Relationships: Origins of communication, self, and culture.* Chicago: University of Chicago Press.

Kravtsova, E.E. (2007). Igra v neklassicheskoi psikhologii L.S.Vygotskogo [Play in non-classic psychology by L.S.Vygotsky]. In Kudriavtsev V. T. (Ed), *Igra v neklassicheskoi psikhologii.* Moscow: Fond L.S. Vygotskogo.

Lindqvist, G. (1995). *The Aesthetics of Play: A Didactic Study of Play and Culture in Preschools.* Stockholm: Almqvist & Wiksell.

Lobman, C. & Lundquist, M. (2007). *Unscripted Learning: Using Improv Activities Across the K-8 Curriculum.* New York: Teachers College Press.

Mages, W. K. (2008). Does creative drama promote language development in early childhood? A review of the methods and measures employed in empirical literature. *Review of Educational Research*, *78* (1), 124–152.

Mikhailenko N. & Korotkova N. (2001). *Kak igrat s det'mi* [How to play with children]. Moskva: Akademicheskij Project.

Nelson, K. (1996). *Language in Cognitive Development.* New York, NY: Cambridge University Press.

Paley, V. (1992). *You Can't Say You Can't Play.* Cambridge, MA: Harvard University Press.

Paley, V. (1997). *The girl with the brown crayon.* Cambridge, MA: Harvard University Press.

Paley, V. (2001). *In Mrs. Tully's Room: A Childcare Portrait.* Cambridge, MA: Harvard University Press.

Reddy, L. A., Files-Hall, T M., Schaefer, C. E. (Eds.) (2005). *Empirically based play interventions for children.* Washington, DC: American Psychological Association.

Sawyer, R.K. (1997). *Pretend Play As Improvisation: Conversation in the Preschool Classroom.* Mahwah, NJ: Lawrence Erlbaum Associates, Publishers.

Sawyer, R. K. (2001). *Creating Conversations: Improvisation in Everyday Discourse.* Cresskill, New Jersey: Hampton Press, Inc.

Singer, D., Singer, J., D'Agostino, H., DeLong, R. (2008). Children's Pastimes and Play in Sixteen Nations: Free-play Declining? *The American Journal of Play, 1* (3), 2–7.

Sutton-Smith, B. (1997). *Ambiguity of play.* Cambridge, MA: Harvard University Press.

Toye, N. & Prendville, F. (2000). *Drama and traditional story for the early years.* London: Routledge Falmer.

Vygotsky, L. S. (1977). Play and its Role in the Mental development of the Child. In M. Cole (Ed.), *Soviet developmental psychology* (PP. 76–99). White Plains, NY: M. E. Sharpe.

Vygotsky, L. S. (1984). On the Problem of the Psychology of the Actor's Creative Work. In *Sobranie sotchinenyi t.6.* [Collected Works, Vol. 6]. Moscow: Pedagogika.

NOTES

1. Acknowledgments: The project was supported by the funding of the Finnish Academy, project 22256.

2. Names are changed.

3. The research laboratory of play "Silmu" (PlayLab).

http://www.kajaaninyliopistokeskus.oulu.fi/tutkimuskonsortio/developunit.htm, is a part of the Research Center for Developmental Teaching and Learning at Oulu University in Finland.

4. The course lasts for two terms (one term is four months).

5. The course lasts one term.

6. The course lasts one term.

Chapter Four

Critical Performative Pedagogy in Urban Teacher Education: Voices from the Field

Ruth Harman and Kristen French

> Exhaustion—after working for three days preparing for the upcoming MCAS test I felt totally exhausted. Not having lunch or taking a break I just wanted to lie down and sleep. Feelings of anxiety crept in also, not knowing if I was truly prepared for the next three days. I thought about what a waste of time this test is. Not only is it consuming for the students but for the teachers as well. And for what? Closing the doors to the MCAS closet, I slowly walked back to my office, sat down and I was reluctant to move. (Angelina's Journal Entry, May 21 '06)

Written during a children's literature course, Angelina's[1] journal entry highlights how frustrated she felt before administering a battery of high-stakes tests to her students. Most urban schoolteachers have been forced in recent years to deal with similar institutional policies and mandated curriculum standards that directly impact their autonomy in the classroom as well as their relationships with students (Darling-Hammond, 2004; Wright, 2005). For example, after the passage of English-only legislation in Massachusetts in 2002, several teachers in the children's literature course said that they were ordered by administrators to stop using Spanish in classrooms and hallways; in one instance, the school librarian was told to "get rid of all the Spanish language materials" in the library. In addition, to avoid sanctions and potential corporate takeover of their schools if their annual yearly progress did not meet government standards (e.g., see regulations of *No Child Left Behind*, 2001), the teachers in River Town, research site of this study, often felt pressured by administrators to focus on test materials and preparation that did not meet the socio-cultural and linguistic needs of their predominantly Latino and African American students (August & Shanahan, 2006; Nieto, 2000; Wright, 2005).[2] To compound these problems, River Town experienced financial difficulties in the years 2004–2006 that led to the hiring of less experienced administrators and lower salary scales for teachers than in nearby suburban school districts. For these reasons, the teachers in River Town, similar to urban teachers nationwide, often felt isolated and demoralized, especially when they lacked collegial or administrative support in challenging what they perceived to be inequitable school policies or practices (Harman, 2007; Gonzalez & Darling-Hammond, 1997).

To support the teachers and students in River Town and a neighboring school district, a federally-funded university-school alliance called Access to Critical Content and English Language Acquisition (ACCELA) was set up among university faculty, school administrators, teachers, and community members in 2002 (Gebhard & Willett 2008; Willett & Rosenberger, 2005). The ACCELA Master's program in Education and Licensure encouraged teachers to teach "against the grain" in their urban schools (Cochran Smith, 2001) by designing curricular units that were academically rigorous and that also incorporated students' cultural and linguistic funds of knowledge (e.g., Dyson, 1993; Nieto & Bode, 2008; Solsken, Willett & Wilson-Keenan, 2000). Similarly, ACCELA instructors designed the Master's courses in ways that incorporated teachers' cultural and professional interests (see Gebhard, Willett, Jimena & Piedra, in press). The final Master's course, "Critical Multicultural Children's Literature and the Puerto Rican Community," was co-taught by Ruth Harman and two other ACCELA instructors.[3] Ruth invited Kristen French, her partner in several other theater projects, to collaboratively design and teach a performance component of the course.

The purpose of this article is to explore the strengths and challenges of using performance in urban teacher education courses as a tool to engage teachers in voicing and reflectively analyzing tensions in their school districts that impact their classroom practices. Specifically, based on a critical sociocultural framework, our guiding questions in conducting this research were the following: Did our use of Critical Performative Pedagogy (CPP) facilitate critical discussion about underlying reasons for administrative and collegial conflicts and tensions (e.g. issues related to institutional policies on high-stakes school reform)? In addition, did these improvisations and discussions support teachers and teacher educators in brainstorming ways to address the underlying issues that directly impact teaching and learning in their urban school classrooms?

The article begins by providing readers with a definition of key constructs and a description of the literature related to CPP, and describes why and how CPP was incorporated into a multicultural children's literature course. Then, using a thematic and discourse analysis of teachers' scenarios and written critiques (e.g. Fairclough, 1992, 2003), the paper discusses how teachers discursively constructed their identities and how the CPP facilitators encouraged analysis of the contextual factors informing these stories. To conclude, the paper reflects on how our future CPP work can be modified based on the findings from this study.

CRITICAL PERFORMATIVE PEDAGOGY

Our development of CPP in teacher education is informed by Boal's Theater of the Oppressed (TO) and Legislative Theater. In his life-long work (1979, 1992, 1998), Boal used theater in Brazil and elsewhere (e.g., France and the United States) to engage communities in embodying and challenging local social inequities. In Image and Forum Theater (Boal, 1979, 1992), participants are asked to re-imagine conflicts from their everyday lives, which the group collectively sees as oppressive, through verbal and non-verbal improvisations. When watching the scenes that revolve around collectively chosen oppressive issues, the Boalian 'joker' (i.e. facilitator) uses "role reversal" techniques to get the audience involved in resolving the problem. Specifically, members of the audience, the 'spect-actors' (Boal, 1979), are encouraged to interrupt the scene's key moments and take on the role of the protagonist when they feel they can embody a more effective strategy to challenge the antagonist. In another rehearsal technique, "Stop and Think," the spect-actors stop the actors and ask them to explain what their motivation or thoughts were at a particular moment in the scene.

In other words, Boalian techniques such as "role reversal" and "stop and think" encourage spect-actors and actors to pause midway through an improvisation and critically reflect on whether other strategies could be used to shift the power dynamics in a particular social context. United by their collective interest in resolving a burning local issue, actors and spect-actors are all, as Jackson (1992) says, "victims of the oppression under consideration; that is why they are able to offer alternative solutions, because they themselves are personally acquainted with the oppression" (p.xxiv).

In Boal's Legislative Theater (1998), Forum Theater was used in Integrated Centers of Popular Education (CIEPs) in Brazil to provide local communities with a forum to re-imagine oppressive events and to vote on what legislation could solve the social issues. For this purpose, Boal was elected as a Member of Parliament in Rio de Janeiro in 1993; In his three years in the legislature, he pushed through some of the suggested reforms.

Our purpose in developing and using a CPP approach is similar to Boal's approach. Through a critical and collaborative use of performance, teacher educators and teachers view social issues from a multi-layered and critical perspective and reflect on how local action might resolve these issues.

CONCEPTUAL FRAMEWORK

This article draws primarily from multicultural and socio-cultural theories of learning and teaching (e.g., Bakhtin, 1981; Ladson-Billings, 2004; Nieto, 2004; Nieto & Bode, 2008; Volshinov, 1994; Vygotsky, 1978). From a socio cultural perspective on learning, dialogic interaction among peers or between students and teacher is a crucial component in mediating understanding of new concepts and disrupting normative discourses (Bakhtin, 1981; Vygotsky, 1978). Connected to this theoretical perspective, multicultural classroom instruction (Nieto, 2004; Nieto and Bode, 2008) is a heterogeneous process that acknowledges and validates the cultural and linguistic backgrounds of *all* students; and that also critically analyzes the socio historical context of normative literacy practices. Ladson-Billings (2004) sees similarities between multicultural education and jazz: both are composites with "infinite permutations that come about as a result of the dazzling array of combinations human beings recruit to organize and fulfill themselves" (p. 50).

Informed by this conceptual framework, CPP is a *dialogic* and *multi-dimensional* process that provides teachers and teacher educators with a rehearsal space to embody and critically engage with local issues that negatively impact meaningful classroom interactions (e.g., Boal, 1979; Harman & French, 2004; hooks, 1994; McLaren, 1995; Pineau, 1998; Rymes, Cahnmann & Souto Manning, 2008). This dialogic approach acknowledges and incorporates student and teacher cultural funds of knowledge as valid multi-voiced contributions. As Shor (1993) states, in articulating his theory of critical pedagogy: "Dialogue is a mutually created discourse which questions canons of knowledge and challenges power relations in the classroom and in society" (p. 87). CPP heightens this process through the use of participants' imagined and "enfleshed" knowledge of different social issues (e.g. Pineau, 1994; Warren, 1999). As hooks (1994) states, the play with the teacher and student body provides a means to deconstruct how "power has been traditionally orchestrated in the classroom, denying subjectivity to some groups and according it to others" (p.139).

As researchers in the field on teacher education have pointed out, however, reflective practices in the classroom do not always challenge dominant practices (e.g. Fendler, 2003). Indeed, as Zeichner and Liston (1996) discuss, reflective activities such as journaling or autobiographical narratives often tend to remain at the individual level and do not include an analysis of how classroom practices are embedded and informed by specific socio-political forces. Distinct from these more individualized reflective practices, CPP attempts to facilitate discussion and collaborative critique of the socio-political context of local discursive events.

CPP in Urban Teacher Education

In our experience working with urban public school teachers (see Harman & French, 2004), the contextualized use of performance in multicultural teacher education courses has been compelling for three interconnected reasons. First, facing threats of pink slips (consistent district layoffs) or administrative intimidation, teachers in urban school districts often are afraid to discuss institutional policies and practices, even when engaged in discussions and collaborative action research that connects to socio-cultural issues. In a previous ethnographic case study, for example, Ruth found that when participating in the ACCELA Alliance, teachers were often reluctant to express and reflect on institutional practices that impacted their classroom teaching not only during course discussions but also in their own school buildings (Harman, 2007). One teacher admitted to feeling powerless and oppressed in her middle school—she was afraid to contest any school policies, even when she knew they were causing emotional and academic havoc among her students. With such issues in mind, as instructors of the multicultural literature course, we felt that integrating CPP might provide teachers with an alternative space to address and challenge some burning local issues in collaborative and embodied ways.

Second, Boalian rehearsal techniques such as "role reversal" and "stop and think" (Boal, 1979, 1992, 1998) are effective ways to encourage participants in critical education courses to participate in active ways in 'real-life' conflicts. From a critical education perspective, the active participation of the spect-actor in the performance connects very closely to Freire's (1998) concept of praxis, where reflection and action are seen as interdependent and always informing each other. Indeed, the hybrid role of actor and audience in Forum Theater can serve as a powerful metaphor and tool for embodied discussions about the role of agency and discursive power relations in multicultural school settings.

Third, by exploring the multiple strategies that 'spect-actors' use in resolving a problem issue in a particular scenario, participants in teacher education courses can be encouraged to adopt a "perspectivalist" approach to local issues. In order to do this, participants can be encouraged to acknowledge the multiple perspectives in texts, some of which are silenced or distorted by institutional discourses (Delgado & Stefancic, 2001). Thus, we used Forum Theater and its rehearsal techniques in a pre-service teacher education course where participants were asked to study how the story of Rosa Parks was represented and repeatedly distorted in children's textbooks (Kohl, 1995). In pre-forum activities, participants were asked to free write on a particularly troubling event where they felt marginalized or pushed to the side in a school context. In groups of four, they were then asked to pick which of the stories would be used for Forum Theater. In post forum discussions, we asked the participants to write about the connection they saw between the eclipsing of multiple narratives by a dominant master narrative in children's textbooks and their own experiences when deciding which group member's story would be re-enacted and in deciding how the group would represent it. Theme analysis of students' journal entries showed that some students began to understand the importance of maintaining a "perspectivalist" attitude in reading history when they saw how quickly their own stories or those of their classmates were altered to fit their groups' needs.

For these reasons, we have integrated the use of performance into urban teacher education courses as opposed to offering stand-alone workshops. The CPP elements encourage us, as teachers and teacher educators, to analyze the socio-cultural context of our own everyday performances along with written texts and multimedia; and to probe the macro- and micro-interconnections among visual, corporal, and textual semiotics (Harman & French, 2004; Greene, 2001).

Other educators in recent decades also have begun to use performance in teacher-education contexts on a systematic basis. For example, Hermann-Wilmarth (2008) uses performance to push pre-service teachers beyond their usual comfort zone in grappling with social issues. An improvised scene in one course, for example, provided the author, the lesbian instructor of the course, and one of her students, a self-identified conservative Christian, with a context to engage in an uncomfortable but productive dialogue about gay and lesbian issues in elementary education. In a professional development initiative, Rymes, Cahnmann, & Souto Manning (2008) discuss how the use of Boalian techniques provided bilingual teachers with a space to embody and critically reflect upon the power dynamics at play in their interactions with parents and other school stakeholders. The enactment and critical discussion of real-life scenarios heightened participants' awareness of the role of language and gesture in challenging or perpetuating oppressive conditions in everyday encounters.

RESEARCH CONTEXT

The purpose of our multicultural children's literature course was to analyze how culturally diverse children were represented in children's literature and to discuss the real-life experiences of students and their families in River Town and other regions of the United States. To illustrate, in discussing Puerto Rican culture, we read representative literature and analyzed the socio-political context (e.g. *The Red Comb* (Pico & Pico, 1994); *Felita* (Mohr, 1979). We also viewed and discussed documentaries about the experiences of Puerto Ricans in Western Massachusetts and New York. In the final part of the course, facilitated by Dr. Matos, an expert on building family/school relationships (Matos, 2008), the teachers designed a family collaborative project in which they invited students and family members to create cultural texts in their home languages as well as in English.

When designing our course, we agreed that the use of CPP would help ensure that teachers' interests would be incorporated into our course in the same way that the family collaborative project would be used to acknowledge and validate students' cultural interests in the teachers' classrooms. In the sessions prior to the CPP module, we used theater games to get teachers accustomed to moving around and playing in improvised and unstructured ways. We then dedicated two and a half sessions in the middle of the course (approximately 9 hours) to Forum Theater and critical discussion.

We started the CPP module by using Reader's Theater to enact a highly tense moment between an African-American teacher (and mother of the novel's protagonist, Cassie) and two racist school district officials in Taylor's *Roll of Thunder* (1976), a book that had been under discussion in the literary analysis module of the course. After watching and discussing the scene, the teachers were encouraged to think about oppressive conditions they encountered in their schools. Teachers spoke mostly of their feelings of frustration and exhaustion. In her free-write, Christa Carlton wrote the following:

> I primarily work with students who are considered significantly underperforming [i.e. ELLs, at-risk learners]. There's this overwhelming feeling of never being able to catch up that's so exhausting in thoughts alone. Despite the fact that the kids are making significant gains, many of them are still below grade level.

After doing some body sculpting and mirroring activities in which participants sculpted their feelings of frustration onto their partners, the teachers did free-writes on particularly pressing conflicts in their workplace that linked to these emotions. With three other teachers, they then negotiated which scene they would use for Forum Theater. The scenarios they selected were rehearsed and performed for the group. They focused on tensions between mainstream teachers, between ESL and content-area teachers, and between a principal of a school and a teacher.

We then distributed worksheets to each teacher, which asked them to analyze their scenarios by using the same critical framework that they were asked to use in analyzing children's chapter books and multimedia.

1. What is the socio political context of the scene (larger forces at play)
2. What are the power relations among the characters and how do they relate to the socio political context? (e.g., does the main character display agency or lack of agency and why?)

3. What type of relationship does the protagonist establish with the antagonist in the scene (give details in terms of language use, gestures, actions she uses)? How about the other characters in the scene?
4. How does the scene end?
5. What other strategies could possibly lead to a different outcome?

In subsequent discussions, we reflected on the different strategies used by the spect-actors and actors in negotiating these conflicts and how they were informed by larger macro events.

METHODS

Our purpose in collecting and analyzing the data in this course was to see how the use of CPP provided teachers and teacher educators with a space to voice and challenge burning local and institutional issues. From March to June 2006 we collected data on the classroom interactions and written texts of the 21 teachers in the children's literature course, which met weekly for three hours over the course of fifteen weeks. The data collected included video and audiotapes of whole-class and small group activities, scanned copies of teachers' journals and free writing, and copies of children's literature and other curriculum resources.

Based on our conceptual framework, we used critical discourse analysis to explore multilayered connections between the teachers' oral performances and subsequent classroom discussions (e.g., see Fairclough, 1992, 2003). Specifically, Ruth conducted a broad thematic analysis of the scenarios and of the free writing conducted in the CPP module of the course to see what discourses informed discussions and performances. She then consulted with Kristen about the validity of her findings. In the second step of analysis, she transcribed CPP scenarios and discussion and used systemic functional linguistics (Eggins, 2004; Fairclough, 1992) to analyze the use of appraisal and transitivity in teachers' texts. For example, by exploring the use of modals and words of appraisal (e.g. use of would, could, will), she was able to determine what type of relationship the protagonist was establishing with the other characters in each scenario.

FINDINGS

This section describes two representative scenarios, performed by the teachers, which illustrate how CPP provided teachers with a space to voice issues of concern. However, they also show how our facilitation rarely led to a group exploration of the connections between these micro-level discursive events and the socio-political context.

Tensions between Grade-Level Teachers

In 2005, Mary Woods moved to the elementary school where she currently works. She was already involved in the ACCELA Master's program and was seen by the principal as bringing a fresh approach to teaching fourth graders (Field Notes, March 2006). Many administrators and teachers see fourth grade as a pivotal grade because it tends to be when, due to more advanced literacy demands, language minority students often suddenly slump in their high-stakes testing performances (August & Shanahan, 2006). Mary replaced a veteran fourth-grade teacher, who was moved to a lower grade. During the 2005–2006 school year, while participating in the ACCELA courses, Mary felt harassed by what she viewed as the continual complaints and gossip that the veteran teacher was spreading about her in the school. In the Forum Theater scenes, Mary and two co-actors, Christa and Paula, first improvised this gossiping. In the scene below, for example, Paula played the role of the veteran teacher and assumed the role of a disgruntled colleague:

> Veteran Teacher (Paula): I'm really upset about that. And you know, they come over here and they just move you out of your room, they take you out of the positions that you're in, I just, you know, and she goes along with it, she doesn't stick up and say, oh, you know, that should be Ms. Dee's position. No! I, I...
>
> Colleague (Christa): So, how do you feel?
>
> Veteran Teacher (Paula): No! I want to be back where I was. That's where I've been teaching for the last 10 years, why can't I be in the fourth grade, you know? What does she do, what does she have that I don't have?

Linguistically, the veteran teacher's pronominal use and the patterns of transitivity (who does what to whom) positioned her as a victim, displaced by an anonymous group: "*They* come over here and *they* just move you out of your room." In the next turn of talk, Paula continued by conflating the new teacher with "them." Pronominally, "they" and "she" have pushed her to the side.

In the next scene, Christa interacted with Mary, who played the protagonist role in the story:

> Colleague (Christa): Ms. Woods, excuse me, can I talk to you in the other room?
>
> New Teacher (Mary): Sure! Hi!
>
> Colleague (Christa): Hi! How are you? I'm soooo tired of Ms. Dee complaining about you!

New Teacher (Mary): She still is?

Colleague (Christa): She is, she just told me she's upset because you took her fourth-grade classroom. Is there something that I am missing? What did you do to her?

New Teacher (Mary): I didn't do anything to her! The principal gave me the job! (inaudible) since the beginning of summer time

Colleague (Christa): But she's talking behind your back, she's saying so many new things about you.

New Teacher (Mary): I don't know what to say, I'm just trying to ignore her, I, I know she's been talking about me, and I've been doing the best I can to ignore her...and I say good morning to her and good afternoon and . . .

Colleague (Christa): You need to do something about it, or talk to the principal.

New Teacher (Mary): I talked to the principal. The principal wants me to talk to her and I try to have a conversation with her but she just doesn't want to listen to me. She wants to blame me because she thinks it's my fault.

In this interaction, as the new teacher, Mary positioned herself as victim in several turns of talk and also emphasized how she had tried different strategies to get Paula, the veteran teacher, to talk to her. In Line 8, she linguistically highlighted how all her strategies with Paula were futile by a repeated use of the pronoun "I" as the point of departure in each clause and her use of action verbs (I talked to the principal; I try to have a conversation with her) which contrasts with the more static mental and emotion verbs used to describe her antagonist ("she just doesn't want to listen; she thinks it's my fault"). Indeed, the linguistic and rhetorical features of Paula's and Mary's discourse show how they polarized each other in terms of social positioning.

To encourage the spect-actors to dialogue with those on stages, Ruth and Kristen decided at this point to use Boal's (1979) technique of "stop-and-think."

Kristen: All right, start it again and every time you want to, stop the performance and ask any of the characters how they feel or what they are thinking. (Actors start scene again)

Veteran Teacher (Paula): I'm sooo! I can't even look at her! I'm so upset with the fact that, you know, she gets my fourth grade. I have been there for TEN years, and all of a sudden, Ms. Wonderful comes in and gets the job!

Colleague (Christa): Are you really that upset?

Veteran Teacher (Paula): Yes! I am! I just don't understand, I, I

VOICE: STOP! Why do you think she's Ms. Wonderful?

Veteran Teacher (Paula): She took over my job! I've had that job for 10 years! Ten years I've had that job. I put all my heart and soul, spent all my MONEY in that room! And the principal just comes and, and changes her! Because she thinks she's all that, you know? She is going to that program, and she's getting her degree, and, I'm sorry, my knees hurt!

VOICE: Stop. Do you have a degree?

Veteran Teacher (Paula): Yes, I do! I don't know, I don't know!! I'm really upset with that, I'm really upset!

VOICE: STOP! Did you speak with your principal about this before?

Veteran Teacher (Paula): Yes! And she told me that that's what she was told… to make changes but I don't understand why she had to move me…

Voice: Stop! Does the teacher have seniority?

Veteran Teacher (Paula): No! I have seniority over her! That's why I'm really upset!

Voice: Not, not about the job, not about the placement of the job but years…

Veteran Teacher (Paula): Years? Yes! I've been in this district for fifteen years! And she's only been in the system for four!!

Voice: Stop! Why are you blaming the teacher and not talking to the principal about it?

Analysis of these interactions shows how the technique of 'stop-and-think' pushed Paula to heighten her construction of Mary as a threat and nemesis. In other words, the technique was not helpful in getting her to perceive other possible avenues for collaboration with her rival teacher. Similarly, as shown below, the use of 'stop-and-think' techniques triggered impassioned responses from the audience about who was 'right' or 'wrong' in the scenario but little discussion of contextual factors that shaped the conflict. The CPP facilitation did not provoke a deeper multilayered analysis of what happened.

Kristen: Ok, stop, what is your, what is your perspective on what really happened? We know what her perspective is, what is your perspective on this?

New Teacher (Mary): Well, my perspective is that the decision was made by the principal and I just did what the principal asked me to do!

Kristen: Did you know that her feelings were hurt by all that?

New Teacher (Mary): Hmm

VOICE: Yes, she did!

New Teacher (Mary): Yes and no. I was told she knew, and I was told she knew a long time before I took the job and the principal told me she knew and then, hmm, I even tried to talk to her and still she wouldn't budge

VOICE: But did you talk to her?

New Teacher (Mary): Yes, I did. Yes, I did. This whole situation really happened.

VOICE: That's how it really happened, ok.

VOICE: Interesting!

VOICE: What are your feelings about that person's teaching ability? Do you feel that you were a better person than (pause) No, not that you are better, that she had difficulty teaching that grade level? Do you think that? (inaudible)

New Teacher (Mary): Well, yeah, in a way but I don't want to get into that because I don't really know, but I just, I just (pause) Actually, yes, I felt it, yes. But I was just, in my mind, I was just doing what the principal had asked me—she just wanted to swap us around. She felt I would do better in fourth and she would do better in fifth, and also I guess there were some things going on in fourth that weren't really working and they wanted to make a change! And the State was also, the whole beginning (inaudible)

Ruth: So in terms of you know, in terms of the multiple layers we're, we're talking about—so that because she was underperforming… New Teacher (Mary): Well, the State is on us, and

Ruth: Oh, so

New Teacher (Mary): The State was saying that the teacher in fourth grade was not licensed in that area. MCAS, MCAS [the high-stakes tests in Massachusetts] You know?

Ruth: We have a real antagonist here

VOICE: YES. It's all about the tests

Ruth: Candy?

Candy: Well, I'm going to play the other side of this because I'm on a waiver [this means Candy does not have licensure yet] and I've been teaching in the same area for the last three years; and I can say that I would be pretty pissed off, excuse my language, if I got kicked out of my position….We're going to pick you up and take you out of a position you've been teaching and put you into whatever, math, social studies, or an area where I don't know the curriculum and I am not familiar

New Teacher (Mary): But for the situation in which someone didn't really cause the situation and for somebody, for the woman to come to me the way she did, and I explained myself the best I could, she still would not get up, and now it's

> May and she still won't get over it. And now she's talking to me, about me, to other teachers in the building, and it's getting back to me
>
> VOICE: Go tell her to get over it!

In this scenario, Mary repeatedly set up the conflict as between Paula and herself and did not shift from this position. Indeed, when Candy compared her own position as a vulnerable special education teacher to that of the veteran teacher, Mary interrupted and made it clear that she did not see any connection to her situation. As CPP facilitators, what seemed most difficult to negotiate in the scenario was that both teachers and their allies kept the same tone and attitude towards each other, even with interventions and concrete suggestions from the audience about other strategies that might be used. At this point, to create a different dynamic, we suggested that the actors create an additional character, the principal, and talk directly to that person who, in the scenes hitherto, had been constructed as the only one with the power to shift the situation:

> Kristen: Okay, this is the scenario where the principal is proactively trying to help you and engage the two of you in some kind of conversation. What would YOU like to say to your antagonist?
>
> Mary (to Paula): I just want to let you know that I respect you as a person and as a teacher and that my intentions are not to come in and just, you know, just take you out of this position. I just want you to help me. You've been here for a long time, I want you to give me some suggestions and some help and answer questions I may have. I really want to (inaudible) being like this. It's stressful (inaudible).
>
> Paula: Yeah. I'm really hurt that they did this to me and I understand it's not your fault, but when you're coming in and I know, I have been here for fifteen years and you've only been here for three.
>
> Mary: And I understand that, I understand that, I'm not trying to take your job, I'm just, yeah, you know trying to do my job?

The inclusion of this new key player in the Mary Woods scenario led to a shift in how Paula and Mary spoke to each other. For the first time, both characters used conciliatory mental and behavioral verbs (e.g. I understand; I know; I respect you) to establish a new footing in their relationship. In discussing this scene later and how it felt to embody this conflict, Mary said that it felt good that others had suggested strategies that she might use in the future. She felt more supported and less alone in her work. She especially felt stronger after the three-party discussion with the principal, an event that had never happened in her real-life context.

Analysis of the identities adopted by the two characters in this scenario reveals how the Boalian use of 'stop-and-think' heightened the tensions between the two characters. However, the improvised technique of bringing in another character (the principal) shifted how the two characters interacted. On the other hand, the actors or spect-actors never discussed how this particular situation or set of strategies could be used to push back against decisions informed by high-stakes testing or accountability policies. As the CPP facilitators in this course, we could have pushed ourselves and the group to analyze alternative "antagonists" in this scenario and explore why the principal chose to replace the veteran teacher, as well as examine other policies and practices that seemed to be coming from the same fear of high-stakes accountability. As CPP facilitators, we ourselves became too involved in the storyline of the antagonistic relationship between the two teachers; we did not step back and probe the underlying tensions that were dictating the principal's decisions.

Tensions between an ESL and Content Teacher

The second scenario focuses on tensions between an ESL teacher and a content teacher. Integration of content and ESL instruction for ELL students is frequently fraught with tensions in both overseas and US contexts (Arkoudis, 2003). This is partially because content and ESL education are grounded in different pedagogical approaches and epistemological assumptions, but also because local issues such as the lack of proper infrastructure and policies often position teachers from the two areas as competitors rather than collaborators.

In this scenario, Clara Rivera, a Puerto Rican ESL teacher, decided to use Forum Theater to embody the tensions she was experiencing with a mainstream teacher with whom she had to co-teach on a daily basis. Usually quite shy and reticent when speaking in public, Clara, who decided to play the part of the mainstream teacher, spent the first few minutes of the performance strutting around the room with her blouse lifted to reveal her midriff. The other teachers laughed and asked her what she was doing.

> Spectator: Why are you dressed the way you are?
>
> Mainstream Teacher (Clara): Because (inaudible)..., no I'm pulling it up because it shows, her, the, the, the clothing
>
> Spectator: Midriff?
>
> Mainstream Teacher (Clara): She doesn't want to do it on purpose, it's just her clothes are too small...

Clara's impersonation of the mainstream teacher highlights how frustrated she was by the large space she felt that the other teacher inhabited in their shared classroom space. In the scene below, the ESL teacher, played by Karen, tried to discipline two students who were fighting. The mainstream teacher, still played by Clara, came into the classroom and walked straight over to the students, ignoring the fact that Karen was dealing with the situation.

> ESL Teacher (Karen): Excuse me! I saw what happened and (*inaudible*) he didn't make the right choice.
>
> Mainstream teacher (Clara): I understand that but, hmm, I'm taking care of the situation from now on, OK? Sweetie? I take care of it. I'm in control, I'm in control… (Applause)

Linguistically, Clara impersonated her problematic co-teacher through repetition (I'm in control, I'm in control) and a condescending use of the term "sweetie." In discussing the scenario, Kristen and I decided that Boal's role reversal technique would be the best one to use in this scene. We invited spect-actors to come in and take over the role of the ESL teacher, the oppressed party in the scene. In the following scenario, Julia, an experienced ESL teacher, decided to come in and intervene:

> ESL teacher (Judy): Excuse me (stands between student and mainstream teacher). Excuse me, I saw what happened, so are you taking the word of the student over me?
>
> Mainstream teacher (Clara): I'm in control here
>
> ESL teacher (Judy): I don't think so because I saw what happened and this is a student and I'm a teacher
>
> Mainstream teacher (Clara): Excuse me, I can handle the situation. I know Anthony and I know Roma
>
> ESL teacher (Judy): Excuse me, but you can't do that! I think we need to see the principal about this. I will document this and we can have a discussion
>
> Mainstream teacher (Clara): Okay, okay, let me handle the situation here now.
>
> ESL teacher (Judy): Then handle it!! Excuse me, excuse me, while you're handling it I'm taking notes. Okay, handle away…(Laughter and applause)
>
> ESL teacher (Judy): And I'm taking a picture of that shirt!

Although the teachers laughed and joked about the intervention and the overall behavior of the content teacher, in the ensuing discussion they contributed insightful comments about how to address the issue and shared similar stories from their own contexts. For example, in the exchange below, a teacher commented on how the institutional lack of policies about ELL and content co-teachers led to these types of conflicts:

Ruth: Does anybody want to share? Whose story it was, or

Teacher 1: I hear this story all the time from ESL or ELL teachers who are working with other teachers,

VOICE: Yeah, yeah.

Teacher 1: ...and they, they, they usually say, that they feel like they don't have any control in that classroom because the other person in the class, almost treats them like paraprofessional

VOICE: Yes, yes, yes.

Kristen: An equal teacher but that's not what they are in the classroom.

Teacher 1: Right, but

Teacher 2: I have a but for that too (pause) I have a big butt (Laughter)... but here's the thing. The city of River Town has *yet* to come up with a plan, especially for the elementary, of how the class is supposed to be set up with an ELL and a regular teacher in the classroom. Once that's set up then they will have guidelines, as of right now, you have, as they say, you have a homeroom teacher who basically does run the classroom, and you have an ELL teacher who has to play second fiddle.

Subsequently, the teachers continued to discuss the lack of guidelines for ESL instruction, their feelings of frustration, and their sympathy for Clara. In a one-to-one discussion with Ruth, Clara admitted to feeling embarrassed about the way she had portrayed her co-teacher but she said her colleagues' support and the shared understanding that it was an institutional issue also heartened her.

Analysis reveals that the use of performance for this particular conflict increased the level of participation and trust among participants. However, analysis also reveals that we, the CPP facilitators, did not use the alternative space in critical ways. In other words, we failed to engage as a group in collaborative analysis of why ESL and Special Education teachers were positioned in this way; and furthermore how institutional discourses and practices in the district tended to isolate teachers and prevent them from collaborating with colleagues.

DISCUSSION

Before discussing the implications of our study, we return to the guiding questions we asked ourselves in undertaking this study. Namely, did our use of CPP provide teachers and teacher educators with a forum to voice burning local issues and did it facilitate critical discussions about the underlying reasons for these conflicts? And did our work help us to imagine action we could take as a group to resolve some of these local issues? To explore these questions, we look first at the feedback provided to us by the teachers after our course.

In their written critiques of CPP, the teachers seemed to find the use of performance beneficial as a tool to collaboratively react to each other's stories and to share painful experiences about daily interactions with administrators and colleagues in their schools. In her written feedback, for example, one teacher commented: "This CPP module/ activity connects and relates very closely to the experiences of most River Town teachers. Most of us related, either directly or indirectly, to every scenario that was presented." Another teacher wrote about how the use of role-reversal, where a spect-actor becomes part of a drama, could be used with children very effectively: "I definitely will use these activities in my class. I think the way students can jump in and try to fix a problem is an excellent way of doing things. It gives people a way of safely and fictionally confronting those who wronged them."

However, the teachers also felt that the use of CPP had only a limited function in helping to resolve conflicts in any real-life way. One teacher wrote:

> At first I thought this was an excellent way to engage people in a hands-on experience and learn new ways of `directing an act' by redirecting and stopping the participants to shift their perspective. Towards the end, though, I didn't feel quite the same. I felt that I shifted from being productive to unproductive as I listened to people complain (including myself) about their current problems with colleagues and other school personnel with no real solutions.

Overall, in their oral and written comments, teachers seemed positive about the possibility of using performance to open up an alternative space to talk about burning local issues but more hesitant to see it as a dialogic way to challenge institutional practices.

Indeed, data analysis of our own discursive practices highlighted a key weakness in our implementation of CPP. Although our intent was to open discussion about how the conflicts related to institutional policies and practices, we remained too fixed on individual conflicts and solutions and failed to focus enough on establishing macro- and micro-connections. Similarly, Salverson (1994), a participant in several Theater of the Oppressed workshops and a theater community worker in Vancouver, notes that often in using Boalian techniques, practitioners "stay focused on individual's personal stories and spend little time linking them to structural or institutional forces" (p. 164).

In addition, much like the teachers themselves, we felt pressured by time constraints to get back to the other parts of the curriculum in our multicultural literature class. Therefore, the CPP module was not sufficiently in-depth to probe the socio-contextual factors at play or to reflect upon possible collaborative action in which we could engage in order to address them. For example, when discussing the conflict between the ESL and content teachers, several of the teachers mentioned that there were no written policies in place about the respective roles of the two teachers in co-teaching, and that this often led to overt marginalization of ESL teachers, who are often seen as not having any content to teach. By focusing on this very real policy issue in a more prolonged CPP module, we might have thought of ways to speak back.

On a more positive note, we did notice in using CPP that the alternative theatrical space provided teachers and instructors with a more dynamic way of relating to each other. Instead of speaking in abstract ways about the issues in children's literature and the real-life experiences of children of color in the River Town school district, we were galvanized by the use of CPP to think about how our own experiences mediated our understanding of the theoretical readings and our roles as multicultural educators in "underperforming" public schools and urban teacher education programs.

Based on our findings from this study, we believe our future CPP work needs to be more systematically embedded into our courses. Ideally, also, our own concerns as public university teacher educators need to be made part of the Forum Theater. Although we took part in the theater games and played minor roles in the teachers' scenarios, we did not put ourselves completely on stage. To disrupt normative practices, however, we need to move into a pedagogy of discomfort (Boler, 1999), where we deconstruct our hierarchical positions within the academe.

Overall, our findings in this study point to the importance of CPP as an instructional tool in teacher education that can be used to incorporate teachers' social concerns and disrupt binary distinctions between teacher and students. If used in a systematic way over the course of a semester or several semesters, it can also be used as a way to re-imagine and collaboratively resolve local issues. In other words, similar to Boal's use of legislative theater, our intention is to use CPP to break the "fourth wall" of the classroom. As Boal (1979) states, "Theater is action! Perhaps the theater is not revolutionary in itself; but have no doubts, it is a rehearsal of revolution!" (p. 155).

REFERENCES

Arkoudis, S. (2003). Teaching English as a second language in science classes: Incommensurate epistemologies? *Language and Education, 17*, 161–173.

August, D., & Shanahan, T. (Eds.) (2006). *Developing literacy in second-language learners: Report of the National Literacy Panel on Language-Minority Children and Youth.* Mahwah, NJ: Lawrence Erlbaum.

Bakhtin, M. (1981). *The dialogic imagination: four essays.* Austin: University of Texas.

Boal, A. (1979). *Theatre of the Oppressed.* (C. McBride & M.O Leal McBride, Trans.). London, UK: Pluto.

Boal, A. (1992). *Games for actors and non-actors.* (A. Jackson, Trans.). London, UK: Routledge.

Boal, A. (1998). *Legislative Theatre: Using performance to make politics.* (A. Jackson, Trans.). London, UK: Routledge.

Boler, M. F. (1999). *Feeling power: Emotions and education.* New York: Routledge.

Cochran-Smith, M. (2001). Learning to teach against the (new) grain. *Journal of Teacher Education*, *52*, 3–5.

Darling-Hammond, L. (2004). Standards, accountability, and school reform. *Teachers College Record, 106*(6), 1047–1085.

Delgado, R. & Stefancic, J. (2001). *Critical Race Theory: An introduction.* New York: New York University Press.

Dyson, A. (1993). *Social worlds of children learning to write in an urban primary school.* New York: Teachers College Press.

Eggins, S. (2004) *An Introduction to Systemic Functional Linguistics.* London, UK: Pinter.

Fairclough, N. (1992). *Discourse and social change.* Cambridge, UK: Polity Press.

Fairclough, N. (2003). *Analyzing discourse: textual analysis for social research.* New York: Routledge.

Fendler, L. (2003). Teacher reflection in a hall of mirrors: Epistemological and political reverberations. *Educational Researcher*, *32*, 16–25.

Freire, P. (1998). *Teachers as cultural workers: Letters to those who dare to teach.* (D. Macedo, D. Koike, & A. Oliveira, Trans.). Boulder, CO: Westview Press.

Gebhard, M. & Willett, J. (2008). Social to academic: University-school district partnership helps teachers broaden students' language skills. *The Journal of the National Staff Development Council, 29*, 41–45.

Gebhard, M., Willett, J., Jimenez, J, & Piedra, A. (in press). Systemic functional linguistics, teachers' professional development, and ELLs' academic literacy practices. In T. Lucas (Ed.), *Preparing all teachers to teach English language learners.* Mahwah, NJ: Erlbaum/Taylor & Francis.

González, J., & Darling-Hammond, L. (1997). *New Concepts for New Challenges: Professional Development for Teachers of Immigrant Youth.* Washington, DC: Center for Applied Linguistics.

Greene, M. (2001). *Variations on a blue guitar: The Lincoln Center Institute lectures on aesthetic education.* New York: Teachers College Press.

Harman, R. & French, K. (2004). Critical performative pedagogy: A feasible praxis in teacher education? In J. O'Donnell, M. Pruyn and R. Chavez (Eds.), *Social justice in these times (*pp. 97–116). Greenwich, CT: New Information Press.

Harman, R. (2007). Critical teacher education: Discursive dance of an urban middle school teacher. *Language and Education, 21*, 31–45.

Hermann-Wilmarth, J.M. (2008). Creating dialogic spaces around controversial issues in teacher education. *Teachers College Record*, Retrieved at URL: http://www.tcrecord.org (ID Number: 15189. Date Accessed: 4/27/2009).

hooks, bell. (1994). *Teaching to transgress: Education as the practice of freedom.* New York: Routledge.

Jackson, A. (1992). Translator's introduction to the first edition. In Boal, A., *Games for actors and non-actors* (pp.ii-xvi). London, UK: Routledge.

Kohl, H. (1995). The story of Rosa Parks and the Montgomery Bus Boycott revisited. In *Should We Burn Babar? Essays on Children's Literature and the Power of Stories*, (pp. 30–56). New York: The New Press.

Ladson-Billings. (2004). New directions in multicultural education: Complexities, boundaries, and critical race theory. In J. Banks & C.A.M. Banks (Eds.), *Handbook of research on multicultural education* (pp. 50–65). San Francisco, CA: Jossey-Bass.

Matos, N. (2008). *Focusing on strength: Building home-classroom connections with Latino families in urban schools.* Unpublished dissertation, University of Massachusetts Amherst.

McLaren, P. (1995). White terror and oppositional agency: Towards a critical multiculturalism. In C.E. Sleeter & P.L. McLaren (Eds.), *Multicultural education, critical pedagogy, and the politics of difference* (pp. 33–70). Albany, NY: State University of New York Press.

Mohr, N. (1979). *Felita.* New York: Puffin Books.

No Child Left Behind (2001). *Mission Statement.* Retrieved December, 2006, from http://www.ed.gov/nclb/landing.jhtml

Nieto, S. (2000). Placing equity front and center: Some thoughts on transforming teacher education for a new century. *Journal of Teacher Education 51*, 180–187.

Nieto, S. (2004). *Affirming diversity: The sociopolitical context of multicultural education* (4th ed.). New York: Pearson.

Nieto, S. & Bode, P. (2008). *Affirming diversity: The sociopolitical context of multicultural education* (5th ed.). New York: Pearson.

Pico, F. & Pico, A. (1994). *The Red Comb.* New York: Bridgewater Books.

Pineau, E.L. (1994). Teaching is Performance: Reconceptualizing a Problematic Metaphor. *American Educational Research Journal*, 31, 3–25.

Pineau, E.L. (1998). Performance Studies Across the Curriculum: Problems, Possibilities, and Projections. In S.J. Dailey (Ed.), *The future of performance studies: Visions and revisions.* (pp. 128–35) Annandale, VA: National Communication Association.

Rymes, B., Cahnmann-Taylor, M. & Souto-Manning, M. (2008). Bilingual teachers' performances of power and conflict. *Teaching Education, 19*, 105–119.

Salverson, J. (1994). In M. Schutzman, and J. Cohen-Cruz (Eds.), *Playing Boal: Theatre, therapy, activism* (pp. 157–171). London, UK: Routledge

Shor, I. (1993). *Empowering Education.* Chicago, IL: University of Chicago Press.

Solsken, J., Willett, J. & Wilson-Keenan, J. (2001). Cultivating Hybrid Tests in Multicultural Classrooms: Promise and Challenge. *Research in the teaching of English, 35*, 179–211.

Taylor, M. (1976). *Roll of thunder, hear my cry.* New York: Puffin Company.

Volshinov, N. (1994) Language as dialogic interaction. In P. Morris (Ed.). *The Bakhtin Reader: Selected writings of Bakhtin, Medvedev, Voloshinov* (pp. 25–37). London, UK: Arnold.

Vygotsky, L.S. (1978). *Mind in society : the development of higher psychological processes*. Cambridge, MA: Harvard University Press.

Warren, J.T. (1999). The body politic: Performance, pedagogy, and the power of Enfleshment. *Text and Performance Quarterly,* 19, 257–66.

Willett J. & Rosenberger C. (2005). Critical Dialogue: Transforming the discourses of educational reform. In L. Pease-Alvarez and S. Schecter (Eds.) *Learning, teaching, and community: Contributions of situated and participatory approaches to educational innovation* (pp.191–203). Mahwah, NJ: Erlbaum.

Wright, W. (2005). Evolution of federal policy and implications of No Child Left Behind for language minority students. Retrieved at http://www.edpolicylab.org

Zeichner, K & Liston, D. (1996). *Reflective Teaching.* Lanham, MD: Erlbaum Publishers.

NOTES

1. All teachers' names, places and school districts are pseudonyms in this manuscript.

2. If a school district fails to meet AYP for four consecutive years, the state can a) ask the school to modify its curriculum program b) withhold Title 111 funds or c) replace the teaching staff at the school (Wright, 2005, p. 26).

3. The course was originally designed by Sonia Nieto and Maria Jose Botehlo for the first ACCELA cohort of teachers in a neighboring mill town. It was co-taught in 2006 by Ruth Harman, Nelida Matos, and Maria Eugenia Lozano.

Chapter Five

Bringing Out the Playful Side of Mathematics: Using Methods from Improvisational Theater in Professional Development for Urban Middle School Math Teachers

Nicole Schectman and Jennifer Knudsen

With such a strong emphasis on testing and accountability in this No Child Left Behind era, and in a nation where more than 60% of the citizens are estimated to be affected by math anxiety (Ashcraft, Krause, & Hopko, 2007), mathematics is not something many people associate with play. In fact, in urban middle school math classrooms, mathematics is typically anything but playful. Such schools are likely to have constrained, procedural-skill-focused mathematics programs in urgent attempts to make quick gains on high-stakes tests (Meier & Wood, 2004; Mintrop, 2004). Many urban districts are underfunded, are low performing by current measures, and serve a high number of students who have special challenges of language, poverty, and cultural differences.

Teachers' interactions with students are typically of a traditional pattern called "teacher initiation, student response, and teacher evaluation" (IRE) (Cazden, 2001; Mehan, 1979). In an IRE interaction, the teacher is the sole authority figure, evaluating the correctness of students' answers and giving feedback when students make mistakes. In classrooms dominated by IRE, the stakes can feel high, correctness can take strong precedence over figuring out concepts, and students are rarely provided an opportunity to generate their own ideas creatively. These students tend to develop a view of their role as passive receivers rather than active constructors and show little confidence in discussing mathematical ideas (Boaler & Greeno, 2000; Chazan, 2000; Lubienski, 2000). In essence, the traditional discursive patterns of the mathematical classroom can foster rigidity in thinking, a lack of conceptual understanding, and low confidence in mathematical skills.

This is in stark contrast to mathematics in the world of the professional mathematician, whose job it is to construct mathematical arguments.

Mathematical argumentation is a fundamental mathematical practice that entails making conjectures and justifying them, generating and evaluating the validity of new mathematical ideas. By its very nature, argumentation requires an element of play or playfulness. As Holton, Ahmed, Williams, and Hill (2001) described, professional mathematicians must spend considerable time experimenting and conjecturing—in other words, playing around with ideas—before they can establish a formal solution or proof. Mathematicians use play at various stages of argumentation, such as trying to understand a problem, making conjectures about possible pathways to solutions, and, once a solution is found, producing generalizations or extensions of the solution to other domains. For productive solution of complex mathematical problems, there must be times when errors are not only acceptable, but also necessary for the flow of problem-solving. Similarly, play is an intrinsic part of the problem-solving work in all the sciences (Jarrett & Burnley, 2007).

The Bridging Project, our program of design and research of teacher professional development (PD), which began in 2004 as part of the National Science Foundation's Teacher Professional Continuum program, seeks to bring the productive play of mathematical argumentation into urban middle school classrooms. In this program, middle school math teachers in challenging urban settings learn to support students in engaging in this fundamental mathematical practice of argumentation during class discussions. In order for teachers to support the cognitively and socially complex practice of mathematical argumentation in their classrooms, Bridging PD helps them develop a deeper understanding of mathematical content, as well as an element of playfulness and a teaching approach that entails facilitative pedagogy.

In this paper, we focus on one of the core components of the Bridging PD approach: using methods from improvisational theater to help teachers develop skills for facilitating classroom mathematical argumentation. We chose to use methods from improvisational theater because it is a domain in which participants are highly trained in some of the critical aspects of play and collaborative co-construction of discourse. We describe in greater detail what exactly classroom mathematical argumentation is; the knowledge, mind-set, and practices that teachers need in order to facilitate mathematical argumentation; and how we adapted and used methods from improvisational theater to support teachers' development of the key mind-set and practices. We then discuss our research and evaluation, presenting two illustrative case studies of teachers enacting classroom mathematical argumentation using skills acquired in the Bridging PD improv activities. We conclude with a discussion of future directions.

WHAT IS CLASSROOM MATHEMATICAL ARGUMENTATION?

Mathematics educators, mathematicians, and philosophers agree that mathematical argumentation is essential for learning mathematics (Kuhn, 2005; Lakatos, 1976; Lampert, 1990; Romberg, Carpenter, & Kwako, 2005; Thurston, 1998; Yackel, 2001). It can provide students with opportunities that enable them to construct conceptually rich understandings and develop a sense of ownership in the construction of knowledge. It can also be empowering to students, enabling them to develop intellectual autonomy and confidence as they become active co-constructors of mathematical arguments, formulating and determining the validity of their own justifications (Yackel & Cobb, 1996). Furthermore, making logical connections between abstract ideas and interacting with others to clarify ideas are both important 21st century skills necessary to an increasing number of STEM (science, technology, engineering, and math) jobs (Partnership for 21st Century Skills, 2008). Indeed, mathematical argumentation is highlighted in national math education policy documents such as the National Council of Teachers of Mathematics' Principles and Standards (2000) and the National Research Council's Adding It Up (Kilpatrick, Swafford, & Findell, 2001), which indicate that generating mathematical conjectures and justifying their validity, are essential to reasoning and communication. These, in turn support the development of essential mathematical proficiencies—conceptual understanding, procedural fluency, strategic competence, adaptive reasoning, and productive disposition.

To create a clear structure for argumentation that teachers can use readily with their students, we follow the model of researchers who have simplified argumentation to two core elements: conjecture and justification (e.g., Erduran, Simon, & Osborne, 2004; Sowder & Harel, 1998; Zohar & Nemet; 2002). We define conjecturing as a process of conscious guessing (Lakatos, 1976) or pattern-finding to create mathematical statements of as-of-yet undetermined mathematical validity (Harel, in press) and justifying as a process of explicating one's reasoning to establish the mathematical validity of a conjecture. Finally, we also emphasize concluding as the process of coming to consensus or agreement about the validity of the conjecture and its justification.

Although mathematical argumentation can certainly be a solitary activity, we are concerned with what we call classroom mathematical argumentation, a process of argumentation that is collaborative in the whole-class discourse among the teacher and students. Argumentation done together within classroom discussion allows students to engage in a rich set of sociomathematical activities: examining multiple conjectures together, trying out justifying or finding counterexamples for other students' conjectures, co-constructing conjectures and justifications, comparing and contrasting alternative conjectures and justifications, and working together to come to agreement about whether their mathematical statements are true or false.

In the research literature, classroom mathematical argumentation is conceptualized as a dynamic interaction of social and cognitive processes (Simon & Blume, 1996). Williams and Baxter (1996) characterized this type of teaching as "discourse-oriented teaching" because the construction of mathematical knowledge occurs through discourse among all participants in the classroom. Discourse-oriented teaching can be contrasted with a more traditional approach (e.g., IRE). It requires a shift in that the students take on significant mathematical authority. The students become responsible for generating and evaluating mathematical ideas in the classroom. The teacher becomes a representative of the mathematical community (e.g., Lampert, 1990) and a facilitator to scaffold student participation, and the students become more active co-constructors of mathematical knowledge (Ford & Forman, 2006).

As an example of classroom mathematical argumentation, we present an episode drawn from a whole-class discussion about similar rectangles in a middle school mathematics class taught by Ms. Esther, a teacher from the Bridging Project. The discussion illustrates how justifications can be co-constructed between the teacher and many students in the classroom. It was preceded by small group work in which students made sets of five similar rectangles (i.e., rectangles that all have the same ratio of length to width) and were asked to consider the method they used and make a conjecture about why it worked. Here, the teacher works with a group of students to help them justify their conjecture, "All perfect squares are similar." They have already established the idea that similar rectangles have sides in the same ratio. (The teacher refers to these ratios as fractions.) Note that the teacher asks the students a series of questions that push them to examine, elaborate, and articulate their own thinking. This questioning also affords the participation of multiple students in this process.

SARA: All perfect squares are similar.

MS. ESTHER: Why?

SARA: Because they are all the same. Their lengths and the widths are equal. So if you reduce any square, if you reduce the proportion or ratio, it becomes 1 by 1.

MS. ESTHER: I don't know what you mean.

SARA: Okay. So let's see. If one of our squares is 3 inches by 3 inches, then the fraction will be 3…uh, okay… 3 is to 3 as 2 is to 2 or whatever. And if you reduce either or both of those, they reduce down to 1.

MS. ESTHER: Are you telling me by definition if I reduce or increase the length of one side, the other sides will automatically increase or decrease proportionally? Is that what you're trying to tell me? Because I understand that. Because it's my words. (Teacher laughs.)

SARA: It's just like...okay. Let's see.

MS. ESTHER: Let me ask. Basically I'm saying you have not convinced me all squares are similar.

EMILY: Um, well, it's a perfect square because if you have one of our squares, the smallest one is 2 ½ inches by 2 ½ inches, and it's, like, even on both sides. So we just make all the squares the same, like 18 by 18, 2 ½ by 2 ½. So they are all similar, all the squares.

MS. ESTHER: Because?

EMILY: Because they are all the same length and …

MS. ESTHER: (Interrupting). Try using the word "as." Because "as" one side?

EMILY: Because …

MS. ESTHER: Doesn't help you. Sorry.

GREG: (Interrupts). Okay, like 2 ½ is to 2 ½ as 18 is to 18.

MS. ESTHER: Because?

GREG: Because they are equal. 2 ½ and 2 ½...

MS. ESTHER: (Interrupts). 2 ½ is not equal to 18.

GREG: No, but the proportions are the same. Both the numerator and denominator of the proportions I guess are equal. No matter what, they're going to reduce to the same thing.

MS. ESTHER: Reduce to what thing? In this case?

GREG: By 1.

MS. ESTHER: By 1?

GREG: 1 is to 1?

MS. ESTHER: Good. How do you get 1 is to 1 from 2 ½ is to 2 ½?

GREG: Divide by 2 ½, divide it by itself.

MS. ESTHER: So in mathematics it's called? Sss (making the "s" sound to give a clue of the first sound of the word) …

GREG: (Whispers to group members).

MS. ESTHER: So are you're telling me if you have 2 ratios, 20 ratios, or there are 100 ratios, and they all simplify to 1, they are equivalent?

GREG: Yes.

MS. ESTHER: Cool. Okay, next group.

FACILITATING CLASSROOM MATHEMATICAL ARGUMENTATION: KNOWLEDGE, MIND-SET, AND PRACTICES

Learning to facilitate classroom mathematical argumentation is challenging for middle school math teachers, especially those accustomed to more traditional IRE approach in which the teacher is more of a "sage on the stage" than a "guide on the side." It requires a constellation of knowledge, mind-set, and practices. First and foremost is mathematical content knowledge. Teachers must have a deep understanding of the mathematics that is the focus of the conversation. They must be able to evaluate student statements for their validity and mathematical precision, interpret unconventional forms or representations that students are likely to make as they construct their understanding, differentiate between colloquial and mathematical uses of language, translate between different representations (e.g., diagrams, algebraic formulas, verbal descriptions), and build connections to mathematics already learned and mathematics to come in the curriculum (Ball, Lubienski, & Mewborn, 2001; Ma, 1999; Shechtman, Roschelle, Knudsen, & Haertel, in press).

However, while improving teachers' content knowledge is necessary, it is not sufficient for teachers to enact more effective classroom practices (Empson & Junk, 2004; Sowder, Philipp, Armstrong, & Schappelle, 1998). For example, a professional mathematician may have deep content knowledge but when faced with a classroom of inner-city middle school students may not necessarily fare well.

A second key aspect of facilitating argumentation is being able to create a classroom culture in which students feel comfortable and empowered to make conjectures. This requires, for many teachers, a change in mind-set. In the traditional mathematics classroom, there is a strong emphasis placed on having the "right" answers. However, conjectures by their nature are not necessarily correct, and argumentation is most productive as a process if students feel they have the freedom to make incorrect statements. Therefore, it is important for everyone in the classroom to be able to take risks and make mistakes.

In the Bridging Project, we help teachers develop a new mind-set by approaching classroom mathematical argumentation as a type of productive mathematical play. We define mathematical play in terms of the essential behavioral factors and necessary social contexts that play theorists associate with play in general: freedom, spontaneity, an element of uncertainty, generating new possibilities, voluntariness of creativity, and active engagement (e.g., Gordon, 2009; Wood, 2009; Yarnal, Kerstetter, Chick, & Hutchinson, 2009). In play, reality is bracketed within its own context in which there are no real consequences for taking risks or making mistakes (Gordon, 2009).

Players know that they are playing and that there is a certain suspension of the constraints of the "real" world in which winning, losing, failing, and succeeding have high stakes and meaning. As Spolin (1963) wrote, "he or she is freed to go out into the environment, to explore, adventure, and face all dangers unafraid" (p. 11). Also in harmonious play, the players agree and cooperate. Players work on teams to accomplish goals together, listening to one another and building off each other's ideas, and supporting one another in taking risks. Such a social context, in which risk-taking is permitted and all participants are involved and collaborating well, can support the behavioral expressions of play.

Mathematical play is a special case of play in that players move freely about a space that is also necessarily bounded by formal rules. Holton et.al. (2001) defined mathematical play as "that part of a process used to solve mathematical problems which involves both experimentation and creativity to generate ideas, and using the formal rules of mathematics to follow any ideas to some sort of conclusion" (p. 403). Bringing playfulness to mathematics is by no means intended to undermine its seriousness. In productive mathematical play, students may have fun experimenting with new ideas, but ultimately they are engaged in important processes in support of deep learning. As Holton, Ahmed, Williams & Hill (2001) described, "mathematical play provides a non-threatening environment where incorrect solutions are not read as mistakes and may lead to better understanding of the problem and/or the confrontation of misconceptions" (p. 404).

However, even the most playful of mathematicians still needs a set of practices to use with students in the moment of instruction. A third aspect of facilitating argumentation that we emphasize is the development of a repertoire of "teaching moves." We use the notion of teaching moves to describe a discrete unit of instructional practice that teachers use to scaffold classroom mathematical argumentation (Jacobs & Ambrose, 2008; Mumme & Carroll, 2007). To support mathematical argumentation, teachers must develop a repertoire of teaching moves that they can use flexibly, responsively, and appropriately given the moment-by-moment needs of the students as they engage in mathematical argumentation.

ADAPTING METHODS FROM IMPROVISATIONAL THEATER FOR FACILITATING ARGUMENTATION

In training teachers in distressed urban districts to support mathematical argumentation, we weave these key elements together—mathematical content knowledge, argumentation as productive play, and a repertoire of teaching moves. Early in the development of the Bridging Project PD, we drew on traditional PD methods for helping teachers develop requisite content knowledge. Previous studies had shown that intensive work with a handful of teachers, sometimes over multiple years, could support deep change in teaching practices (e.g., Cobb, Confrey, diSessa, Lehrer, & Schauble, 2003; Lampert, 1990). However, little prior work indicated how to frame argumentation as play or support in necessarily short term PD the development of a repertoire of teaching moves for argumentation.

An approach we began to develop was the adaptation of methods from improvisational theater. In improvisational theater, a group of performers works collaboratively to create an unscripted performance that emerges spontaneously on stage in front of an audience. Groups may specialize in doing short-form scenes that take only a few minutes or long-form work in which entire plays are created on the spot. Improvisational actors collaborate skillfully to spontaneously co-construct elaborate characters, scenes, and storylines that unfold in the moment. Through a variety of "improv games," they are trained in the elements of character and narrative, as well as the discipline of spontaneity, active engagement, and productive cooperation. The humor and fun of improvisational theater elicits intense emotional experiences of joy for actors and audience alike. This art form has been popularized in recent years on the television show "Whose Line is It Anyway?" in which improvisers create a series of spontaneous skits in front of a live studio audience. Sawyer (1997), in his book on children's pretend play as improvisational performance, pointed out that the first improvisational theater group in 1955 formed around a series of children's games and later grew into the well-known Chicago-based group The Second City, from which eventually grew the television show Saturday Night Live.

While the connection to math teaching may not seem obvious at first glance, prior to the Bridging Project a number of researchers had begun using improvisational theater as a metaphor for understanding how discourse and learning unfold in the classroom. For example, Sawyer (2003) framed effective classroom discussion as improvisational because the flow of discourse unfolds in an unpredictable manner and emerges dynamically from the actions of the teacher and students working together. Drawing on observational and interview studies of improvisational actors, he used the term "collaborative emergence" to describe both classroom discussion and improvisational theater because they are both emergent (i.e., the outcomes cannot be predicted in advance) and collaborative (i.e., the outcomes are collectively determined by all participants). Similarly, Borko and Livingston (1989) used the metaphor to capture the fact that teaching requires improvisational responses as lessons unfold in the moment to adapt to what students know and can do.

They demonstrated that expert teachers, compared with novice teachers, are better able to both stay on track with a lesson and respond improvisationally to students in a productive manner.

Lobman and Lundquist (2007) discussed and demonstrated how improvisational methods can be used to create productive learning environments. A hallmark of improvisational theater is that it offers a safe environment in which mistakes are acceptable and even expected, and all players must work together through listening to one another and working cooperatively. A core improvisational method is setting up an environment that is collegial, safe for making mistakes, and supportive of collaborative cooperation. Improvisational actors work with a set of guiding principles that underlie all improvisational work, for example: (a) use "Yes, and…" by acknowledging what others have said and then contributing something new; (b) make each other look good; (c) make big mistakes; (d) pay close attention, listen, and remember; (e) participate fully; (f) share responsibility; and (g) take care of each other (Johnstone, 1979; Lobman & Lundquist, 2007; Madson, 2005; Sawyer, 2003). In the classroom, improvisational theater methods could be used to create a learning environment in which students would feel safe to take risks and would have the facility to co-construct new understandings together.

Likewise, several researchers had already begun to explore how improvisational methods could be adapted for teacher training. For example, Sawyer (2004) and Lobman (2007) used research on improvisational theater to provide practical suggestions and tools for creating social norms in both the classroom and teacher PD supportive of effective collaborative practice, as well as specific activities to establish a classroom environment in which teachers and students learn the skills necessary to interact collaboratively and take on powerful roles for sharing ideas and taking risks. We saw in these associations an opportunity to bring innovative methods into our work to help teachers learn to support classroom mathematical argumentation.

Across the various American improv traditions, there are hundreds of improv games, most of which tend to be intrinsically fun to participate in and watch. Many games are also designed primarily for improvisational training so that players can develop various aspects of their theatrical repertoire. There are games in which improvisers can develop their skills at inventing characters, developing narrative, or creating songs. Many games constrain players to a small set of rules that allow them to experiment with a particular improv skill. For example, in Word-at-a-Time Story players stand in a circle and construct a narrative by going around and contributing one word each until a story emerges. This allows actors to practice contributing to the development of a narrative without "stockpiling" (i.e., planning ideas ahead of time).

We saw two uses for improv games in mathematics teachers' professional development: First, together with norms, they can be used to create a nonthreatening environment to support the development of productive mathematical play in professional development and ultimately the classroom. Second, in the same way that improvisational actors develop a toolkit of fundamentals for building scenes together, analogous games could be used to help teachers develop a toolkit of fundamental building blocks to facilitate argumentation—teaching moves.

Parallel to improv games, we created a series of teaching improv games (TIGs) in which teachers could develop flexibility in using the teaching moves required to facilitate classroom mathematical argumentation. We focused on the types of teaching moves that the research literature indicates are important in facilitating argumentation. Such moves include encouraging students to take ownership or responsibility for a mathematical position, helping students to clarify their ideas through questioning, using paraphrasing or re-voicing to help ensure that everyone understands the ideas on the table, eliciting agreement or disagreement, eliciting counterexamples or alternative solutions, providing content, and finally concluding arguments by bringing the correct solution, fully explained and justified, into the discussion (Forman, Larreamendy-Joerns, Stein, & Brown, 1998; Lobato, Clarke, & Ellis, 2005; Silver & Stein, 1996; Stein, 2001; Wood, 1999). The games embedded these moves in the three-part structure of argumentation that we had set up for teachers—conjecturing, justifying, and concluding.

The Bridging PD Workshop

The Bridging PD has been implemented as a 2–week summer workshop designed to foster intensive teacher learning. The training in the first week focuses on deepening mathematical content knowledge, while the training in the second week builds on this knowledge and uses improvisational methods to develop the pedagogical aspects of facilitating mathematical argumentation. We implemented two iterations of this workshop in the summers of 2006 and 2007. Across years, the workshops were designed to be complementary such that teachers could participate in any one summer only or obtain increased learning from participating both summers. Several teachers participated in only one or both.

Week 1: Deepening Mathematical Content Knowledge

The focus of the first week was on deepening mathematical content knowledge. Proportional reasoning and coordinate geometry, central and cross-cutting themes in middle school mathematics (Hiebert & Behr, 1988), were core conceptual themes. Teachers, as adult learners, developed their understanding of mathematical argumentation, proportionality, coordinate geometry, and their roles in the curriculum. As Stein (2001) pointed out, a strong support to classroom argumentation is the selection of activities that prompt students to find different solutions and take different positions. We gave Bridging teachers curriculum units with a series of activities on proportionality and coordinate geometry with open-ended questions that support conjecturing and justifying. Using adult versions of the classroom units, teachers learned to make mathematical arguments for themselves, while deepening their understanding of the mathematical concepts. They analyzed brief classroom scenarios focusing on students' mathematical thinking. Teachers learned to make their whole-group arguments in terms of conjecturing, justifying, and concluding.

An important principle in this first week was that the workshop facilitators modeled with the teachers how to facilitate argumentation in the classroom. They used the same pedagogical strategies to facilitate the teachers that would be the focus of learning in the second week. This allowed teachers to begin to experience firsthand what it would be like to be a participant in classroom mathematical argumentation. It also provided an important authentic learning opportunity as teachers began to formulate how they might facilitate argumentation.

To begin to structure argumentation as a discussion, the facilitators established a sequence of explicit steps that could be used as guidelines for beginners. We asked teachers to "do" argumentation a step at a time, generating and clarifying conjectures before moving on to justifying them. We thought it important for beginning arguers to get ample opportunity to make conjectures, and this step ensured that several teachers got to make conjectures before we moved into arguing for or against one. Additionally, concluding seemed important as a separate step because arguments can tend to trail off in conversation, leaving conjectures dangling, not yet established as true or false. We concluded arguments by loudly "stamping" each conjecture with a sticker saying "true" or "false." This seemed to provide some logical, as well as emotional, closure to an argument.

Providing playful opportunities was also an important design consideration in creating the activities in this unit. For example, in *Find Your Similar Rectangle* each teacher is given a paper rectangle and instructed to find the person who had a similar rectangle. When actually doing this activity, teachers had informal definitions of similarity, but they had not been taught a mathematically precise definition. The teachers wandered the room to find the person carrying the rectangle similar to their own. They may have been looking for a match to the skinniness of their own rectangle in another rectangle that was much larger or smaller. There could be quick matches, long searches, and opportunities for humorous mismatches as pairs of teachers held their rectangles up at a distance and then got closer to verify similarity. We watched teachers' interactions vary from tentative approaches to quick scans—both of which produced spontaneous laughter.

Week 2: Facilitating Classroom Mathematical Argumentation Using Improv Methods

The focus of the second week was on how to use this mathematical knowledge in the actions of teaching to facilitate mathematical argumentation in teachers' classrooms. We moved between three complementary methods to help teachers observe, experience, analyze, and plan for using teaching moves to facilitate mathematical argumentation in their classroom discussions: (1) improv games and TIGs, in which teachers worked with a more playful mind-set and experimented with new teaching moves; (2) script read-throughs, in which teachers analyzed teaching moves in fictionalized classroom transcripts; and (3) lesson planning, in which teachers composed detailed lesson plans with step-by-step anticipation of classroom action and where they might use their newly learned teaching moves.

We began by first introducing the fundamental principles of improv as ground rules for all the improv activities that teachers would do in the program. As improv was new to all of the teachers and was met with significant trepidation by many, we began with a series of warmup basic improv games that would help teachers gain experience and confidence in their own ability to participate in this new modality. One such game was Giving a Gift, which is a traditional improv game in which players present each other with pantomimed gifts and tell stories about them. Another such game was Freeze, in which players take turns pantomiming simple two-person scenes. Both of these games help players practice the "Yes, and…" rule, learn to build off of each other's ideas, and begin to gain confidence in their capacity to generate creative ideas spontaneously. Almost all of the teachers participated fully and expressed enjoyment of the activities.

In the workshop, once we had established the supportive, collaborative, and playful environment, teachers engaged in a progression of TIGs that built upon each other. In the first games, teachers further developed their own argumentation skills, emphasizing construction and critiquing of ideas. Next, they tried out constrained sets of classroom facilitation moves, emphasizing questioning and orchestrating participation. In the culminating game of the workshop, teachers integrated these skills to improvise facilitating simulated whole-class mathematical argumentation.

In an early game, *Why, Why, Why?*, triads of teachers experimented with generating explanations and using the one-word inquiry, Why? There were three roles: an explainer, a questioner, and an observer. Each role had associated rules. The explainer had to describe a given mathematical concept. The questioner could ask only why but could ask this question as frequently as desired. The observer was to take notes on what happened, so that the players could stay fully engaged in the game, but all three could participate in a debrief afterwards.

We had teachers play *Why, Why, Why?* with a focus on a concept central to proportionality but sometimes not deeply understood by teachers: a justification for why cross-multiplication works for evaluating the equivalence of fractions. The game often unfolded in an interesting manner. Teachers first had the opportunity to explain their initial conceptions but were then pressed to examine these further. Several rounds of Why provided the opportunity to find the gaps in their reasoning, deepen the explanation, and explore different facets of the concept. After a few rounds, the question why encourages mathematical play because it invites a creative explanation for a claim or conjecture. Eventually, many teachers experienced a boundary between "why" as a useful question and "why" as humorous and even absurd. This was often accompanied by playful laughter. Furthermore, the context of the game allowed them to engage in the inquiry without feeling they were exposing a lack of knowledge.

Basic Argumentation was the next TIG. This game allowed teachers to formulate justifications and began to introduce the dynamics of having a "constructor" and a "critiquer" of an argument. As Ford and Forman (2006) discussed in their explication of scientific discourse, in collaborative argumentation participants take on the roles of constructing arguments and critiquing ideas. These roles are dependent upon each other, and participants move fluidly between the roles. In *Basic Argumentation*, teachers worked in groups of three. They were assigned to be constructor, critiquer, or observer. The players chose one untested conjecture that would be the object of their argument. The constructor would begin the game by articulating a justification for the conjecture. The critiquer, whose role was not described in detail, would give some kind of feedback, such as discussing where the reasoning may or may not have made sense, providing a disconfirming counterexample or simply negating the constructor's statements. Players were to keep their roles until the constructor could no longer argue for the conjecture, and then they would switch roles.

In the workshop, teachers played *Basic Argumentation* with conjectures they had made about proportional relationships among similar geometric shapes. In addition to the initial intentions of the game, an opportunity emerged to explore how the rule "Yes, and…" can be important in collaborative argumentation. In playing the role of critiquer, sometimes teachers presented constructive criticism, but sometimes they simply negated what constructors said. The players could then experience how constructive criticism supported sustained argumentation, even when initial justifications were incorrect, but negation tended to simply close an argument down. This was similar to the improv notion of "blocking," in which one player fails to take up another player's bid for the next sequence in a scene. Improvisational scenes cannot flourish when blocking occurs, and argumentation will be curtailed by simple negation.

Progressing further toward classroom practice, proceeding TIGs focused on teaching moves for facilitating others to co-construct mathematical arguments. In each game, 4 to 12 teachers would participate. In addition to constructors, critiquers, and an observer, each game now included a facilitator. The role of the facilitator was to draw out reasoning and orchestrate participation for the constructors and critiquers. One or more of the stages of argumentation were included in each game. Constraints on these stages provided different purposes for each game.

In the games *Closed-Ended Only* and *Open-Ended Only*, one teacher facilitated a pair of players who could move between constructing and critiquing roles in developing a justification. A new rule was that the argument had to be mediated by the facilitator. The constructor and critiquer could not respond to each other but only to the facilitator. The games were played successively, each focused on the same mathematical conjecture. The only difference was the rule that in *Closed-Ended Only* the facilitator could only ask closed-ended questions, and in *Open-Ended Only* the facilitator could only ask open-ended questions. Closed-ended questions are those that require simple responses, such as a yes or no, or one number. They are usually designed to elicit a specific piece of information and are often used by teachers to determine whether the student knows the answer. Open-ended questions call for a more elaborate response that the teacher may not be able to fully anticipate in advance. No one would actually teach using only one of those types, but the constraints in the games made it possible for teachers to compare the affordances and drawbacks of each—and have the experience of using them in initiating and sustaining classroom argumentation.

Teachers drew some important conclusions after playing these two games. One teacher noted that it was easy to generate correct statements of content for all to hear by asking closed-ended questions, but she was left unsure about what any individual student actually knew about that information. Another teacher said that using only closed-ended questions left the teacher doing all the work. Teachers had more difficulty with playing and analyzing *Open-Ended Only*. They found themselves asking closed-ended questions despite the rule not to. We wondered why. While they had critiques of using only closed-ended questions, it is possible that this game was closer to their actual practice than the game of asking open-ended questions. Despite the spirit of suspending reality through games, teachers' reality is still an important influence on their participation in games based on their vocation.

In the culminating game, *In the Classroom*, teachers integrated all of the teaching moves in a final improvised simulation of an entire lesson that they would actually teach back in their classrooms. Each teacher was given 30 minutes to practice teaching with the curriculum materials we had used in the first week of the workshop. They chose part of the materials and part of the argumentation process on which to focus. We introduced here another method from improvisational theater, character endowment, which is declaring that someone in the game is a particular person or kind of person. The lead teacher endowed her or his fellow teachers as students with specific qualities that were similar to those of the students in their real classrooms. For example, teachers endowed others as shy, know-it-all, and extremely tired. Endowing teachers with specific student qualities helped avoid a syndrome we had seen in year 1 of our workshops: Our teachers, when asked to play students, automatically played quite ill-behaved students and created a disastrous scene. If working out frustration is one function of play, we can guess at what was going on.

This game served as a transition between games and classroom. Thirty minutes was time enough for teachers to develop one stage of argumentation thoroughly (i.e., conjecturing or justifying) or to practice moving between one stage and another. They could also cover a fair amount of a specific curriculum activity. Most important, this TIG enabled teachers to practice in an unconstrained manner the teaching moves they had analyzed, observed, experienced, and used themselves in previous TIGs.

In each of these games, in combination with the other activities in the workshop—analyzing fictionalized classroom transcripts of idealized episodes of argumentation and making concrete lesson plans for their classrooms—teachers engaged in the playful practice of argumentation and developed teaching moves to facilitate their students' argumentation. We observed that in the process, teachers experienced a wide variety of emotions. The games sometimes evoked strong feelings, ranging from playful joy to sheer frustration. This may be an important part of teaching games: this chance to experience both the excitement and unpleasant feelings that accompany change, within a supportive environment of having adventures in argumentation together.

RESEARCH AND EVALUATION

In this early design phase of the Bridging Project, we implemented the PD within the structure of a small-scale 2–year randomized experiment impact study with complementary in-depth case studies. Data collection focused on teachers' mathematical content knowledge and the mathematical argumentation that occurred in their classrooms when teachers used the Bridging curriculum materials during each school year following summer workshops. We used these data to inform the iterative development of the PD, to investigate broadly the feasibility of the program for impacting teachers' practice, and to understand the different ways that teachers' practices could be affected.

While the more general results are documented elsewhere (e.g., Knudsen, Michalchik, & Kim, 2010; Shechtman, Knudsen, & Stevens, 2010), here we describe the overall research design and present two case studies that trace different ways that teachers enacted in their classrooms some of the playfulness and teaching moves that were the focus of the teaching improv games (TIGs).

Overview of Research Design

Teachers were recruited from high-poverty urban districts in the San Francisco Bay Area and randomly assigned to either a treatment or control group. Each year, teachers in the treatment group received the full 2–week Bridging intervention. Teachers in the control group received only the Bridging week 1 mathematical content training but not the week 2 training using improv; in the second week, these teachers participated in a different workshop of equal duration and professional value, examining how mathematical content is coordinated across grade levels. A total of 35 teachers attended the workshops. During each school year, all teachers in both groups taught the curricular materials used in the week 1 workshop that summer. All teachers were observed and videotaped teaching these units over a 2– to-4–day period. The whole-class discussion portions of these videotapes were transcribed verbatim.

The main hypothesis of the experiment was: The classroom discourse of treatment group teachers (compared with that of control group teachers) will have more argumentative talk. In other words, we hypothesized that additional professional development with a focus on teaching practices using improv techniques would help teachers foster more mathematical argumentation in their classroom than professional development focused mostly on content. To test this hypothesis, we developed a coding protocol to analyze systematically the transcribed classroom discourse, the Mathematical Arguments as Joint Activity in the Classroom (MAJAC) coding protocol (Shechtman,

Knudsen, & Kim, 2008). This protocol was used on verbatim transcripts of whole-class discussion to locate and count the number of substantive student statements and teaching moves made in the episodes of mathematical argumentation.

Overall, there was support for the main hypothesis: in both years, we observed more argumentative talk in the treatment classrooms than in the control classrooms, in terms of both student statements and teaching moves. This difference was statistically significant in year 1 and marginally significant in year 2.

Using quantitative methods at such an early stage of a program's design means that our qualitative studies are important for understanding what happened in teachers' classrooms as they returned to them after our workshops and how ideas and techniques from the workshops were taken up in the classroom.

Development of the Case Studies

On the basis of initial impressions from these broad analyses, we selected a subset of teachers whose classroom discourse had important contrasting qualities that would highlight different aspects of the PD and the use of improv methods. Here we present the illustrative cases of Ms. Stephanie and Ms. Peg who exhibited how argumentation can be enacted in ways that were quite different yet both aligned with the intentions of the TIGs. They both taught in the same urban middle school, which had a high level of student poverty and the lowest possible ranking for the state academic performance index. Both told us that argumentation was new to their practice.

In the highlighted excerpts, the teachers' classes were doing the same week 1 Bridging activity from the coordinate geometry unit. Students draw four rectangles (all aligned with the axes) on a coordinate grid and label the coordinates of the vertices (corners). They then look for patterns in the numbers that make up each pair of coordinates. Patterns can then be formulated as conjectures, which serve as the basis for argumentation.

MS. STEPHANIE: THE STERN NOVICE TEACHER WHOSE STUDENTS ARGUED ENTHUSIASTICALLY

Ms. Stephanie did not have the odds in her favor for successful enactment of mathematical argumentation. When she attended our workshop, she had been teaching for only one year. As a new teacher in a tough school, she was in the high-risk category for teachers who leave the profession within five years. A typical challenge, and one that we observed for other novice Bridging teachers, is basic classroom management—making sure, for example, that students take turns talking and stay in their seats as necessary. Without this basic classroom order, mathematical argumentation might never be an option. Ms. Stephanie, however, had clearly mastered an effective set of management skills. Her style was quite stern and seemingly unplayful—so much so that one researcher, on seeing a videotape of her establishing order in the beginning of class, predicted that little student argumentation could possibly happen.

Yet a considerable amount of rich argumentation happened in Ms. Stephanie's class—in fact, she told us that she reserved each Friday for argumentation and that her students looked forward to it each week. This was well above and beyond what we had asked the teachers to do. When we observed in her classroom, we saw that the students actually quite enthusiastically participated in elaborate argumentation. She brought many of the workshop moves back to her own classroom, much as the workshop facilitators had modeled and she had rehearsed in the TIGs. She had already established norms that were supportive of argumentation.

It was clear that Ms. Stephanie took the structure of argumentation as we presented it quite seriously and used it with the students as an organizing frame of reference. Prominently displayed in her classroom was her own version of a poster that looked quite similar to the one that we had used in the workshop. As shown in Figure 1, our poster outlined the phases of argumentation according to the project's theoretical framework. Ms. Stephanie used this physical resource in her classroom to guide and structure the discussion as it unfolded.

Here we discuss an episode that includes all the phases of argumentation and in which Ms. Stephanie used a variety of teaching moves to draw out

Mathematical argumentation is a conversation in 3 parts.

- Conjecturing
  - Boldly stating what MIGHT be true
  - Clarifying (vocabulary and logic)
- Justifying
  - Figuring out together if it is true
  - Logically connecting the dots
- Concluding
  - Deciding if the conjecture is true or false
  - Building new conjectures

Figure 1. Ms. Stephanie's Stages of Mathematical Argumentation Poster.

student reasoning and orchestrate participation. The excerpts also clearly illustrate that Ms. Stephanie had previously created a classroom environment in which the students could be playful in their argumentation and were eager to participate, contribute, and voice opinions. This is supported through a combination of rewards for participating (i.e., points for math argumentation) and teaching moves to orchestrate participation so that students could listen to one another and contribute. Students were playful in coming up with new ideas, and they built off of each other's thinking. They even spontaneously went up and wrote on the board and called on each other to speak. While there was enthusiastic participation, Ms. Stephanie always remained in control of the classroom.

In the previous class period, students had worked in small groups to make observations about patterns they saw in four rectangles they had drawn on a coordinate plane. They then used these observations to make a conjecture about coordinates. The teacher then had each group report out on their conjecture and had the class vote on which conjecture they would like to justify together as a class. The conjecture they chose is illustrated in Figure 2.

The episode begins with the conjecturing phase of argumentation. Ms. Stephanie has Jason write his group's conjecture on the board. She reminds the class that the purpose of this is for everyone to have a clear understanding of the conjecture before people decide if they agree or disagree.

MS. STEPH: Jason, before you write, can you say that out loud again?

JASON: If you have a coordinate plane and you put a point to the left and below the origin, then it has to be negative, negative.

MS. STEPH: Okay. (Jason writes this on the board, "If you have a point on a coordinate grid to the left and below, it is a negative, negative.").

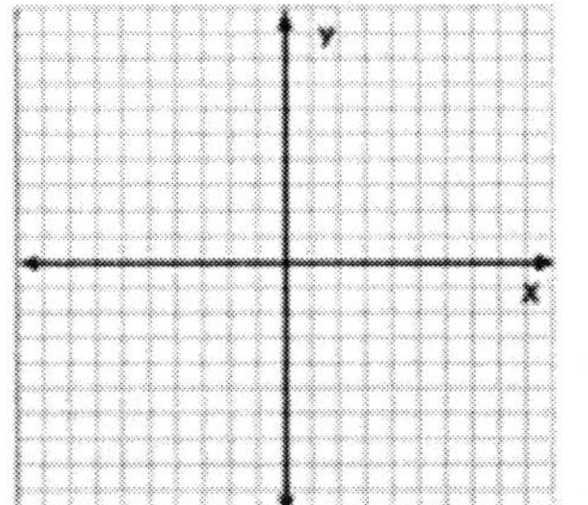

Figure 2. The Conjecture Discussed in Ms. Stephanie's Classroom. Conjecture: On a coordinate plane, any point to the left of and below the origin will have two negative coordinates.

DENIS: But that's pretty much what the conjecture is.

MS. STEPH: Uh, Denis we are clarifying. We are making the sentence clear for everybody. (to the whole class) I want you to think about what Jason is writing on the board and decide if you understand what it says now, so we can move on to justification.

MS. STEPH: (After Jason has finished writing) Okay. Read it to us, Jason.

JASON: If you have a point on a coordinate grid to the left and below it is a negative, negative.

MS. STEPH: Okay. Do we understand what the conjecture is?

STUDENTS: Yeah.

MS. STEPH: Put your hand up if you don't understand what the conjecture is. (no hand goes up) Okay let's move on then to justification. Now you are going to argue that this is true or this is not true. (Many students raise their hands.)

MS. STEPH: You are going to argue this is true or not true. Remember to get your points for math argumentation, you need to be participating.

They then move into the justifying phase. Given the nature of the conjecture, much of the argument is focused around graphing conventions, which are taught almost every school year throughout middle and high school.

VENESSA: I think it's true because they said that this is…I think it's true because of the positive up there on the right side, the negative number is left side.

MS. STEPH: Okay, so you think it's true? (Many students raise their hands.) Harrison.

HARRISON: Um, I think it's also true because you have your coordinate plane, and this is negative, negative corner right? To make it into a positive, then you'd have to bring it up here. (Indicating the upper part of the plane).

MS. STEPH: Okay. Ozzy.

OZZY: Um, I think it's true because what Jason said in his statement was like the top top right part is positive, positive and the left lower part is negative, negative. And the other two is negative, positive, positive, negative. And it is true. To me. (Many students raise their hands).

MS. STEPH: Okay. Martin.

MARTIN: Yes I agree, too. (A pause. Some students laugh.) Um, all right. That's all I got.

MS. STEPH: Irene?

IRENE: I think it's true. Can I write up there while someone else talks? Because it's going to take kind a while if I write it.

MS. STEPH: Write what?

IRENE: Why I think it's true.

Note that in an analysis of argumentation, Sowder and Harel (1998) described appeals to authority (i.e., "this is true because it is the convention") as a particularly weak form of justification. But in many classrooms, the text is the authority—and teachers and students, as well as parents (when helping with homework) accept its authority without question. The majority of what mathematics textbooks demonstrate are the details of mathematical conventions, the way things are commonly done, said, and pictured when doing school mathematics. But in this episode, several students come up with ways or reasons the conventions could be wrong. One student, Kennyn, for example, introduces the idea that there could be a "whacky coordinate plane" on which this conjecture would not be true. Later, when Ms. Stephanie prompts for disagreement with the conjecture, Denis and Andy come up with their own playful ways of falsifying the conjecture.

DENIS: If you rotate like this... (Draws arrows on the board showing how if the axes are rotated 90 degrees, the point could still be in the lower left, but the coordinates would be different.)

JASON: It's still the same grid. (Students discuss this amongst themselves).

ANDY: Denis, call on me.

MS. STEPH: Okay. Denis. Thank you. Okay, Andy.

ANDY: The thing is that if you rotate it like this, then it won't be true. And also in other countries, they may have different grids.

SAM: What country, Andy?

ANDY: [The conjecture] says if it's left and below the origin, it didn't say what country. It didn't say what country we are in.

SAM: I don't think other countries have different grids. (Students discuss this among themselves.)

ANDY: Why not? They have the metric system.

MS. STEPH: Thank you. Thank you. Ozzy.

OZZY: I agree with Andy, because some other countries do have different ways of doing math or grids, whatever you call it, so yeah.

Eventually, Ms. Stephanie moves to the concluding phase of the argument by pushing the class for a final consensus on the conjecture.

MS. STEPH: Okay. We are trying to conclude, and I am asking you basically if you agree with this (points to the conjecture, which has been revised based on the discussion). Unless you have anything you need to add before we can agree. If you have something you need to add before we can agree, that's what I'm looking for here. Otherwise you can say, do we agree with this. If you have your hand up, I'm going to assume you have a thing to add.

The students discuss the conjecture for another few minutes. Some students take issue with the revision that had been made to the conjecture, saying it was not necessary. Kennyn gets so engrossed in and upset by the discussion that he uses profanity toward Denis. Ms. Stephanie ends the episode with a vote.

MS. STEPH: All right, guys. We are going to stop. If you agree with the conclusion, the statement, it is true. This. Our original conjecture was, "If you have a point on a coordinate grid to the left and below, it is a negative comma negative." Raise your hand if you agree with our conclusion that it is true. (Many students raise their hands.) Raise your hand, please, if you agree that it is true. (Counts hands. Many students talk simultaneously and argue whether it is true or not).

MS. STEPH: Okay. Hands down. We have 18 that I counted. We had 18 out of 27 who agreed with it. It is the majority but hardly. It is more than half of you who agreed with it. At this point and time, it's going to be the best we can do. Half of you agreed with it. That's the best thing we can do.

In sum, Ms. Stephanie's case clearly shows how a teacher appropriated both the playfulness and teaching moves that were modeled and developed in the workshop. In this difficult urban setting, she impressively engendered playfulness, eager participation, and critical mathematical thinking. During the workshop, her turn at In the Classroom foreshadowed many of the moves we observed in her classroom. Many of her moves for orchestrating participation were among those modeled by the facilitators, but, interestingly, not among those explored in the TIGs. In particular, she herself asked few probing open-ended or closed-ended questions but rather left all mathematical content up to the students. Her class was one of the few we observed in which students were actively arguing with each other. There were also many moves that she invented on her own, such as giving students points. We hypothesize that the moves she learned in the workshop were sufficient for this new teacher to support argumentation because, unlike some other new teachers, she had sufficient classroom management skills to make it possible for argumentation to happen, but her practice was still malleable enough to take on new practices.

MS. PEG: THE VETERAN TEACHER WHO USED TEACHING MOVES FROM THE TIGS

Ms. Peg was a veteran teacher with over a decade of experience who participated in both years of our program. However, given her fairly traditional background, mathematical argumentation was a new way of doing mathematics for her. She was highly engaged in the workshop, working diligently to learn the basics and asking many questions about the meaning of terms and how to carry out argumentation in her classroom. Her active participation in the workshop was particularly evident during the TIGs and the discussions held just after the games.

When we examined Ms. Peg's classroom discourse, in comparison to Ms. Stephanie she seemed more specifically influenced by her participation in TIGs. In the excerpt from classroom dialogue below, Ms. Peg used a combination of open- and closed-ended questions to help her class make conjectures and justifications. This, of course, echoes our two games *Open-Ended Only* and *Closed-Ended Only*. We had expected the game to enable teachers to contrast the use of these questions in order to find a blend that was suitable for a given situation, and this is in fact what we saw in Ms. Peg's classroom. We know that in our first year observation of her class, her students made only a few arguments and Ms. Peg's support of those arguments seemed tenuous. The excerpt below is from observations made in the second year of the project, after Ms. Peg had participated in new TIGs focused on questioning techniques.

As this episode begins, Milla has examined her four rectangles on the coordinate plane and makes an observation about the vertical lines—specifically about the endpoints of these lines, which are vertices of the rectangles. Her conjecture, stated more precisely than it was in the classroom, was that the x coordinates of the two endpoints of any one vertical line are equal. Ms. Peg's restatement of her conjecture is that the two vertical lines have the same x-coordinate, a different and, as it turns out, false conjecture. Another student makes a move to provide a counterexample.

MS. PEG Okay, go ahead and state your conjecture. What do you think?

MILLA Okay, I say my patterns are—12 and the 10. My other is—12 and the 4. The pattern is—12.

MS. PEG So which … which coordinate is it? The x or y?

MILLA X.

MS. PEG So you're saying that you're noticing that your two x [coordinates]—in the vertical or horizontal line?

MILLA Vertical.

MS. PEG Has to be the vertical, are the same. Can you write that down? (looking at another student) Two vertical lines share the same x. Raise your hand if you made that observation. (Some students raise their hands) Do you agree with what your data is? That your x's are the same. Is that true in every single rectangle?

STACY No.

LUANNE Yeah.

MS. PEG It's not true. Stacy has got a counter. And Stacy we may have you show that on a grid paper, a counter, and I'm going have you do it right here. (hands Stacy a transparency) Somebody else, an observation they made. Mike?

Let us look closely at what questions Ms. Peg uses to elicit and support argumentation. First, she instructs students to state a conjecture and uses the open-ended question, "What do you think?" Milla responds, not with a conjecture (i.e., a statement that could be true or false) but with seemingly disconnected numbers. Ms. Peg asks the student a couple of close-ended questions about which coordinates and which lines on the rectangle she was referring to in her conjecture, thus connecting the numbers to mathematical terms that could form a conjecture. Ms. Peg states her own version of the conjecture: "Two vertical lines share the same x." Then, she asks the entire class to consider the truth of the conjecture, prompting them to find counter-examples with, "Is that true of every single rectangle?" Technically this is a closed-ended question, because the answer is yes or no. In context, however, it occurs as an open-ended question, as if "why" were appended. This suggests that the class had been developing norms of argumentation for some time. Ms. Peg's version of the conjecture is not true, perhaps fortunately, because this provides a student with the opportunity to offer a "counter" (i.e., a counterexample). A counterexample is a particularly efficient form of justification, establishing that a conjecture is false by providing one example where it is not true.

In sum, Ms. Peg combines open- and closed-ended questions to facilitate a classroom argument that started with formulating a conjecture and progressed to a justification for or against the conjecture. Her case indicates promise for the intended purposes of the TIG—in the workshop she had played with the teaching moves introduced in the game, and in her classroom we observed her using these teaching moves flexibly to foster mathematical argumentation.

DISCUSSION

The mission of the Bridging Project is to provide middle school math teachers in challenging urban settings training to support students in engaging in the fundamental mathematical practice of argumentation in the discussions in their classrooms. As classroom discussions in this type of setting are traditionally dominated by IRE types of interactions, the program seeks to leverage scarce professional development resources to help teachers make small shifts in practice that provide significant new opportunities for students to actively participate in constructing their own understandings. The Bridging PD training emphasizes the development of both a deeper understanding of mathematical content and pedagogy for facilitating discussion. Mixed results from our small impact study suggest that the Bridging PD has promise for helping teachers do more argumentation in the classroom.

In this paper, we examined one of the central components of the PD: using methods from improvisational theater to foster mathematical argumentation as productive mathematical play and as an approach to developing teaching moves for the classroom. As part of our 2–week summer program, we developed and implemented a range of games, both drawing from the theater tradition and creating new specialized teaching games. Through close observation of the discourse in teachers' classrooms in the subsequent school year, we found important traces of the approach and tools that teachers learned in the workshops. One case study example showed a teacher who engaged students' enthusiastic participation in argumentation following the structure we had provided, and another case study illustrated at a more fine-grained level how the teaching moves in the teaching games may be enacted in discussion.

This project continues to build the literature illustrating the utility of using improvisational theater methods for teacher professional training. Just as in prior work (e.g., Lobman, 2007; Sawyer, 2004), we found that improvisational games can be used to establish social norms of safety and collaboration in which teachers can be relatively uninhibited in exploring new knowledge and practice. This can be particularly important in developing new practices around facilitating highly dynamic discussions that require teachers to be on their toes, in terms of both mathematical and pedagogical skill. These methods can provide a safe environment in which teachers can experiment and admit where knowledge is lacking.

Another implication is that methods from improvisational theater, particularly the use of strategically designed improvisational games, can be used for the development of specific teaching moves to be used in mathematics classroom discussion. Both teaching and improvisational theater share a collaborative emergence in which there is a complex set of moves and dependencies that can shape the way a discussion or scene unfolds. In the math classroom, such unfolding can have a significant impact on the learning opportunities that students are provided and the ways in which students engage with mathematical ideas. In the Bridging PD, our teaching improv games focused on the moves teachers can make for shaping argumentative discussion in the classroom. There are a multitude of other types of teaching moves that unfold in the mathematics classroom. For example, Hill et al. (2008) discuss the notion of Mathematical Quality of Instruction, which includes, among other aspects of pedagogy, a number of in-the-moment moves that math teachers make that are likely to influence student learning. Such moves include how teachers respond to student errors and misunderstandings, the degree to which teachers acknowledge student ideas, and the use of precise mathematical language in conversation. Furthermore, Pierson (2008) showed that the manner in which teachers responded to student ideas in conversation was directly related to student learning of complex mathematics. Teaching improv games can potentially provide simple and direct ways for teachers to practice applying the mathematical knowledge they have to the process of engaging in important discursive moves that shape student learning.

A next step in the Bridging Project program is to develop improvisational games that teachers can use with their students to enhance mathematical play in the classroom. We will develop a series of student improv games (SIGs) to support students in feeling safe to take risks and collaborating productively with one another. We will focus in particular on developing games that will engage students who are traditionally disenfranchised in mathematics classrooms, such as girls and ethnic minority students. For example, in *Classroom Conject-a-thon* students will brainstorm conjectures about a mathematical object and be encouraged to make some deliberately bad ones so that making a false conjecture loses its stigma. Drawing on our experiences with Ms. Stephanie, we will also create the game *Argument-of-the-Week.* In this game, students will spend an allotted time each week generating a conjecture and justification for some aspect of the content in their current unit. We will also build on the games outlined by Lobman and Lundquist (2007) that support students in taking on new roles in the classroom, such as *Compulsive Math Gal/Guy* and *Captain Precision.*

Mathematics is traditionally not associated with play, especially in challenging urban schools in which the focus tends to be on testing and accountability. Yet just as in the work of professional mathematicians, play can have an important place in the math classroom. When teachers are trained to bring an element of serious playfulness to their classrooms, students can be provided the opportunity to work together without fear of failure to experiment with developing their own conceptual understandings.

REFERENCES

Ashcraft, M. H., Krause, J. A., & Hopko, D. R. (2007). Is math anxiety a mathematical learning disability? In D. Berch & M. Mazzocco (Eds.), *Why is math so hard for some children?: The nature and origins of mathematical learning difficulties and disabilities.* Baltimore, MD: Brookes Publishing Company.

Ball, D. L., Lubiensky, S., & Mewborn, D. (2001). Research on teaching mathematics: The unsolved problem of teachers' mathematical knowledge. In V. Richardson

(Ed.), *Handbook of research on teaching* (4th ed., pp. 433–456). New York, NY: Macmillan.

Boaler, J., & Greeno, J. G. (2000). Identity, agency, and knowing in mathematics worlds. In J. Boaler (Ed.), *Multiple perspectives on mathematics teaching and learning* (pp. 171–200). Westport, CT: Ablex Publishing.

Borko, H., & Livingston, C. (1989). Cognition and improvisation: Differences in mathematics instruction by expert and novice teachers. *American Educational Research Journal, 26*(4), 473–498.

Chazan, D. (2000). *Beyond formulas in mathematics and teaching: Dynamics of the high school algebra classroom*. New York, NY: Teachers College.

Cazden, C. D. (2001). *Classroom discourse: The language of teaching and learning* (2nd ed.). Portsmouth, NH: Heinemann.

Cobb, P., Confrey, J., diSessa, A., Lehrer, R., & Schauble, L. (2003). Design experiments in education research. *Educational Researcher, 32*(1), 9–13.

Empson, S. B., & Junk, D., (2004). Teachers' knowledge of children's mathematics after implementing a student-centered curriculum. *Journal of Mathematics Teacher Education, 7*, 121–144.

Erduran, S., Simon, S., & Osborne, J. (2004). Tapping into argumentation: Developments in application of Toulmin's argument pattern for studying science discourse. *Science Education, 88*, 915–933.

Ford, M. J., & Forman, E. A. (2006). Redefining disciplinary learning in classroom contexts. *Review of Research in Education, 30*(1), 1–32.

Forman, E. A., Larreamendy-Joerns, J., Stein, M. K., & Brown, C. A. (1998). "You're going to want to find out which and prove it": Collective argumentation in a mathematics classroom. *Learning and Instruction, 8*(6), 527–548.

Gordon, G. (2009). What is play?: In search of a definition. In D. Kuschner (Ed), In *Children to Red Hatters: Diverse images and issues of play, play & culture studies, volume 8.* Lanham, MD: University Press of America.

Harel, G. (in press).What is mathematics? A pedagogical answer to a philosophical question. In R. B. Gold & R. Simons (Eds.), *Current issues in the philosophy of mathematics from the perspective of mathematicians.* American Mathematical Association.

Hiebert, J., & Behr, M. (1988). Introduction: Capturing the major themes. In J. Hiebert & M. Behr (Eds.), *Number concepts and operations in the middle grades* (pp. 1–18). Hillsdale, NJ: Lawrence Erlbaum.

Hill, H. C., Blunk, M. L., Charalambous, C. Y., Lewis, J. M., Phelps, G. C., Sleep, L., & Ball, D. L. (2008). Mathematical knowledge for teaching and the mathematical quality of instruction: An exploratory study. *Cognition and Instruction, 26*(4), 430–511.

Holton, D., Ahmed, A., Williams, H., & Hill, C. (2001). On the importance of mathematical play. *International Journal of Mathematical Education in Science and Technology, 32*(3), 401–415.

Jacobs, V., & Ambrose, R. (2008) Making the most of story problems in teaching. *Teaching Children Mathematics, 15*, 260–266.

Jarrett, O. S., & Burnley, P. C. (2007). The role of fun, playfulness, and creativity in science: Lessons from geoscientists. In D. J. Sluss & O. S. Jarrett (Eds.), *Investigating play in the 21st century, play & culture studies, volume 7*. Lanham, MD: University Press of America.

Johnstone, K. (1979). *Impro: Improvisation and the theatre*. New York, NY: Routledge.

Kilpatrick, J., Swafford, J., & Findell, B. (2001). *Adding it up: Helping children learn mathematics*. Washington, DC: National Academy Press.

Knudsen, J., Michalchik, V., & Kim, H. (2010). *Three cases of argumentation in urban classrooms*. Manuscript submitted for publication.

Kuhn, D. (2005). *Education for thinking*. Cambridge, MA: Harvard University Press.

Lakatos, I. (1976). *Proofs and refutations*. Cambridge, England: Cambridge University Press.

Lampert, M. (1990). When the problem is not the question and the solution is not the answer: Mathematical knowing and teaching. *American Educational Research Journal, 27*(1), 29–63.

Lobato, J., Clarke, D., & Ellis, A. B. (2005). Initiating and eliciting in teaching: A reformulation of telling. *Journal for Research in Mathematics Education, 36*, 101–136.

Lobman, C. (2007, April). *The developing teachers fellowship program: Exploring the use of improv theatre for the professional development of inner city teachers*. Paper presented at the annual meeting of the American Educational Research Association conference, Chicago, IL.

Lobman, C., & Lundquist, M. (2007). *Unscripted learning: Using improv activities across the K–8 curriculum*. New York, NY: Teachers College Press.

Lubienski, S. T. (2000). A clash of class cultures? Students' experiences in a discussion intensive seventh-grade mathematics classroom. *Elementary School Journal, 100*, 377–403.

Ma, L. (1999). *Knowing and teaching elementary mathematics: Teachers' understanding of fundamental mathematics in China and the United States*. Mahwah, NJ: Lawrence Erlbaum.

Madson, P. R. (2005). *Improv wisdom: Don't prepare, just show up*. New York, NY: Bell Tower.

Mehan, H. (1979). *Learning lessons: Social organization in the classroom*. Cambridge, MA: Harvard University Press.

Meier, D., & Wood, G. (Eds.). (2004). *Many children left behind: How the No Child Left Behind Act is damaging our children and our schools*. Boston, MA: Beacon Press.

Mintrop, H. (2004). *Schools on probation: How accountability works (and doesn't work)*. New York, NY: Teachers College Press.

Mumme, J., & Carroll, C. E. (2007). *Learning to lead mathematics professional development*. Thousand Oaks, CA: Corwin Press.

National Council of Teachers of Mathematics (NCTM). (2000–2004). *Principles and standards for school mathematics: An overview*. Reston, VA: Author.

Partnership for 21st Century Skills. (2008). *21st Century skills, education & competitiveness: A resource and policy guide.* Tuscon, AZ: Author.

Pierson, J. (2008). *The relationship between patterns of classroom discourse and mathematics learning* (Unpublished doctoral dissertation). University of Texas at Austin.

Romberg, T. A., Carpenter, T. P., & Kwako, J. (2005). Standards-based reform and teaching for understanding. In T. A. Romberg, T. Carpenter, & F. Dremock (Eds.), *Understanding mathematics and science matters* (pp. 3–26). Mahwah, NJ: Lawrence Erlbaum.

Sawyer, K. (1997). *Pretend play as improvisation: conversation in the preschool classroom.* Mahwah, NJ: Lawrence Erlbaum.

Sawyer, K. (2003). *Improvised dialogues: Emergence and creativity in conversation.* Westport, CT: Ablex Publishing.

Sawyer, K. (2004). Creative teaching: Collaborative discussion as disciplined improvisation. *Educational Researcher, 33*(2), 12–20.

Shechtman, N., Knudsen, J., & Kim, H. (2008, March). *Classroom mathematical argumentation as joint activity: A new framework for understanding an important classroom practice.* Paper presented at the annual meeting of the American Educational Research Association, New York, NY.

Shechtman, N., Roschelle, J., Knudsen, J., & Haertel, G. (in press). Investigating links from teacher knowledge, to classroom practice, to student learning in the instructional system of the middle school mathematics classroom. *Cognition and Instruction.*

Shechtman, N., Knudsen, K., & Stevens, H. (2010, April-May). *The Bridging Teacher Professional Development Program: Supporting mathematical argumentation in distressed urban middle school contexts.* Paper presented at the annual meeting of the American Educational Research Association, Denver, CO.

Silver, E. A., & Stein, M. K. (1996). The QUASAR Project: The "Revolution of the Possible" in mathematics instructional reform in urban middle schools. *Urban Education, 30*(4), 476–521.

Simon, M., & Blume, G. (1996). Justification in the mathematics classroom: A study of prospective elementary teachers. *Journal of Mathematical Behavior, 15*, 3–31.

Sowder, L., & Harel, G. (1998). Types of students' justifications. *Mathematics Teachers, 21*, 670–675.

Sowder, J., Philipp, R., Armstrong, B., & Schappelle, B. (1998). *Middle-grade teachers' mathematical knowledge and its relationship to instruction.* Albany, NY: SUNY.

Spolin, V. (1963). *Improvisation for the theater: A handbook of teaching and directing techniques.* Evanston, IL: Northwestern University Press.

Stein, M. K. (2001). Mathematical argumentation: Putting umph into classroom discussions. *Mathematics Teaching in the Middle School, 7*(2), 110–112.

Thurston, W. P. (1998). On proof and progress in mathematics. In T. Tymoczko (Ed.), *New directions in the philosophy of mathematics: An anthology* (pp. 337–355). Princeton, NJ: Princeton University Press.

Williams, S. R., & Baxter, J. A. (1996). Dilemmas of discourse-oriented teaching in one middle school mathematics classroom. *The Elementary School Journal, 97*(1), 21–38.

Wood, T. (1999). Creating a context for argument in mathematics class. *Journal for Research in Mathematics Education, 30*(2), 171–191.

Wood, E. (2009). Conceptualising a pedagogy of play: International perspectives from theory, policy and practice. In D. Kuschner (Ed), in *Children to Red Hatters: Diverse images and issues of play, play & culture studies, volume 8*. Lanham, MD: University Press of America.

Yackel, E. (2001). *Explanation, justification and argumentation in mathematics classrooms.* In M. van den Heuvel-Panhuizen (Ed.), Proceedings of the 25th conference of the International Group for the Psychology of Mathematics Education (Vol. 1, pp. 9–24). Utrecht, Netherlands: Freudenthal Institute.

Yackel, E., & Cobb, P. (1996). Sociomathematical norms, argumentation, and autonomy in mathematics. *Journal for Research in Mathematics Education, 27*(4), 458–477.

Yarnal, C. M., Kerstetter, D., Chick G., & Hutchinson, S. (2009). The Red Hat Society: An exploration of play and masking in older women's lives. In D. Kuschner (Ed), *From children to Red Hatters: Diverse images and issues of play, play & culture studies, volume 8*. Lanham, MD: University Press of America.

Zohar, A., & Nemet, F. (2002). Fostering students' knowledge and argumentation skills through dilemmas in human genetics. *Journal of Research in Science Teaching, 39*(1), 35–62.

Part II

PROMOTING HUMAN DEVELOPMENT USING PERFORMANCE

Chapter Six

Play as a Staging Ground for Performance and Life

Sally Bailey

"To be one who plays is to be one who bravely adventures through life."

—McKenna Hall (2009)

Play has been seen by developmental psychologists as the work of childhood: the way children best learn, test reality, practice skills, and express themselves (Bodrova & Leong, 2007; Brown, 2009; Pelligrini & Smith, 2005; Piaget as cited in Flavel, 1963; Russ, 1993; Vygotsky, 1978; Weininger, 1979, 1988). However, once they enter formal schooling, with each passing year students are given less and less support for playing due to the accepted mainstream belief that play is not a valuable academic tool and will not be needed in their futures. The responsibilities of adulthood are not thought to require play much beyond the physical benefits that participation in sports provide. However, research shows how crucial play is as a developmental, educational, recreational, and therapeutic tool for people throughout the lifespan (Bodrova & Leong, 2007; Brown, 2009; Sawyer, 1997; Smilansky, 1968; Vygotsky, 1978; Weinninger, 1979, 1988).

As a theatre artist whose work includes playing in the rehearsal hall and on the stage, as a drama therapist who has used play to heal traumatized lives, and as a teacher of young adults who are developing social-emotional skills, I have found that dramatic play is essential for people of all ages. Play is at the root of imagination, creativity, and the ability to think and create metaphor, social connection, and healing (Brown, 2009). It is a stress-relieving activity *par excellence*, which regenerates and revives the weary body, mind, and spirit (Bailey, 2004, 2008; Brown, 2009). Moreover, dramatic play provides a safe haven in which players can rehearse skills and behaviors that transfer directly to performance on all of life's stages (Bailey, 1993; Emunah & Johnson, 2009; Moreno in Fox, 1987; Sternberg & Garcia, 2000).

THE DEVELOPMENTAL NATURE OF PLAY FROM INFANCY THROUGH ADULTHOOD

We begin playing almost as soon as we are born, exploring our world through sensorimotor play (Piaget as cited in Flavel, 1963). Within hours of birth, babies initiate mirroring and imitating others. Between the ages of 1 ½ and 3 years all children begin to engage in dramatic play (Piaget as cited in Flavel, 1963; Weininger, 1979). This form of play becomes a major avenue through which we observe how society functions, reflect on the world around us, and practice doing what we see. Play is found in all human cultures (Pelligrini & Smith, 2005; Brown, 2009). It appears that humans are "biologically wired" to play, just as we are "biologically wired" to learn language. Dramatic play is one of our innate learning modalities (Brown, 2009; Vygotsky, 1978; Weininger 1988).

If we are lucky, we have parents and siblings who encourage our play by playing *with* us, scaffolding and encouraging our basic "hardwired skills." Children who have missed opportunities to play—whether because of neglect, poverty, isolation, disabilities, or sickness—lack certain cognitive skills, socio-emotional understanding, and physical abilities (Bailey, 1993; Brown, 2009; Vygotsky, 1978). The richer a child's play, the more connections are generated among the neurons in her brain, the more pathways are developed to connect brain regions, and the more problem-solving resources are available to her in school and in life (Brown, 2009).

In the 1930's Russian psychologist Lev Vygotsky identified dramatic play as the leading educational tool for pre-school children (Bodrova & Leong, 2006). Vygotsky (1978) felt that dramatic play allowed children to develop crucial beginning cognitive structures that later mature into abstract reasoning. One of the outcomes of dramatic play is the creation of imagination—a symbolic state in which children can explore reality through a system of signs to learn about thinking, problem-solving, and functioning with others under the rules of society. In dramatic play these symbols are the imaginary characters and situations that are enacted. He sees dramatic play as the first move from external (sensorimotor) to internal (abstract reasoning) learning. Without dramatic play experiences, he believed, children would have difficulty coming to understand and develop social roles, the rules of behavior, cultural competence, impulse control, and the symbolic manipulation of ideas (Bodrova & Leong, 2006; Vygotsky, 1978).

Vygotsky was not the only psychologist who saw play as a central component of healthy learning and growth. Otto Weininger (1988) conceptualized imagination as the ability to pose questions and think about "what if?" "What if I were one of King Arthur's knights?". He identified the ability to pretend as acting out a particular role in dramatic play: behaving "as if" one were someone else or using an object "as if" it were something else. In his model, imagination and pretend, while different processes, are intimately connected to and build on each other reciprocally.

The ability to use the "as if" does not go away with age; it continues to be a skill we can access at any time. Constantin Stanislavski taught actors using his method to develop their "as if" abilities to a fine degree (Stanislavski, 1961). Stanislavski's acting method continues to be used by contemporary actors. "As if" can also be applied to the classroom and the workplace to assist the invention of new skills, ideas, solutions to problems, or ways of interacting with others. The "as if"(dramatic play) provides a staging ground on which "what ifs" (imagination, ideas, images, or hypotheses) can be explored.

The "as if" and "what if" involved in play do not exist in reality—they are imaginary constructs that are generated and shared between human minds in real space and time. This dynamic creates an interesting juxtaposition of real and non-real interacting simultaneously. D.W. Winnicott (1971) described play as happening in a liminal, symbolic space which he called *potential space*, a realm that is physical and real, but also imaginary and full of possibilities. Today Winnicott's term *potential space* is referred to as *transitional space* (Johnson, 1999), the metaphorical place where reality transitions into imagination and both co-exist. In dramatic play, transitional space is where children can become medieval knights and slay fire-breathing dragons. In theatre it is where the actor makes the transition from himself to his character and the audience allows a "willing suspension of disbelief" to come over them in order to accept fiction as truth and enjoy the play as a temporary reflection of reality. In therapy it is where the client can heal and change by revisiting and transforming past experiences, trying on new roles, and practicing new ways of being.

The transitional space is co-created by all the participants and creates a safe space in which anything can happen. That safety is guaranteed by the good-enough mother, the good-enough teacher/director, or the good-enough therapist who facilitates the creation of the play space and ensures that whatever happens, even if it might be scary part of the time, is not ultimately traumatic and damaging. The ability to have one foot in reality and the other in an imaginary world is one of the unique abilities homo sapiens have that, so far as we know, no other living creatures with the capacity to engage in play also have (Brown, 2009).

While some forms of play are done alone, most forms of dramatic play are done in groups and, therefore, provide the opportunity to learn social skills and how to interact with others. Through the give and take of play—particularly through the complex symbolic replications of life made possible through dramatic play—we learn how to share, compromise, listen to, and respect each other. We can open up and honestly be ourselves, because we feel we will be accepted. As a result, we get to know ourselves better, we get to know our playmates deeply, and our playmates get to know us.

DRAMATIC PLAY IN THE COLLEGE CLASSROOM

Despite positive results identified by psychologists and educators who have researched the benefits of play in the classroom (Bodrova & Leong, 2006; Sawyer, 1997; Smilansky, 1968; Vygotsky, 1978; Weininger, 1988), dramatic play by and large has been neglected as a teaching resource in the vast majority of our elementary, secondary, and collegiate educational environments. I have always felt more comfortable presenting information in an interactive, dramatic manner, rather than in a lecture mode, and during the last ten years as I have focused on teaching college students, I have come to believe that it is not only more enjoyable for me to deliver and for students to receive instruction through dramatic play, it is also more effective. Students who learn through action and then reflect on that action are making their own discoveries, which they retain longer than facts which are presented to them already "packaged" by their professor. I have observed that students tend to learn in more depth and breadth as well: incorporating social and emotional information in addition to facts, theories, and other objective course content. This seems to me to be appropriate as the university educational mission at Kansas State University, where I teach, identifies knowledge, critical thinking, communication, diversity, academic and professional integrity, developing human potential, and enriching cultural expression as priorities for student learning outcomes (Kansas State University, 2009). One course that clearly demonstrates my observations on the value of play for preparing young adults for life is Creative Drama.

Creative Drama at Kansas State University

Each semester for the past ten years I have taught Creative Drama, a course which is open to undergraduate and graduate students across the university. The class meets twice a week for an hour and fifteen minutes. A typical class has 24 students enrolled: a combination of undergraduates in social work, biology, speech pathology, political science, psychology, business, agriculture, English, and theatre, along with graduate students in accounting, family studies, counseling, and drama therapy. Because this assortment of students is not the usual cohort of theatre and education students who take Creative Drama in order to learn how to teach it to young children, I focus the class on exploring play and creativity personally through actually engaging in play dramatically.

The course is organized into four units beginning with theatre games and improvisation, moving to storytelling, then to story drama, and ending with puppetry. The stated goals of the course include developing students' creative imaginations, self-expression, self-knowledge, and social relatedness through working with others in a creative group enterprise focused on dramatic activities (Bailey, 2009a). This class has provided me with an environment in which to observe, assess, and reflect on what dramatic play has to offer young adults and to allow my students to do the same. I ask my students to focus on re-discovering how to use their imaginations, connecting with others, and collaborating to create effective improvisational dramatic experiences. While the class does not specifically focus on the potential of play to promote healing, the students report that it consistently generates personal as well as educational and aesthetic growth for them.

As the first assignment of each semester I ask students to write their definition of play. Most definitions are short and simple, ranging from "having fun" to "acting on a stage in a performance" to "playing games with friends." They keep a daily journal about what we did in class and reflect on the activities and their experience of them critically. After spending fifteen weeks immersed in a variety of forms of dramatic play, I ask them to write a 6 to 8 page paper on what they have discovered about play through the semester. When they first receive the assignment, their reaction is usually, "How can anyone write 6 pages about *play*? There's nothing to *say!*" But when they turn in their papers, I am always amazed at what they have discovered and articulated.

A pattern of responses has appeared over the years that mirror my own experiences in play as a child and as an adult. Students speak of common obstacles, constructed by cultural stereotypes, they had to face and overcome before they could join the play. They are able to point out which aspects of the class allowed them to do so. These structural components are safety, permission to take risks, and acceptance by the group. When these are in place, a transitional space can be created and students willingly and fully enter into the play process.

Students talk about experiencing growth in a number of areas of their lives once they have become deeply involved in play. They talk about learning more about themselves and developing relationships with others. They identify practical skills in problem solving and communication that they have learned and how they have integrated those skills into their performance in other classes, jobs, and personal relationships. They regularly report that they experience the natural healing power of play and leave class rejuvenated, refreshed, and renewed. Their insights validate for me that what I have observed is a common experience of play. Their responses, often eloquent and deep, resemble various observations made by psychologists and philosophers of play, even though my students have only been exposed to those ideas briefly. However, for these insights to be achieved, students need to be prepared in the beginning weeks of the semester to step out of their inhibited comfort zones, let go of their prejudices about play as being "childish" or "silly," and allow their "creative juices" to flow as freely as when they were younger. Without time spent investing in the creation of an environment for play, no play will happen, or if it does, it will be half-hearted at best. In this chapter I will identify key elements that encourage the development of a play community and the impact of the class on the students. Because I have students do reflective writing via journals and papers, many students' experiences are shared in their own words, quoted here through their permission.

Creating the Environment for Play

In order to play whole-heartedly students need to feel they are in a safe space where they can succeed, where they will be welcomed, accepted, and respected by the leader and the other participants, and where they will have the freedom to express themselves within clear boundaries so they can share their ideas without offending or being offended by others. When these criteria are achieved, a play community forms and co-creates a transitional space in which they are able to play.

The Transitional Space Must Be a Safe Space

Being college students—few of them drama majors—the types of play my students still engage in rarely incorporate dramatic play or make-believe. Recreational time tends to be devoted to partying, drinking, video games, watching entertainment, and participating in or watching sports. Motivating students to let go of their inhibitions enough so that they can play dramatically means creating a space in which they feel safe enough to trust me, and each other.

As the group leader I work hard at creating a fair and respectful framework in which students can interact with each other. I set clear parameters, laying out expectations so players know what the boundaries are for their own and for others' behavior. For each activity I identify, not just the rules, but also the goals. For instance, if I introduce a game that relies on cooperation, I mention that as a goal that ideally should be an outcome of following the rules. This, I think, helps frame the experience for people from a culture where winning at any cost is often the unspoken value assumed for any team-based interaction.

My players acknowledge that this clear framework that supports their play creates the safety of the transitional space. Anna Beck expresses it this way:

> We were given a framework, much like a picture frame, and asked to fill it in. Sometimes, the picture frame was smaller than others (we were given more specific instructions), and other times the frame was quite large…But the fact that we were given a frame allowed the painting of a masterpiece inside. Without a frame, we would all have had different ideas of what to create and the very play itself would have become chaotic. (Bailey, 2008)

While I want students to experience freedom for self-expression, one of the basic general class ground rules is to respect the others in the group and think through how your actions could affect them. Many contemporary professional improvisation groups push the boundaries of good taste and go for shock value, but these players have extensive training and have often worked as an ensemble for a long time. In my creative drama class, students are beginners learning to work together. Before we jump into improvisation, I like to say:

> We can do wild and crazy things in class, but before you take a flying leap into the unknown, take a second to evaluate if you would feel comfortable doing this activity or telling this story in front of your mother or your younger sister. If they wouldn't be offended, then you are probably not going to be embarrassed and you won't embarrass another member of the group.

I do not see this request as censorship or even self-censorship, but as encouragement to take the tastes and sensitivities of others in the group into respectful consideration. I like to remind people before a game that involves a lot of spontaneity to "make sure everything you do is within the bounds of good taste." On rare occasions when insensitivity occurs, I step in and gently, but firmly say, "That was inappropriate. Try something else," or "Whoops, let's rewind that and make a different choice."

Without a framework held together by a trusted and trustworthy leader, players cannot feel safe and will tend to avoid crossing into the transitional space. As Anna Beck, one of my graduate students, said, "I believe there is a moment, right before we consciously decide to enter the world of play, and that moment is much like jumping off a cliff. However, a safe environment and basic structure provide a safety net, and that will allow you to jump without fear, and enjoy the feeling of flying" (Bailey, 2008).

Another student has pointed out the importance of the leader being aware of the emotional and imaginative states of the players. Derek Schneweis says, "The leader has to enter the minds of the actors and take them on a journey" (Bailey, 2009b). If the players are not prepared to go with the leader, they will not follow; however, if the leader has prepared the players and has a good sense of the current state of their abilities, openness, and imagination, they will follow willingly. An effective leader plays along with the group of players, as opposed to controlling the group from a position as an outside manipulator.

Risking Becomes Possible in a Nonjudgmental Atmosphere

In order to feel free enough to take risks, students need to let go of their fears of others judging them negatively as well as fears of the voices of their own "inner critics." Whenever feedback from one player to another or one group to another is necessary, I request comments to be framed constructively and supportively. I encourage the sharing first of "what works," not only so that those on the receiving end can feel good about their performance, but also because when we are not aware of what succeeded, we often throw away what is most exciting, fresh, and valuable along with what was ineffective. Additionally, hearing positive comments first opens up the listener, so she can later take in the aspects of the scene or story that need to be worked on.

When someone is framing comments on what did not work, the use of objective observation skills and critical thinking go hand-in-hand. When a recipient of feedback is able to stand back and look at the work from a distance as a "transitional experience" that was "just pretend," suggestions for improvement become easier to accept without defensiveness. Feedback can be offered in terms of what the character did in the scene as opposed to what the player did. Evaluations can be couched in terms of what could make the scene more effective, more expressive, or more exciting when replayed. Students can be reminded that, unlike many real life situations, in play there are many chances for "do-overs," and because of that, players often become more open and relaxed about taking risks.

Participants need to develop an internal locus of evaluation, so they are not inhibited by external judgment from either the leader/adult/therapist/teacher or the other players. Darin Brunson says, "Ridicule is an enemy of creativity and play" (Bailey, 2008), whether it is real, imagined, or just anticipated from others. Trash-talking is not acceptable during game playing nor are put-downs or "laughter at" instead of "laughter with" the actors in response to improvisations.

Achieving an internal locus of evaluation for all the individuals in a group can be difficult in a class for which a grade must eventually be assigned. As the leader I try to put the emphasis and value on full and joyous participation, rather than on holding players to a specific level of aesthetic achievement. I find that when the pressure for "performance value" is taken off, the level of achievement often improves on its own because students feel free to take the necessary risks to excel. In short, they allow themselves to stop judging themselves and start playing. In my grading system more points go toward participation and reflection activities than performance benchmarks.

I also ask them to list at least three personal goals to achieve during the semester, whether that be to make new friends, learn new games to use at summer camp, or simply get an A. Darin Brunson identified that maintaining a sense of individual control seems to make it possible for everyone to "hover outside their comfort zone" through their own choice (Bailey, 2008). Ironically, once players are focused on playing in the moment and not on judging themselves or others, they often effortlessly achieve artistic heights they never expected they could reach.

The Transitional Space Must Be a Place of Welcome

Players need to feel unconditional positive regard from others in the group and experience give-and-take in terms of empathic understanding (Rogers, 1954 cited in Russ, 1993). Each player must come to believe that when she joins the others, she will be accepted. "Come and play" is one of the most joyous invitations that can be extended. Unfortunately, all of us, at one time or another in our lives have experienced the isolation of being excluded from the play space or not being picked for the team. That is a lonely and sometimes traumatic experience—for anyone of any age. As Ryan Robinson (Bailey, 2008) puts it, "Those five words, 'Do you want to play?' can change your life....Those words represent a gift to an outsider...acceptance of their presence, a welcome gesture to be part of a group. Our life is all about making connections with others."

The appreciation for each other quickly becomes an important aspect of the class. Comments like McKenna Hall's "I wish I could convey to everyone how deeply I am affected by our time together this semester. I looked forward to class each and every day to hang out with our group and to learn together what it means to be an adult who truly embraces play," are common (Bailey, 2009b).

We play different name games for at least three or four periods in the beginning of the semester until everyone has a good grasp of everyone else's name. This is not a small thing for a class that ranges in size from 20 to 26, but it is crucial in order for individuals to feel as if they belong within the group. To be seen and accepted as a valuable, named contributor starts connections that grow. Many students have told me that Creative Drama is the only course they have had in four years of college where they knew the name of every person in the room and where, in turn, the professor knew their names.

In addition I make sure that everyone has worked with everyone else at least once during the first unit by randomly dividing into smaller working groups for each activity. This facilitates the learning of names and allows each person an opportunity to personally interact with as many of the others as possible. The more social connections that are made, the more known and the safer each person tends to feel. By the time we start the storytelling unit, students feel as if they are part of a community.

Avoiding competition with a group of players beginning to develop a playing relationship also creates a safer, more accepting play space. I start with cooperative team building games and improvisations whether I am working with a theatre class, therapy group, or theatrical troupe. If I introduce competition at all, it is in small doses and long after the group has become a cohesive whole. This, along with the emphasis on learning names early, and the small group mixing method, ensures that by the time several weeks have passed, no one is a stranger; everyone has become each others' playmates.

Student Learning Outcomes that Result from Play in the Classroom

Students' participation in a semester of play teaches objective content, such as Aristotle's six elements of drama, the theories of play as a sociological and psychological construct, how to prepare and tell a story, the theatrical skills required for improvisation, and a variety of methods for constructing puppets. These outcomes result in specific dramatic skills, which can be utilized in their professional and personal lives. Students also develop larger, more general outcomes targeted by the university, such as enhanced critical thinking, improved communication, wider awareness of diversity, expanded human potential, enriched cultural expression, and academic and professional integrity. These outcomes have been targeted as desirable for all university courses to address. In terms of the Creative Drama course, I believe the achievement of these wider outcomes ultimately focuses on the development of a deeper understanding and appreciation of self and a wider range of social and emotional skills for use when interacting within a community.

Learning about the self

Play helps the player learn about herself and develop her own identity. As one succeeds in a group and has contributions accepted and valued, confidence and self-esteem rise; fears abate. New ideas, roles, and abilities can be experimented with and extended. Darin Brunson says it is "ok to take chances and sometimes even completely flop" (Bailey, 2008). The group and the leader are there for support and encouragement.

Within the structure of a game, "winning" and "losing" is temporary. One game ends and the next begins. Rachel Massoth reported, "I never remembered who the winners and losers were, I just remembered different parts of the game, and the creativeness of the people involved" (Bailey, 2004). Your position can change from leader to follower or from loser to winner, even within successive rounds of the same game, providing the opportunity to experience a variety of roles and expand the repertoire of roles available for you to play in life. While making improvisational scenes, situations can be replayed in different ways or roles can be reversed in order to experience the other character's point of view, extending and expanding everyone's point of view and empathy. When this is done, new insights result.

Developing problem-solving skills

Problem-solving skills are enhanced in play, in part because of the symbolic capacities of the form. Divergent thinking skills, which are typically not practiced frequently in traditional schooling, can be re-learned and with them intrinsic motivation for problem-solving can be re-ignited. Any object one plays with can be used metaphorically "as if" another and any situation can be explored through "what if." Within the realm of the imagination, a variety of choices can be played with safely, and therefore, the potential consequences of those choices can be experienced and evaluated in the "laboratory setting" of the classroom before being tried out in the "real world" where those consequences might be harmful and irreversible. Ashley Gibbs expressed her insights into this process in this way:

> Not only does play enable people to use their real life experiences to organize concepts of how the world really operates; through play one can see how new experiences are related to previous learning. Much of what we learn cannot be taught directly (as in many of the lectured college classes), but must be put together in our own way through our experiences. We all understand that feeling of "ah-ha!" when we finally understand something. By using play to learn new things, we are more likely to have that feeling… (Bailey, 2009b)

Play provides emotional and intellectual distance so that difficult issues can be experienced and experimented with. Much of play is done within a distancing structure of some kind. Rules of behavior that are followed within a game apply to everyone and create a level playing field in which skills can be tested without risking actual loss of status, money, or life. Fictional characters that are played out within dramatized scenes under the guise of "just pretend," allow players to put themselves into the shoes of people very similar or very unlike themselves. Even improvising a situation one might actually experience is within a protected, distanced structure, because the improviser knows she is in a scene. When the scene is over, each improviser leaves the "transitional reality" of the scene and goes back to being herself within the larger group.

Developing self confidence

The confidence that develops through playing is a key element in the ability of players to become performers whether on the transitional space of the theatrical stage or in the real world. Playing with others in a group allows one to be seen as an active agent and valid contributor. At first some shy or unconfident students may feel shame or embarrassment at being "seen" in the group. In the beginning they experience stage fright and worry that they will not be "good enough," but as they experience success through the play process, their ability to enjoy standing out in the group grows. Gretchen Hammes, a graduate accounting student, reported, "When we first started the class, I was afraid to even speak out in front of the class and by the time my group performed "The Three Billy Goats Gruff" [in the story drama unit], I was wearing faux horns and grazing on the stage" (Bailey, 2003).

Laura Taylor reported:

> This class has let me discover ways to feel safe havens by completely opening up…not only being honest to myself, but with my classmates as well! My "secret space" in which I can be safely alone and give myself over to needed fantasies and adapt to the challenging world is right here in this very classroom where judgment, vulnerability, and self consciousness is left at the door when you walk in! It has allowed me to discover…a sense of trust and well being that would allow play to emerge….The ability to play is in all of us and transformative when it's rediscovered! Free yourself of fear! (Bailey, 2009b)

Feeling free enough to be oneself with others because one feels accepted is an example of what humanist psychologist Carl Rogers called "unconditional positive regard" (Rogers as cited in Russ, 1993). Rogers felt it was necessary for each human to experience unconditional positive regard in order to feel loved and to be able to grow and thrive in relationships (Rogers, 1970). This leads us naturally to a discussion about the self in relationship with others, which requires the development of social and emotional skills.

Social and Emotional Skills

Developing relationships through play

Dramatic play is done in groups and, therefore, provides the opportunity to teach social skills and how to interact with others. In order to care about learning social skills, one has to care about developing a positive relationship with the others with whom one interacts. In a cohesive, trusting group we can open up and honestly be ourselves. As a result, we get to know our playmates deeply and they get to know us. Amanda Hoffman expressed her understanding of how play and relationships are connected through the following analysis:

> Play is a process acted out through relationships. This process builds new ones and strengthens the ones already in place….I believe, if people took more time to play and build relationships, many of the problems and miscommunications we have within our world would not be so strained and serious. Playing would allow people to break down their fears and struggles and relax more. Playing would allow people to express their true personalities and not be so afraid of speaking out or taking a stand. Play would unite people together because we would not be so afraid of what people would think about us. This would improve society in so many ways—one of the most important, I believe, would be in respecting diversity. (Bailey, 2004)

Stuart Brown (2009), a psychiatrist and clinical researcher, sees this connection between play and relationships as well. He says, "Play modulates deep psychological fears and insecurities that threaten emotional closeness" (p. 163). He believes that long term friendships and romantic relationships develop from and are sustained through play. The flexibility, joy, and spontaneity that play creates keep interactions interesting and smoothes out conflicts that inevitably occur when two or more people are together.

Stress relief

Play helps release tension and promotes relaxation. Putting aside the everyday grind and pressures to focus on an intense, enjoyable, short-term goal with others gives players a break from the vicissitudes of daily life and allows them to think more clearly when they go back to work. Student players remark quite often that dramatic play is a welcome break from their academic burdens and learn that when they are stressed, taking a "play break" can actually help.

> I used to not deal with stress very well….Now when I have a huge project come up, I have learned that stressing and worrying about it will not get the project or paper written any sooner….I have also found out that the less time you stress about a situation, the more clear your mind, which in turn makes it easier to come up with ideas. Since I have learned how to de-stress myself [through play], it has cut the amount of time it takes me to do my school work. I no longer have to stay up until the wee hours of the morning. I am getting better nights of sleep, and I'm becoming more productive in my other classes…people ask me how I'm able to accomplish so much when I have a lot going on. I tell them that when I find I am starting to stress, I take a break or go play. (Bailey, 2004)

Adam Hamor concurs, "…play can help focus a person or group. When I stress over an assignment, taking a break to play or be creative helps a lot to re-focus my attention on what needs to be done"(Bailey, 2004). Functioning effectively or fully when stressed is difficult; play breaks or playful approaches to work and interactions allows ideas, communication, and energy to flow freely within an individual's system as well as within a social system.

Social support

Even in the worst of times, approaching life with an attitude of playfulness can make a major difference in a person's ability to handle the stresses and struggles of life. One fall, early in the semester, while driving home for the weekend, Amy Bosomworth was pushed off the road by another vehicle. Her car rolled four times and she broke the second vertebrae in her neck. As she says, "It was a miracle that let me walk away from that accident. Looking at pictures of the car now, I can't believe how lucky I am to have survived" (Bailey, 2004). She was in a lot of pain and spent several weeks in bed. She says that even when she could not sit up longer than a half an hour, "I wanted to be in Creative Drama, I wanted to listen to the stories and remember how fun it was to be active." She practiced her story for her dog and "played with him as a recovery tool." Returning to school was far more challenging than she had imagined due to pain, physical limitations, missed lessons, and fear of failure.

> Some people were mean and others were exaggeratedly nice. I was the same person—why was I suddenly feeling like I would never fit in again? But I hadn't been to Creative Drama yet….my classmates showed me that it is okay to make fun of myself. Laughing is really one of the best medicines, and laughing happens when you are playing. (Bailey, 2004)

Her story drama group always found something she could do in each story that would not hurt too much and frequently incorporated humor that played with her situation. For their scary Halloween story drama she decided that she would go Trick or Treating as a crash test dummy.

> Without the ability to make fun of myself and play, I would have been a wreck—a sad, lonely, cranky mess of a human being. The ability of playing gave me the opportunity to feel as if I could live again, even with a collar around my neck, cast around my hand, weeks of homework to make up, and people who stare and ask too many personal questions. My opinion of play changed from "adults don't have time for it," to "adults better find time for it—everyday!" (Bailey, 2004)

Human beings are social animals. We crave the support and encouragement of our kind. There is no doubt in my mind, after reading about Amy's experience, that the social support the other members of the class offered made all the difference in the world to her ability to heal emotionally and physically from her accident. Without it, she might not have made it out of her bed by the end of the semester and quite possibly may have fallen into a deep depression.

PLAY: THE PERFECT REHEARSAL

As one student articulately put it, "Play is cross-training for adult life," in terms of physical, mental, and emotional education (Bailey, 2004). What is learned in play at any age can be put into practice at school, at work, at home, and in the community. The skills learned through the process of play are then transformed into the product of performance outside of the transitional play space in the real world in real time.

Creative drama is an approved professional elective for Communication Science Disorders (CSD) majors at Kansas State University because dramatic play skills can be directly applied to future speech therapy clients. Nothing is more motivating for a child—or for any of us—than play. Clients will practice a skill that is fun many more times than they will one that is boring. They will pay attention to information that is novel and presented in a way that appeals to their imagination. Quite a few Communication Science Disorders majors have echoed this CSD student when she reported, "Many children with speech impairments are not very confident or outgoing in their attempts to make friends or just in being themselves. This reminds me of myself at the beginning of the semester quite a bit and I think a little bit of play in their lives prior to the speech therapy could increase their confidence and give their personality a boost as well"(Bailey, 2008).

Creative drama is also an approved elective for graduate accounting students in the College of Business and for students in the Leadership Studies minor. Skills developed in playing are immediately applicable to brainstorming in a corporate environment and to developing teams that can work effectively, respectfully, and creatively together in the workplace. Students who have interviewed for summer internships in a number of accounting firms in Kansas City have told me that when they report to certain potential employers that they have taken Creative Drama at K-State, they are seen as having an advantage, because they have already developed into team players who can creatively think outside of the box and bring a positive attitude into the office.

Even the ability to get a job can be enhanced through the confidence and skills taught through play. Ryan Young, a graduate accounting student, was, by his own admission, shy and introverted. His first experience of interviewing for summer internships in the recruiting done on campus by CPA firms each October was not successful. He felt awkward meeting new people and portraying his personality in a favorable light. He believed that because he held back, he was not offered a position (Bailey, 2004). However, after taking Creative Drama, he reported that he had learned how to confidently and genuinely encounter other people. So when he went to the recruiting day the next year, he says,

> After attending several social events that the CPA firms hosted, I knew that Creative Drama had made a difference. I actually enjoyed meeting the different people from the firms and felt that they were mutually interested in me. I was much more relaxed, less shy, and more out-going around all of these strangers. I was invited to four different CPA firms to have an office interview. By the end of the process, I had two offers to choose from....By being able to better understand play, I believe that I was able to obtain a full time position. (Bailey, 2004)

Ryan's employment saga may or may not have related to his personal growth in the Creative Drama class, we have no way to know for certain; however, what is significant is that he was able to identify what was different about his approach to his job interviews pre- and post-class and where he learned those skills.

CONCLUSION

Just as preschoolers find dramatic play to be an emotionally supportive, natural vehicle for learning, college students also thrive when they are presented curricular material through play. Any educator, administrator, or non-playing individual of any age who suggests that play belongs only to childhood because it has been replaced by "higher, abstract thinking abilities" of the formal operations period is ignoring basic learning theory from developmental psychology. Gardner (1991) makes a strong case in *The Unschooled Mind* that learning modes from sensorimotor, pre-operational, and operational stages of cognitive growth are not extinguished as we age, but are merely overlaid and enhanced by newly developed cognitive abilities. Students never stop using earlier learning modes, even if teachers neglect to employ them.

Growing older does not negate the need to explore the world through dramatic play's "as if" and "what if." If anything, the creativity demanded by the workplace of the 21st century requires these abilities even more. Daniel Pink, author of *A Whole New Mind* (2006), identifies play, story, empathy, design, symphony (i.e., the ability to work harmoniously with others), and meaning as the six senses that all workers will need in order to succeed in business in the Conceptual Age we have entered. The brave new world of enterprise requires workers to incorporate high tech, high touch, and high concept in order to stand above the crowd.

Play encourages participants to connect proactively with others, engage in the team concept, and perform at a high level. In a play community all play their parts as effectively as they can for the enjoyment and betterment of themselves and the group. Shy, awkward individuals are challenged in a nurturing, supportive way to step beyond their self-limiting boundaries into new, freer, more powerful identities.

Stuart Brown, founder of the National Institute for Play, says, "I sometimes compare play to oxygen—it's all around us, yet goes mostly unnoticed or unappreciated until it is missing" (Brown, 2009, p. 6). People of all ages must be made aware of the need to incorporate play into their jobs and relationships daily. This will ensure their ability to continue to learn and grow, to make healthy connections with others, to release their stresses and worries, and to continue to be mentally and physically healthy adults.

Perhaps my favorite student quote about play and the doors it can open for everyone who participates in it comes from Ryan Robinson. He says, "Play is the freedom to live your dreams in consciousness…in play we can make our dreams come true" (Bailey, 2008). Play into performance; imagination into reality; all we have to do is trust in the process, believe in our innate creative abilities, and we can manifest the imaginative process into aesthetic and practical products.

REFERENCES

Bailey, S.D. (1993). *Wings to fly: Bringing theatre arts to students with special needs.* Rockville, MD.

Bailey, S.D. (2003). [Citations from course papers]. Unpublished raw data.

Bailey, S.D. (2004). [Citations from course papers]. Unpublished raw data.

Bailey, S.D. (2008). [Citations from course papers]. Unpublished raw data.

Bailey, S.D. (2009a). *Creative Drama.* Unpublished class syllabus, Department of Communication Studies, Theatre and Dance, Kansas State University, Manhattan, KS.

Bailey, S.D. (2009b). [Citations from course papers]. Unpublished raw data.

Bodrova, E. & Leong, D.L. (2007). *Tools of the mind: The Vygotskian approach to early childhood education, 2*nd *ed.* New York, NY: Prentice Hall.

Brown, S. (2009). *Play: How it shapes the brain, opens the imagination, and invigorates the soul.* New York, NY: Penguin Group.

Emunah, R., & Johnson, D.R. (Eds.). (2009). *Current approaches in drama therapy, 2nd ed.* Springfield, IL: Charles C. Thomas Publisher.

Flavel, J.H. (1963). *The developmental psychology of Jean Piaget.* New York, NY: D. Van Nostrand Company.

Fox, J. (Ed.). (1987). *The essential Moreno.* New York, NY: Springer Publishing.

Gardner, H. (1991). *The unschooled mind: How children think and how schools should teach.* New York, NY: Basic Books.

Johnson, D.R. (1999). *Essays on the creative arts therapies: Imaging the birth of a profession.* Springfield, IL: Charles C. Thomas Publisher.

Kansas State University, Manhattan, Kansas, *About the university: Mission statement.* Retrieved December 31, 2009 from the Kansas State University Web site: http://catalog.k-state.edu/content.php?catoid=13&navoid=1403.

Pelligrini, A.D., & Smith, P.K. (2005). *The nature of play: Great apes and humans.* New York, NY: Guilford Press.

Pink, D.H. (2006). *A whole new mind: Why right-brainers will rule the future.* New York, NY: Riverhead Books.

Rogers, C. (1970). *On encounter groups.* New York, NY: Harper and Row, 1970.

Russ, S.W. (1993). *Affect and creativity: The role of affect and play in the creative process.* Hillsdale, NJ: Lawrence Erlbaum Associates, Inc.

Sawyer, R.K. (1997). *Pretend play as improvisation.* Mahway, NJ: Lawrence Erlbaum Associates, Inc.

Smilansky, S. (1968). *The effects of sociodramatic play on disadvantaged preschool children.* New York, NY: Wiley & Sons.

Stanislavski, C. (1961). *Creating a role.* New York, NY: Theatre Arts Books.

Sternberg, P., & Garcia, A. (2000). *Sociodrama: Who's in Your Shoes? 2nd ed.,* Westport, CT: Praeger.

Vygotsky, L. (1978). *Mind in society: The development of higher psychological processes.* Cambridge, MA: Harvard University Press.

Weininger, O. (1979). *Play and education: The basic tool for early childhood learning.* Springfield, IL: Charles C. Thomas Publisher.

Weininger, O. (1988). "What If" and "As If": Imagination and pretend play in early childhood. In K. Egan & D. Nadaner, (Eds.), *Imagination and education.* New York, NY: Teacher's College Press, Columbia University, 141–52.

Winnicott, D.W. (1971). *Playing and reality.* London: Routledge.

Chapter Seven

Playing with Asperger's Syndrome: "We're not supposed to be able to do this, are we?"

Paul Murray

This chapter gives examples and analysis of the results of three years of playing at a small residential school in England for children aged 11 to 16, all of whom had been diagnosed as having Asperger's Syndrome. Being a theatre-maker, my practical efforts are represented here not in the form of traditional analysis or case study but as a series of scenes. Each scene tells a story of what I consider to be particularly important events, which took place at the school during my time there and each is concluded with a short account of why I deem these events to have been significant to my own learning. Each scene is entitled with one of ten characteristics of theatre-making that I have used elsewhere (Murray, 2009) as a frame of reference for better understanding and developing the ways in which Devised Theatre works. In practice, however, each of the following characteristics are perhaps more accurately described as aims that I attempt to realize.

- Entertainment: The theatre maker's underlying motivation is to entertain. She or he uses the theatre form in an attempt to share his or her own amusement in a particular facet of human existence.
- Facilitator: The work of the facilitator is to unearth the inherent creativity that lies within a society, or a group and those people which make it up.
- Group: Devised Theatre relies on a group of people working effectively together. The ability of the group to perform in such a manner depends upon the co-creation of a creative environment.
- Dialogue: The heart of theatre is the encounter. Dialogue, the direct encountering of others in a mutually curious manner, is the only process by which the creative environment can be co-created.
- Story: The story is the central operation of the theatre. I aim to develop with others essentially imperfect and provisional theatrical stories in order

to reveal the essentially imperfect and provisional nature of all (even real world) stories.

- Politics: Both the manner in which I create Devised Theatre and where I choose to create makes it a political act. An acknowledgement of this is essential in assessing its impact.
- Educational: Devised Theatre does not necessarily concern itself with the needs of formal educational systems. However it is concerned with education in a wider sense, due to its belief that all learning and all meaning is constructed and develops from relational activity.
- Individual: All individuals have equal rights within the devising process and have the ability to make a valuable contribution to the making of theatre and society.
- Relevance: Developing increased understanding of Devised Theatre and its relevance to society as a whole, requires the active seeking out of opportunities to dialogue with wider audiences and alternative modes of understanding.
- Playful: "By considering the whole sphere of...culture as a play sphere we pave the way to a more direct and more general understanding of its peculiarities than any meticulous psychological or sociological analysis would allow" (Huizinga, 1950, p. 25).

SCENE I: ENTERTAINMENT

At the beginning of this chapter the reader might be asking themselves: what would a theatre-maker find entertaining about working in a school for children with Asperger's Syndrome? The simple answer is that I have spent my career making theatre in contexts which I have found baffling, in order to better understand both them as well as the potentials and limits of theatre as a tool for human development. Inherent in this work is a dialectic between the theatre being created and the specific site in which it is situated. It is this dialectic and the events that unfold as a result of its practical development that I find entertaining; much in the same way that theatre-maker Bertolt Brecht alluded to in the following:

> The theatre...is in a position to make dialectics into a source of enjoyment. The unexpectedness of logically progressive or zigzag development, the instability of every circumstance, the joke of contradiction and so forth: all these are ways of enjoying the liveliness of men [sic], things and processes, and they heighten both our capacity for life and our pleasure in it. (cited in Willett, 1964, p. 277)

Devised Theatre

I am a professional actor, director and theatre teacher practicing the art-form known as Devised Theatre. For those of you unfamiliar with this term, it represents a particular method of theatre-making. "Rather than starting from a play text that someone else has written… devised theatrical performance originates with the group and is generated from people working in collaboration" (Oddey, 1994, p.1). The demands of Devised Theatre on the performer are arguably greater than those of more traditional or mainstream theatre where the contributions required of its actors are largely limited to playing specifically assigned roles and reciting specifically assigned lines. In contrast to this kind of treatment of the performer, Devised Theatre places increased responsibility and offers greater opportunity on the part of the actor to play a more central part in the theatre-making process. As Oddey again states, the Devised Theatre form "provides wider possibilities for all the members of the group…it offers a different route for the actor, which is often associated with having greater status and input within the overall creation of the theatrical product" (Oddey, 1994, p.11). Unlike in the mainstream theatre, the product that is created through this type of collaboration relies totally on the input of the performers within the group. My aim in creating a Devised Theatre piece is that the performance reflects as much as possible the views, opinions and creative ideas of all participants, for without their contribution to this process a truly collaborative product is unobtainable.

Very often the theatre-making activity that I undertake (or facilitate) does not (and is not designed to) result in the kind of theatrical product which is commonly played out on a stage in front of an audience. In my most recent work I have come to regard the whole experience of theatre-making as the "performance product" with all participants included as co-authors, performers and devisers. This does not mean to say that audiences for this kind of theatre performance do not exist. Throughout the devising process participants are encouraged to become their own audience; acting and performing with a degree of self-reflection and reflexivity towards not only their own actions but those of others within the group, and the performance generated by them.

Within the devised form of theatre-making previously "taken for granted" concepts such as *the performance, the actor (or performer) and audience* are challenged and expanded, as development of the form becomes entwined with the development of the participant. Defining Devised Theatre partly by its aim to aid the development of participants as performers, actors and human beings places those of us who practice this form, in direct or indirect contact with other professions and methods that similarly attempt to promote human development. Many Devised Theatre directors/facilitators recognize this feature of their work but few are keen to make specific reference to the role that the art-form may play in promoting human development. This may be due to artists' unwillingness to enter into the kind of justifications and quantifications that they believe would be required of them for their claims to be taken seriously by other professions.

There are of course exceptions: one of them being the renowned and increasingly recognized within the theatre field French theatre-teacher Jacques LeCoq, who has stated that:

> [My] sights are set on theatre, but theatre education is broader than theatre itself. In fact my work has always nurtured a dual aim: one part of my interest is focused on theatre, the other on life....My aim, perhaps utopian, is for... [participants]...to be consummate livers of life and complete artists on stage. (Lecoq, 2000, p.18)

Whatever LeCoq means by the phrases "complete artist on stage" or indeed "consummate liver of life" in a macro sense, it is clear from examining a variety of literature concerning Devised Theatre practice that there are a common set of skills which the director believes could distinguish a "strong" and competent performer.

The following list summarizes the skills that I aim to develop within all the participants in order to more effectively achieve a successful and truly representative theatre performance:

- Complicity or attunement: the ability to work sensitively with others.
- The ability to trust and be trusted.
- Playfulness: the ability to play with others as well as ideas and concepts.
- Imagination: the ability to reframe everyday understandings and offer new possibilities.
- Self-belief: to believe that one has an important contribution to the devising process.

Despite the fact that the theatre-making process aims to foster, encourage and promote the above skills in all participants, the individual participant is valued unconditionally from the outset as a performer (this statement applies even if the skills outlined above are not learned or demonstrated). Their value is similarly not judged by how productive or useful they may be to the wider society; it is only their contribution to the micro theatre-making process that concerns the theatre-director. Essentially what we are talking about here is contribution; fostering and promoting the reality that no matter what is thought of them in other contexts, each participant has a unique and valuable contribution to make to the creation of a shared group performance.

Playing with Asperger's Syndrome

Having suffered from what is commonly described as depression throughout my life, I have become acutely aware of the way in which behavior deemed by those in power to be at best *different* and at worst *deviant* has become judged by the values inherent within a system of economic production. A cursory glance through the history of mental health (and illness) would suggest that the relationship between diagnosis, confinement and productivity are inextricably linked.

This belief has drawn me to the conclusion that what stands in the way of many individuals being able to contribute to mainstream society is the fact that they are deemed incapable of adding to the overall economic wealth of the society. From my experience in working with the diagnosed and confined, it is also my conclusion that this perspective becomes appropriated within the belief system of many individuals who have been treated in this manner. I find the dominant system of diagnosis and treatment that is used to explain or contain "those of difference" to be a less than humane way of treating human beings and less than helping as a means of promoting overall human development and understanding.

Whether or not mainstream psychology has had a positive or negative effect in producing these effects remains to be seen, however what is clear is that the diagnosis of Asperger's Syndrome remains on the increase (Autism Society, 2010). If one examines the features or behaviors which combine to produce a diagnosis of Asperger's Syndrome (AS), one can see that the condition is largely identified by behaviors which stand in opposition to those that are regarded as being necessary for normal or productive human relations. According to medical literature (Klin, 1995), those suffering from AS do so because they display:

- Paucity of empathy.
- Naive, inappropriate, one-sided social interaction, little ability to form friendships and consequent social isolation.
- Pedantic and monotonic speech.
- Poor nonverbal communication.
- Intense absorption in circumscribed topics such as the weather, facts about TV stations, railway tables or maps, which are learned in rote fashion and reflect poor understanding, conveying the impression of eccentricity.
- Clumsy and ill-coordinated movements and odd posture.

This particular diagnosis is of interest to this theatre-maker, mainly because many of its features stand in direct opposition to those I am trying to promote in the Devised Theatre performer. If this explanation of these individuals were accurate it would strongly suggest that individuals diagnosed with AS do not have the capacities necessary to make a meaningful contribution to the theatre making activity. However, through my experience of working with children diagnosed with AS I am in no doubt that the behaviors they display can be somewhat out of the ordinary, but in no way have I found any of them incapable of making a valuable and unique contribution to the making of theatre.

The particular educational establishment in which much of this work took place is called Tinely House School (THS). It is an educational establishment operating within a mainstream school structure, with each child following the requirements of the national education curriculum. This educational model is delivered and supported by a number of teachers and teaching assistants. Outside the school day THS operates as a residential care institution for 38 weeks of the year with a separate staff of care and social workers. Crossing both aspects of the school is a team of therapists, psychologists and psychiatrists who are responsible for developing treatment programs for the children both within school and care time. I was asked into the school in order to deliver theatre and drama classes with each class for 45 minutes per week. Each of the 6 classes that I taught every Wednesday contained up to six children and between one or two teaching/care assistants.

Throughout this creative process the ability of many children to perform as theatre-makers shocked those that had previously believed them incapable of contributing to any form of social activity. In this chapter I work to communicate some of the experiences that have led to these reactions. It is my hope that the following scenes will not only help the reader to better understand the work which was undertaken, but may open the door to Devised Theatre being better understood and appreciated as a way of unlocking the potential of those we sometimes easily discount. It may be that it is only within the micro context of theatre-making that these young people have a meaningful contribution to make, but maybe not?

One final note with regard to the actual activities undertaken in pursuit of a theatre performance: what actually transpires in the theatre-making space. These activities are almost entirely comprised of simple group improvisation games. Such games will be familiar to many by the work of mainstream Improv theatre groups and television shows such as "Whose Line is it Anyway?" All of these games and exercises are designed to promote and develop "intuition, spontaneity, and an accumulation of ideas" (Oddey 1994, p.1), without which no theatre performance of any quality or originality could be generated.

The underlying principle of each game is commonly known in theatre circles as "yes and..." Every contribution made within the workshop, every idea put forward is accepted as being a meaningful and creative part of the overall performance; it is my job as director to play with and incorporate all ideas and suggestions presented rather than dismissing any of them as not being worthy or valuable contributions.

Finally before we move to scene two, I have to acknowledge the support and cooperation of the staff and students of Tinely House School, who accepted all offerings I made in pursuit of the Devised Theatre process we were all involved in performing/creating.

SCENE II: FACILITATOR

I remember clearly walking into the first class I ever taught at THS. Those in the room included five rather large and lively boys of 15–16 years and a rather small but equally lively teaching assistant. I began the class as I normally began initial drama sessions, with some general games and exercises to find out the abilities of the group in terms of such things like trust, concentration and imagination.

It is relatively normal procedure for a theatre facilitator to begin the process of theatre-making in this kind of way, attempting to focus the group in order that they can better ascertain the skill levels of the performers. It was clear however that after three weeks of trying to engage this particular group in a number of different activities, they were bored with what I was suggesting and would clearly rather be playing their own games. They did not seem to see the point of the trust or name games that I was trying my hardest to get them to play. I remember being increasingly frustrated that they wouldn't do as I wanted them to, and in my head I kept saying to myself that unless they did what I asked of them there is no way we would ever be able to make theatre together.

On reflection however, I noticed that in the times in between me trying to get them to play the games I wanted them to play, they would often play at shooting each other. It suddenly dawned on me; they were demonstrating quite clearly that they were already capable of performing together. Not only that, but if I had taken the time to see, I would have witnessed them demonstrating all the skills of *trust, concentration and imagination* that I could ever have hoped to teach them. I decided that if I couldn't beat them I would join them and picked up my imaginary gun.

As a result of doing this, I was now accepted into the group and the pattern of all following sessions developed. After a few more weeks we had got to the point where on entering the room, the first thing that was expected of me was to come out with the first line of an improvisation: such as "quick it's going to explode" or "how many times have I got to tell you don't come in here without the sausages?" The resulting improvisations would often continue for the length of the entire lesson. Occasionally we would stop to discuss how it was going and where we wanted to make changes, but essentially we improvised for 45 minutes each week. As a group we never really communicated with each other outside the fictional narrative apart from saying "goodbye" or "see you next week": I guess the intensity and meaning contained within these shared creative experiences made was clear to us all.

As stated in the introduction to this chapter, the skills that the facilitator is trying to teach or unearth from participants centre on complicity, trust, playfulness, imagination and self-belief. It is often the assumption of the facilitator that (whether working with those diagnosed with AS or not) that she is working with a set of "blank canvasses" or "empty vessels" to be filled with knowledge learnt from their expert director. The above story taught me clearly that not only are these skills alive and well in all human beings, but there is no reason why anyone should be expected to somehow "prove them" to an outsider if that outsider is not the kind of person that they wish to share them with. When I think of the typically intimidating situations a child finds themselves in when undergoing assessment for AS, I wonder how many choose not to demonstrate those qualities and abilities which would lead to them not being diagnosed?

Pharmaceutical Facilitation of New Performances

As a sub-scene, I must share what it feels like when one of the group is put on medication or has his medication changed. This happened to Jim. He came into the class one week acting like a zombie, completely devoid of any of the qualities that he had displayed in our sessions previously. He was usually so lively and enthusiastic, sometimes a little boisterous but always full of fun and enthusiasm. In contrast to this, the quality of his performance on his new medication was slow and stilted; he now performed as someone who found it hard to concentrate, engage, or see the point of playing with the rest of the group. On his new medication, Jim was much more quiet and reserved than he had been before, which was perhaps the intention of him being prescribed it. Maybe his new performance style made life easier for other members of the school to deal with him, but the opposite was true for the co-devisers of his drama group. Following his medication the original Jim was never seen again. He had lost the capacity to perform as anything other than quiet and stilted.

Dealing with children that are heavily medicated is particularly difficult when one has known and built up relationships with and enjoyed them in their previously unmedicated state. Whatever medication Jim was on it caused him to behave in ways much more symptomatic of somebody with AS than he had ever done previously.

SCENE III: GROUP—SITTING ON A CHAIR DOING NOTHING

I had been working with this particular group for a year. One group member however had not shown any signs of wanting to join in with any of the theatre-making activities. In the first few months in which I worked with this group he had stayed in the class for only a short amount of time and then would leave. As time went on I had managed to persuade him to stay in the room for the whole class even though he would always spend this time sitting on a chair doing nothing, looking in the other direction from where the drama was taking place, and invariably yawning.

I had tried everything I knew in an attempt to try to get him to actively engage in the play-making activity but had come to the conclusion that on this occasion Adrian was one of those rare children incapable of meaningfully participating. I had also decided that any further attempts on my part to encourage him to do so would end up in him leaving the room and not wanting to come back. I decided that for this particular group-member *sitting on a chair and doing nothing* was the most I could aspire to on his behalf.

On the day in question the group started to work on creating a performance based on *Romeo and Juliet*, which they had adapted to Romeo and *Graham*. One of the characters that emerged in the play was the Prince. As the improvised performance developed the Prince decided that he really needed an assistant. He asked me if this was ok I and said that it was a good idea, but there was no one left in the room who was free to play the part.

As I was busy thinking if he, I or someone else could play this extra role, the person playing the Prince approached Adrian with a proposal:

Prince: Do you want to be my assistant?

Adrian: What would I have to do?

Prince: Nothing. You just have to sit on a chair and do nothing. Can you do that?

Adrian: (after some thought) Yes.

Prince: Good, then you can be "sitting on a chair doing nothing Prince's assistant"

Adrian: OK.

Adrian played the part of "sitting on a chair doing nothing Prince's assistant" for the rest of the session. Halfway through the following session in which the group was still developing the Romeo and Graham story, Adrian, who had spotted an empty plastic bottle in the room asked me, "Can I be "sitting on a chair doing nothing Prince's assistant" with a plastic bottle?" The group and I agreed to the character's proposal, at which Adrian got out of his chair picked up the bottle and sat back down again. He spent the rest of the session playing the part of "sitting on a chair doing nothing Prince's assistant with a plastic bottle'' which I must say he did very well.

Halfway through the following session Adrian asked, "Can the "sitting on a chair doing nothing Prince's assistant with a plastic bottle" hit people on the head from time to time as long as it doesn't hurt them?" Again we all agreed and again Adrian played this part very well, getting up from time to time from his seat when the prince needed him, in order to gently hit people on the head with his plastic bottle. From this point on Adrian would often actively join in the theatre-making activities the rest of his group were involved in.

This scene demonstrates the power that the group (as a separate entity to the facilitator in this case) can have on its individual members. Again however I feel the central lesson contained here relates to the limits of our capacities as facilitators or directors, and how often we are trapped within the limitations of our own expectations and judgements. The above experience helped me to learn to be more comfortable to be in a place or position of not-knowing, and trust that someone else in the group may be able to deal with certain situations that I cannot.

On many occasions I have heard from colleagues and other professionals that the most stressful thing about being in a position of authority is the expectation on all sides that one should "know what to do." For some, any admittance of "not knowing" would represent some kind of professional failure. As far as I am concerned, if the environment in which one is working/facilitating is such that other members of the group enjoy the freedom to solve situations one cannot overcome, this reflects well on the facilitators' capacity to co-create such environments.

SCENE IV: DIALOGUE—"IT TAKES TWO TO TANGO"

Theatre is created through dialogue, and can be created anywhere. Any space can become a "creative space" but it firstly requires a space within which to create. When I first arrived at Tinely House School I was shown a number of potential spaces to play in and eventually it was agreed that the school hall would be our permanent playground. It was ideal in terms of size, although it did have what I considered at first to be an unhelpful characteristic of two glass walls. Although these walls had some blinds, which were *supposed* to be able to cover the glass, very often they were broken and we would find ourselves being peered at by anybody who happened to be passing.

But as is often the case, those things that at first we may regard as being counter-developmental or counter creative turn out, if accepted (in true "yes and..." fashion) to actually prove to be more conducive to creative dialogue than one may first have thought. In time I found that the school hall and its goldfish bowl like qualities turned into a useful device for sharing the work we were doing with the rest of the school. Always being able to see out on two sides, and nearly always being the subject of curious eyes from the playground meant the work was not taking place in a physical or conceptual vacuum.

An example of the unforeseen positive impact of this situation happened one day when I was working with just one student since the rest of his class had gone on a school outing, which he didn't want to go on. He told me that he was a good dancer and asked if he could go to his room and get his CD player in order to show me the routines he had been working on. He had worked out very precise routines to a number of popular music songs and danced with such concentration that I found it very difficult to keep a straight face; the juxtaposition between the intensity of his movements and expressions and the whimsical nature of the music was intensely entertaining.

After a while I saw him starting to crack a smile and focus his attention on something behind me. I turned around and saw that outside the window in the playground was Dan, one of the few boys in the school who had flatly refused to even enter the drama space. He said he didn't like moving about with other people and thought the whole idea of it was rather silly. To my surprise Dan was copying Liam's dance moves as though in a mirror. He was as concentrated and as engaged as Liam. I acknowledged Dan so he acknowledged me with a wry smile. He did not stop dancing and was edging closer and closer to the glass door of the school hall. I walked over to the door and opened it, and then sat down again. Dan entered, still dancing. He danced with Liam for the rest of the 30–minute class. After this session Dan came to drama classes with the rest of his group and showed himself and others that he had a real aptitude and enthusiasm for the subject.

Very often we professionals (particularly theatre professionals) find ourselves demanding certain conditions within which to practice our work, often we will seek places of isolation free from the peering eyes and other distractions of the outside world. Very often it is only when we have developed some kind of finished product that we are satisfied with that we are happy for our activities to be put on display to an outside audience.

What the above series of events taught me was that it is not only possible to undertake intimate and creative work under the prying gaze of the outside world, but that somehow this situation may prove even more conducive to creative development. Many of those who would linger outside those windows observing our strange activities had previously expressed no desire to be involved in drama, however many of them chose to participate after seeing what "drama" actually looked like in this context.

To some extent there will always be some separation existing between art and life; between those happy to create and those content to observe, those who believe they belong either "inside" or "outside" of the creative space. Either position is of course valid, however by placing our activities more in the public gaze we offer the chance to those who are attracted by it to make the small step from being cultural observers to cultural producers. Under such conditions sometimes all we as facilitators need to do to promote wider involvement, is to stand up and open a door.

SCENE V: STORY—NEW AND IMPROVED DAVE

Dave (aged 16) was not known for his patience, he had also showed little skill in sharing ideas and activities with other people in the group. He usually worked in a group of six other young people and while he showed good levels of imagination he often would find it a real challenge to control his excitement. This would lead him to find it difficult to accept others' ideas and "take it in turns" with other group members. Dave's fellow group members would get frustrated with him for not being patient, and in turn he would get frustrated with them for not being quick or confident enough with their contributions…this was an ongoing story.

I heard from other teachers that Dave spent most of the rest of his days in the school being very isolated and aggressive; he would not normally stay in the classroom and was often "getting himself into trouble" for one reason or another. It had got to the stage where the drama sessions were the only "classes" in the school that Dave was attending. For this reason one of the other teachers asked me if it would be possible for Dave to attend a second drama session on the day I was in the school.

As the classes were normally separated by age group, the practical option for him was to participate in either an older or younger group than his own. The younger group were very keen on drama, but they still felt a little self-conscious about playing some of the games that were being proposed. I thought that Dave could be a real asset in this situation, as *self-consciousness* was not really in his repertoire. I also knew that the younger children also looked up to Dave as being one of the "cool kids" in the school; I had a feeling that if they saw Dave playing, they would be more inclined to overcome their own fear of creative expression.

Of course the major concern to me was whether or not Dave could contain his own excitement. I had a chat to him beforehand and told him how I hoped his presence in the class would benefit the younger children. He told me that he understood my aims and he was happy to try and make them a reality. He too was worried about his own ability to curb his enthusiasm but said that so long as he was able to act as he normally did within his regular class-group he should be able to perform differently with the younger children.

When the younger group (and Dave) met for the first time Dave was like a different boy. He was still very good at the games and was able to play them in a manner that was full of imagination and lacking in self-consciousness but he was now doing all of this with a level of patience and support of others that I had not thought him capable. In this environment, where he felt as though he had some responsibility for helping others to learn, he demonstrated the qualities of a skilled facilitator: being able to play and be imaginative at a moment's notice, while at the same time maintaining a consciousness and sensitivity for the needs of others in the group.

The result of placing Dave into this new group seemed to benefit all concerned, but it was the change in Dave's performance that was most noted in amazement by the teaching assistants in the group and the members of the therapist team that came to see what had happened to him. As a result of this and after several visits to witness the *new Dave* in action, it was decided that Dave might be able to help out as a teaching assistant at the local mainstream primary school. This decision did not surprise me in terms of the ability that Dave had shown with the younger children, but it did pleasantly surprise me that the staff of THS and the local primary school came up with this idea. Dave ended up working very successfully in the local primary school and with the younger group at THS until he eventually left the latter some weeks later. He was expelled for some sort of violent behavior in another class, the details of which I never found out about.

One of the main aims of any theatre is to make unfamiliar (by means of representation) real-life events that are otherwise regarded to be "inevitable" or "natural" narratives. In this scene the narrative in question was the character of Dave. What we have witnessed in the above scene is how under the right conditions a person is able to alienate others from the familiar view previously held of them. Without witnessing Dave's performance in the drama group with youngsters, neither I nor any of the other staff at the school would have thought it possible for Dave to perform a different story to the one he usually played out.

The significance of this story to me is not whether or not Dave's new behavior could be constituted as "improved" or not, but that under certain conditions people have the capacity to perform "other than" in the manner an audience may have thought inevitable. If these alternative performances are not maintained outside the confines of the theatre-making environment, we need to ask ourselves the question: under which given circumstances were certain performances created and destroyed?

SCENE VI: POLITICS—AN INSPECTOR CALLS

On one of my days in the school I was informed that in a couple of weeks, the school was to be visited by an inspector from the Office for Standards in Education, Children's Services and Skills (OFSTED) and one of my classes was to be observed. One of the requirements the school made in preparation for this visit was that each member of the teaching staff who was to be inspected should draw up a lesson plan that would be passed to the inspector prior to the visit.

I found this task problematic because I did not normally write lesson plans. Not only was this because I am not a trained teacher, but because the course of the activities undertaken with the children could not be predicted from one week to the next. This improvisational approach evolved as an attempt to remain truly responsive to the particular circumstances of each class situation. In deciding upon an activity I always try to respond to what I regarded to be the needs of that particular group on that particular day: predetermining activities can impose a logic which is not attuned with the mood or desire with which one is engaged.

In this particular circumstance however I felt as though I had to make an effort to put something down on paper given that the school considered this important and since they had been supportive of me not having to do such things under normal circumstances.

I decided to plan to play a game that was as general and basic as I could think of, one that may be useful to wherever the group may be on that particular day in their creative process. The game I decided upon is one in which the group sits in a circle and passes an object around which is transformed by each person into something that it does not seem to be. For example, I could pass a pen around, and it may get transformed by someone into a telescope by them putting it up to their eye and pretending to look through it to the stars. When explaining the "rules of the game" in the lesson plan I included the very important rule that we as a creative group had developed and rigidly adhered to: that all those present in the room should be encouraged to participate in the playing of the game.

At the beginning of the lesson, which was visited by the inspector, I sat with the group in the circle while the examiner took a seat at the edge of the room with a folder of papers on her knee. At this point one of the children invited her into the circle to participate in the game and despite some clear trepidation on her part she came and sat with us and put her folder underneath her chair.

At the beginning of the game the object (a pool triangle) was passed around the group with each of us successfully turning it into another object. The inspector was participating fully as an equal member of the group and had so far turned the triangle into an earring and a television, however, as the game progressed she felt inspired to pick up her folder from under her chair to write in. At this point the triangle had been passed to Geoff (a very large boy who took his drama and the rules of the game very seriously). As he saw the inspector pick up her folder, he threw the triangle with a great force into the corner of the room and stated, "If she ain't [expletive] doing it I ain't." He then sat in his chair with his arms folded staring at me. At this point the inspector had adopted a similar position, both presumably curious to know how I would deal with the "troubling behavior" of the other.

I chose to deal with it by suggesting to the inspector that I thought that Geoff had a point, even if his way of communicating it was rather aggressive. His point was that the rules of the game and of the class were fair, and that if one person chose not to follow them the class could not function properly. With this the examiner apologized to both him and the group as she was not quite aware of the impact writing in her folder would have. Once he had heard this Geoff arose, went over to the corner of the room where the triangle lay, picked it up, came back to the circle and we all continued playing the game.

This was my first experience (since university over twenty years before) of having the work I was doing inspected against a set of criteria other than an aesthetical one. The introduction of an outsider, particularly one who has the task of judging the work against what is ultimately a set of politically driven criteria can be perceived as a threat; to both the immediate creative experience and the continued existence of the work at all.

What the experience of this scene demonstrated to me was the power of the micro situation to diffuse any actual or perceived political macro threat. Geoff's challenge to the inspector was not done on the basis of what he knew about her or what she represented, it was done purely on the basis of what he regarded to be fair and appropriate human behavior. His actions however represented to me a way in which we can consciously and developmentally confront those who we may believe threaten our activities. We are talking here about breaking down the barriers and promoting shared activities between those in control and those controlled, even if it is only in one small room in one small school in one small country.

Following the class the inspector's feedback to me was framed not in relation to any outside criteria which was written in her folder, but purely in relation to the impact of her personal experience. In her official report she awarded the class the highest grade possible, stating that what the children were demonstrating was a high degree of learning in respect to the conditions necessary for mutual learning to take place.

SCENE VII: EDUCATIONAL—"I WOULD HAVE GOT AWAY WITH IT IF NOT FOR THOSE PESKY TEACHERS..."

A newly qualified teacher had just started working at the school and wanted to come and join in "the drama" (as it had become known). A few minutes into the first class she participated she started looking troubled. We were doing an improvisation about being lost at sea in a big ocean liner, we had hit an iceberg and panic had broken out amongst the crew and passengers as the great vessel began to go sink. As you can imagine under such extreme circumstances the level of energy in the room had reached an extremely high level.

At the end of the class the teacher asked if she could speak to me about some concerns she was having. She said that she felt that what we were doing was not appropriate and that we were working in a way which was counter to many of the school rules that she had a responsibility to uphold. I had not been made aware of these school rules before, but apparently they included: no running around, no swearing, no shouting, no touching, no interrupting etc. As she was sharing her concerns with me I remember being very frustrated and concerned that she was going to try and impose the rules of the school within the drama sessions. If this had happened I have no idea what kind of theatre would have been made, but I am sure that its nature would have suffered as a result of these restrictions.

That night I went out for a drink with a friend of mine and began to moan about the teacher (in a rather clichéd manner): "The kids are great" I said, "it's the teachers who are the problem, if it wasn't for them we would all get along fine." To these points my friend asked whether he was right in believing that I always said that I worked towards fostering and promoting *inclusion*. He asked me why I was able and willing to tolerate fears and anxieties among the children but not, it seems among the staff.

It was at this point that I realized the slightly hypocritical nature of my reaction to this new teacher/group member. I had been treating her as though she was somehow a special member of the group who did not have the right to reflect on experiences like the rest of us. As a result of this conversation I began to realize the extent of some of my prejudices against both this teacher and the kind of rules that I thought she was looking to impose.

The following week I asked to talk to the teacher before the class and listened more intently to her reflections about the previous week. I also shared with her my own reflections, explaining to her that the class *did* have rules and what I understood them to be. I also told her that the head-teacher had taken part in a number of such classes and was happy to let the school rules slide within the theatre-making environment. This seemed to put the new group-member's mind at rest and she was able then to join in freely the activities without being hindered by her previous anxiety, at the same time as I was (hopefully) less hindered by my own prejudice.

Throughout any experience of facilitating group activities we are faced with situations that confront our own prejudices. In the above scene I was faced with some deep-seated resentment for the way in which many educational establishments I had attended as a pupil had operated: these kind of rules always seemed to be to be inhumane, Draconian and unworkable.

I believe that the above story demonstrates that what an educational environment could or even should look like will depend on a number of complex factors to do with tradition and subjective preference. It is impossible to objectively describe the defining features of an educational environment, however with time and effort it is possible to accommodate all opinions in this ongoing debate as we attempt to create conditions for education which best suit the specific learning and development needs of all participants.

SCENE VIII: TREATMENT OF THE INDIVIDUAL—"HE IS NOT SUPPOSED TO BE ABLE TO DO THIS."

I received the following letter at the end of my second year of working at THS, it was written by one of the teachers who was about to leave the school for another position:

> Sam is one of the boys with very poor literacy levels of approximately half his chronological age of 15. He has approximate age appropriate verbal skills but lacks the age appropriate reasoning ability. He has extreme anger management problems and is also very tall for his age. He has been temporarily excluded on occasions for violent outbursts. He has ADHD [Attention Deficit and Hyperactivity Disorder] and is very self-conscious regarding all of these things. In English, the main subject that I teach, Sam is limited as to what he can do and becomes very frustrated. I was genuinely amazed to see the extent of imaginative narrative Sam had in his mind when he was invited by Paul to improvise his own piece in mime and we had to guess what he was doing. I can't remember the exact framework that Paul had given him to work but I can vividly remember the resulting improvisation even though it is now 6 months since he performed it: it had such an impact on me.

> It would be impossible for Sam to produce the written narrative of what he performed, even if he was able to tell someone and they scribed for him. Sam would not have the ability to formulate in coherent narrative with sufficient detail and specific sequencing of events in conjunction with the descriptive detail and omniscience required to narrate both thought and action together (or separately) sufficiently for it to be possible. Any attempt would result, I am certain, in frustration and panic. When Sam is describing a joke or event to you he often gets things out of order or forgets bits.
>
> Sam's improvisation featured a high tech burglar with a suitcase of special gadgets-a little akin to James Bond or Tom Cruise in Mission Impossible. It started with him opening the suitcase and looking around furtively and then selecting a gadget and carried on taking his character through a series of chambers each offering a different challenge to the character thus requiring a new gadget. It was one of the longest pieces of improvisation that any of the boys have done to date. If I had not had the opportunity of working with Paul at Tineley I would only know these boys by what they can produce on paper or in English lesson. I would have no idea of the depth of their emotions, imagination or indeed any real insight into their lives or true personalities.

The one thing that keeps surprising me in the work we do is how exercises which are designed to develop the imagination and communication skills of a theatre performer result in audience responses which ascribe significance to them which reach far beyond the scope or bounds of theatre itself. I often wonder how effective these exercises would be if I were to attempt to replicate them for the same purpose that they have been ascribed by others. I think part of the power that this work has is the fact that what takes place usually happens through accident rather than design. Certainly I believe the children I was working with would have been resistant to undertake any activities, which they felt, were designed (as they have said) to "cure" or "improve" them: they have had a lifetime of such activities thrust upon them.

SCENE IX: RELEVANCE—THE THERAPISTS' CONVENTION

As a result of the good working relationship I had built up with the therapy team, I was asked to present a paper on the playing I had been doing at THS at a regional therapists' convention. This was the first time I had been asked to present anything to an outside audience about my work at the school and the request presented me with my first taste of how difficult it is to capture in any real sense, the quality of practical work in any form other than itself. In the first place, how could I find a way of representing in any real sense the quality of the work we had been doing? And in the second, what could I say or present that would not be in danger of misrepresenting those people from the group who were *not* asked to present? I felt a great sense of responsibility on both these levels.

Despite these reservations, my decision to accept the offer was based on a desire to begin to share with a wider audience the perspectives that the work within the school had offered me. I was not under the impression that such a presentation would change to any great degree the paradigm of therapeutic understanding of which I have been so sceptical, but I felt that by not accepting this invitation for dialogue I would be in danger of isolating myself and further isolating the children. As the day went on however, I increasingly felt like a "fish out of water." My presentation was scheduled to be the final one of the day and would follow what turned out to be a series of more clinical-based presentations, which addressed such subjects as brain dysfunction and other deficit-based ways of viewing the kind of children I was making theatre with.

I realized that what I was stating would be at odds with much of what had gone before. I consider myself to be non-confrontational by nature and normally in these kind of situations I will do everything I can to head off any potential conflicts or feelings of awkwardness, either on my own or anyone else's behalf. However, in this case I felt that I had no choice but to face these uncomfortable feelings, as I suddenly did not feel as though I was only responsible for my own well being.

I may still not have been sure about the accuracy or ethics of my presentation or even my attendance at this event, but I knew even more clearly that failing to say what I had come to say (or more accurately saying anything else for the sake of short-term appeasement) would have not been fair on those members of the theatre groups who were not here to speak for themselves. I imagined all the children of the school in the audience of the conference and tried to imagine their reaction if I failed to at least fully represent *myself*.

The following is a summary of the presentation I delivered. First I showed a slide of the identified features of Asperger's Syndrome (as they appear earlier in this article), I then showed a slide of the individual characteristics identified as being useful skills for the Devised Theatre actor to have (also shown here in Scene I). I then showed them a short film of some of the playing that we had done at THS, which seemed to suggest (to me at least) that these children were performing in ways which according to many of the audience they should not be able to. Finally I told the following story which highlights this contradiction in a way in which I could never hope to:

> Sam's Story:
>
> At the end of one group improvisation with a group of six 14 year olds and one teaching assistant the following conversation took place between myself (Paul) and the children:
>
> Sam: Paul, do you think what we have just done was good?
>
> Paul: In what way?
>
> Sam: Well, do you think it was imaginative and creative?
>
> Paul: Absolutely.
>
> Sam: That's what I thought. I also thought that we are not supposed to be able to do what we just did.
>
> Mary: What do you mean?
>
> Sam: Well according to some people we are not supposed to have a good imagination, be able to play with other people, or empathize.
>
> Brian: Who says that about us?
>
> Sam: Experts.
>
> Mary: And what would those experts say if they saw us do what we have just done.
>
> Sam: They would call us an anomaly.
>
> Brian: What does that mean?
>
> Sam: They'd say we are the exception that proves their rules.

Somewhat to my surprise the reaction to the presentation was very positive. On the whole people were very curious about the work we had done and somewhat accepting of their role in maintaining the contradiction that Sam had highlighted. Many members of the audience also seemed visibly shocked at the way in which these children (who were known to them in other contexts) were performing.

My lasting impression of this experience is two-fold: firstly how easy it is to prejudice and underestimate any group of people purely on the basis of their group identity: be they therapists, those diagnosed with Asperger's or anybody else. Secondly it showed me how much the deficit model of macro understanding dominates therapeutic work at a micro level; and how much the medicalized explanation of these children seems to be taken as fact. The fact that children were doing what (in relation to the diagnosis criteria) they were not supposed to be capable of is not a contradiction for the theatre-maker or many of the children I worked with. The contradiction only exists if one believes that the AS diagnosis truly represents the capacities of the child.

SCENE X: PLAYFUL—GETTING TO THE HEART OF THE MATTER

This scene offers some examples of what I consider to be significant acts of playfulness which took place over the course of the three years at the school.

The Driving Test

We were busy playing when the interviewees for a new therapist position came to visit the hall to see what we were doing. According to tradition the five of them were invited to participate in the activities we were all involved in. On this occasion we were playing status games, playing around with performing high and low status characters. I paired up one of the young people with one of the interviewees and told them to play a scene where one was a driving examiner (high status) and one was the student (low status) taking their driving test. Once this scene was complete I asked them to keep the same characters and scenario but swap status.

At the beginning of the scene, the boy playing the examinee (now high status) turned to examiner and said that he wanted to swap seats. The rest of the scene involved the playing out of the examiner taking the test for the boy, giving himself instructions and undertaking them. At the end of the scene, the examiner who had been driving turned to the examinee and told him that he had passed his test.

The Animalizing Machine

At the end of a long improvisation, the story had reached a point where the group, in character as biologists, decided it would be good to invent a machine that could turn them into the animals they wanted to study. The first two biologists who used the machine were successfully transformed into a dog and a bear. The third biologist wanted to study frogs, so that is what she wished for as she stepped into the machine. Unfortunately for her, due to someone not putting enough money into the electricity meter, the machine stopped working halfway through the process and she end up just having frog's legs; on which she hopped through the rest of the lesson and into the playground at the end.

The Great Dustmite Massacre of 1892

Apparently, according to one of the students who was playing an expert on such matters there was a terrible dustmite massacre which took place in Southampton in 1892. It took place as part of a plan by cleaners to get rid of their sworn enemies once and for all. The cleaners gathered in the town hall square armed with brushes and chemicals and began to slaughter all dust-mites with no concern for the dustmites' families or children. Unfortunately much like the spreading of myxomatosis in Australia some years before which was designed to get rid of the troublesome rabbit population, it was discovered that 1% of the dustmites were immune to the brushes and the chemicals and so in time a new variety of *super dustmite* was created, the ancestors of which are busy making dust in our homes today.

The Clash of the Royal Body Guards

We were halfway through the third week of creating an improvised story where one royal family was having a feud with another from a neighbouring kingdom. We were all playing two characters in this story, one from one royal family, one from another. Consequently as of halfway through week three no members of either family had directly confronted one another.

However, halfway through week three's class both families came to the conclusion that they should fight each other, but none of the royals wanted to get their hands dirty. Instead they decided to send a representative to fight on their behalf. Both families chose to send their bodyguard, played by the same actor. The war between the two families manifested itself as one actor playing two characters simultaneously having a duel with himself for about five minutes.

The People's Army of the Chinese Republic

I suggested a scene in which each student plays a character at a picnic. The first few suggestions offered were: a mother, a cook, a driver and a teacher. The fifth student's suggestion took me somewhat by surprise: Adam wanted to be the People's Army of the Chinese Republic, "Fine" I said "great idea"… he spent the rest of the improvisation as the entire People's Army of the Chinese Republic, speaking in Chinese and guarding the picnic from invaders and protesting against his mistreatment as an organization.

What I learned from participating in these devised spontaneous theatrical performances was much the same as the therapists learned from watching the DVD of this activity in the previous scene: that no matter what one might believe of children with AS, their ability to be imaginative, creative and collaboratively creative is clear for all those who take the time to see and pursue their abilities.

EPILOGUE

My inspiration and interest in working with the children at THS came from a bafflement and distress with the way in which some young people whose behavior is considered somehow inappropriate to a dominant "norm" are treated. From my experiences of working and playing in an environment designed to both confine and treat such children I have become acutely aware of the relationship between how they are regarded on a macro level and how they are treated on a micro one.

The connection between the macro explanations (diagnosis) of individuals and the micro treatment to which it can lead are most clearly expressed in the words of R.D Laing:

> Man [sic] can be seen as a person or a thing. Now even the same thing, seen from different points of view, gives rise to two entirely different descriptions, and the descriptions give rise to two entirely different theories, and the theories result in two entirely different sets of action…To look and to listen to a patient and to see "signs" of "disease", and to look and to listen to him [sic] simply as a human being are to see and hear in radically different ways. (Laing, 1959, p. 20)

In the above stories I have chosen not to analyze any of the individual children I worked with in direct relation to the AS diagnosis, not because I do not believe that some of the features described within it do not describe accurately some of the performances these children are capable of demonstrating, but because I do not regard it as being a useful frame of reference with which to analyse the activities which I undertook.

As a theatre maker this kind of diagnosis is of no interest to me other than a social construction that can be used as a means by which to justify the separation (either physically or pharmaceutically) of certain people from society. If I had taken seriously the AS diagnosis as being an accurate description or explanation of the identity of the children I was to work with it would have made little sense to work with them at all. There exists such a clear dichotomy between the behaviors these children are deemed to be lacking in and those required of the Devised Theatre maker that any attempts to engage them in a Devised Theatre making process would surely have proved fruitless. As a theatre maker I am never concerned with whom a person thinks themselves to be or what others see them as being, but rather who (or who else) they can become; this was my motivation for the work described above.

It is not the task of the theatre or the aim of this article however to try and convince anyone that children with diagnosis of AS are "just as capable as he rest of us to perform and contribute to the development of society." Equally I am not interested in using theatre to try and convince anyone in a didactic sense of anything with regards to what freedoms of opportunity should be offered to such children. As Kershaw states in the following:

> What I am interested in centrally then, is not the ways in which radical performance might *represent* such freedoms, but rather how radical performance can actually *provide* such freedoms, or at least a sense of them, for both performers and spectators, as it is happening." (Kershaw, 1999, pp. 18–19)

As already stated the only or most effective way in which the theatre can tackle perceived injustice or inequality is to represent or reframe previously held views or stories which have come to be regarded as being the norm. By housing my theatre making activities in those very systems that I seek to reframe, I am aiming to both make unstable some of dominant ways in which children diagnosed with AS are known and treated and provide some possible alterative approaches.

My desire to continue practicing and developing this form of art is inspired not only by the developmental potential I feel it has as a means of viewing and commenting on the world but by also by its potential to practically alter it. At the beginning of this chapter I stated that the contribution required of mainstream theatre actors is largely limited to playing specifically assigned roles and reciting specifically assigned lines. Adherence to these roles and these rules assures directors of such theatre that the authority of the playwright will not be challenged and the status quo of the theatre will not be challenged.

It is often hard for audiences of mainstream theatre (or television) to believe that their favorite actors have a life, which is different to the role that they so faithfully portray on the stage or screen. Is it perhaps equally difficult for some to believe that for those children cast in the roles of AS sufferers that another kind of life or performance is possible for them. The only way to find out for sure if these individuals are performing to the extent of their repertoire or potential is to first recognise them as performers and secondly meet and play with them. If at first one does not believe that the individuals you meet are capable of performing anything other than in ways that their diagnosis may lead you to expect, my advice on the basis of my experiences at THS would be...keep playing!

REFERENCES

Autism Society. (2010). *What's unique about Aspergers Disorder?* Retrieved from http://www.autism-society.org/site/PageServer?pagename=life_aspergers

Huizinga, J. (1950) *Homo ludens.* London: Routledge and Kegan Paul.

Klin, A. & Volkmar, F. (1995). Asperger's Syndrome: Guidelines for assessment and Diagnosis. *Learning Disabilities Association of America*, June.

Kershaw, B. (1999). *The radical in performance.* London: Routledge.
Laing, R.D. (1959). *The divided self.* London: Penguin Books.
Lecoq, J. (1999). *The moving body.* New York: Routledge.
Murray, P. (2009). *Playing with mental health.* Unpublished doctoral thesis. University of Winchester, U.K.
Oddey, A. (1994). *Devised and collaborative theatre.* London: Routledge.
Willett, J. (1964). *Brecht on theatre.* London: Hill Macmillan Publishers.

Chapter Eight

Social Therapy with Children with Special Needs and Their Families

Christine LaCerva and Christine Helm

Play has been used in therapeutic settings for many years going back at least as far as Anna Freud (1965) and Melanie Klein's (1932) work in child psychotherapy and later, Virginia Axline's (1947, 1950) person centered non directive play therapy influenced by Carl Rogers. Play in this tradition is a vehicle used to transmit a child's unconscious experiences, desires, thoughts and emotions. More recently, play therapists including Moustakas (1997) and Schaefer (2007), have developed models following Axline that integrate elements of systemic family therapy, narrative therapy, solution focused therapy and cognitive behavioral therapy. Play-based techniques have also been developed for work with autistic children. In approaches such as Floortime therapists, or often parents, learn how to help children develop relationships and social/communication skills starting with the autistic children's own interests or obsessions (Greenspan & Weider, 2009).

In this chapter you will read an interview with a practitioner of social therapy on her work with children and families. Among the many ways one might describe social therapy, play therapy is an illuminating choice. This innovative and practical postmodern approach originated in the 1970s in part as a critique of mainstream diagnostic and individuated psychotherapy through the work of philosopher and psychotherapist Fred Newman (Holzman & Mendez, 2003). In this mode of play therapy the purpose is not to get inside a child's mind nor is it instrumental and child-centered as in techniques developed to teach social/communication skills to autistic children. Indeed social therapy was not developed expressly for children but for people of all ages. In social therapy with families, both the parent and the child participate in creating the conditions for their therapy through play and performance. The social therapeutic method is based on the idea that we, children and adults, are fundamentally social and always creating things together. Although the work with children, as described in this chapter, can be more unambiguously playful, all social therapeutic practice draws upon our capacity to play and perform. It is a group practice focused on emotional growth.

Social Therapy's radical humanism is manifest in this understanding that people are social beings who perform, improvise, and create their lives together. The individual is understood in a dialectical relationship to others; the self-contained, isolated individual is an illusion. It is by virtue of this relationality—the connectedness and the collaborative nature of human activity—that people grow and things get done.

Life then can be seen as a series of stages upon which groups (ensembles) create the millions of scenes of their lives. These scenes are created through performing, pretending, playing and improvising. Social therapy emphasizes the *ensemble activity* of creating the performance and in this way differs from psychoanalytic, psychodramatic and group dynamic approaches. It taps into our capacity to work and play, learn from and teach, and create well with others.

Vygotsky's (1978) understanding of children's play as the engine of development is highly relevant to the social therapeutic process. As in children's pretend play, group participants are engaged each week in doing what is familiar to them and at the same time things that are brand new—beyond them. They are being themselves and other than themselves at one and the same time. They are becoming. Following Vygotsky, development/growth is not something that happens to us but something we create. It is a not the external manifestation of an individualized, internal process but a cultural activity that we engage in together—and one of the discoveries of social therapy is that we can engage in this activity and grow throughout life (Holzman, 2009; Newman & Holzman, 1993). Indeed, social therapy explicitly strives to revitalize the capacity to grow through play—a capacity that we typically leave behind once we are socialized, "grown."

At first glance, an observer might see little difference between an adult social therapy group and a group engaged in another form of "talk therapy." Most people come to group seeking help and they talk about their problems. The difference is a powerful shift of focus from the content (what is being said) to the human interaction. Group participants create and play with their talk. The job of the group is not to interpret or analyze what is said (although this can certainly go on), but to find a way to contribute to the group's creative process. Participants in a social therapy group struggle to listen in a new way. Rather than listening to hear something they agree or disagree with, to assess the "truth value" of what is said, to size up the speaker, or to hear the pause that signals "it's my turn now," they learn to listen as improvisers—to create scenes in each week's play. The group performs new conversations together.

In the interview that follows LaCerva offers examples of scenarios with children that are unlikely to be observed in therapy with adults (including games co-created in the therapy and evolving like children's first games). On the social therapeutic playground, the goal is to take the truth referential rug out from under discourse—magically transforming "who we are," "how things are," "what really happened," "explanations," "justifications," and so on into the raw material for creativity and the activity of talking with each other into performance. In working with children and adults alike, the therapist's role is that of organizer/director, helping the group choose to create their own play. In social therapeutics there is an important distinction made between power and authority—the power of the group's creative process versus the authority of the therapist, diagnosis, roles, "how things are." Each week is a struggle for the group to reject authority in favor of the group's power; to reject a problem/solution model in favor of play. Indeed, at its most effective social therapy is caring, intimate, creative, and pointless activity. What emerges? New emotions, new ways of seeing, and new social units—indeed the group itself.

For all, adults and children alike, the playful social therapeutic process is an environment that lets the other in. The group activity is an opportunity to eschew the habitual desire to "know," "get to the bottom of," "express feelings" in favor of participating in an emergent process. With nothing more than the assorted ugly, painful, exciting, unnerving, humiliating debris of their lives, groups can transform rigidified roles, patterns and identities, create their development, and live less alienated, more joyous lives. In the following interview, social therapist Christine LaCerva describes how she and the therapists she supervises work with children and families in the context of multi-family groups comprised of both families and children, as well as in individual therapy sessions that support that group work. The examples she shares demonstrate how the parents, children, and families with the support of the group are able to create new performances and perform beyond themselves, breaking out of habitual scripted ways of relating.

Q: Over the years, as a therapist, you've worked with kids who have some kind of developmental, cognitive or emotional issues, or they might have been diagnosed before they came to see you. They might not have. Can you tell me about some of the young people you've seen over the years?

Christine: We've seen children starting at age four through their teenage years—up to eighteen. But I've worked predominantly with younger children, ages four through twelve.

Kids are often diagnosed before they come to see us, most often with either attention deficit disorder (ADD) or attention deficit disorder with hyperactivity (ADHD). These are the more popular diagnostic categories that we started to see about five or six years ago. Most children who go in to see a psychiatrist, if they're having problems sitting in their seat or focusing in any way, are almost immediately diagnosed and prescribed medication.

Q: So by the time they get to you, most of the kids you've seen have been diagnosed?

Christine: Yes, they've been diagnosed. Some parents will come sooner—as soon as the school recommends some kind of evaluation—because they're concerned whether to go through with an evaluation. They're wondering if they should go to their doctor. They don't want their child on medication. Some people come knowing that the diagnosis is on its way towards them. In the last five years there's been an increase in children diagnosed with autism spectrum disorder, which is an umbrella term that includes autism and the newest category, Asperger's Syndrome.

We've had an increase of children ages five through nine who have been diagnosed with Asperger's. Most therapists will see ADD or ADHD kids, but not the Asperger's kids. They believe that Asperger's is an educational issue that needs to be handled by educational specialists to help these children learn. I don't even like using the language of "Asperger's," but that's part of the territory.

Q: So you're saying that Asperger's is typically seen as a learning disorder?

Christine: Yes. It's not so much viewed as a psychological label as an educational label. Very often, when children are diagnosed with Asperger's parents ask, "What am I supposed to do? How do I get help with this?" They're told to put their child in a special-ed classroom, where there's more support for learning. The only therapeutic help generally recommended, if any, includes cognitive behavioral approaches like reinforced learning that can be used in the classroom and at home.

Q: What about the other autism labels? What are the range of diagnoses and some of the thoughts about appropriate treatment?

Christine: There's some differentiation among the autism labels. For example, high-functioning autism is very controversial. Some practitioners don't even believe it exists. Children labeled high functioning are sometimes referred to behavioral therapists—but *not* to psychotherapists. The prevailing belief is that these children do not have the capacity or the interpersonal skills to function in psychotherapy. Children with more extreme autism, labeled low functioning, are sent to educational learning specialists.

Q: So before they come to see you, a social therapist, parents might have been told that therapy was of no use?

Christine: Yes.

Q: But they come anyway?

Christine: They do. Parents hear about us through referrals or our website. Typical comments include, "I heard you work with Asperger's kids. I've been trying to find somebody. Nobody will take my child. What can you do to help?"

Q: What's your response to them?

Christine: We respond to families the same way we respond to everybody. We relate to everyone as having the capacity to develop. We don't pathologize them. We support the human capacity to perform: to be both who you are and *other than* who you are. And we relate to that child and that family as having the capacity to organize what's happening in a more creative and developmental way. We support organizing environments where relationality is key. In essence, social therapy helps all concerned look at the impact they are having on other people. In some cases, that means recognizing that there *are* other people.

Once a diagnosis has been established, it limits what parents and others do with that child. In the case of autism spectrum disorder, parents are told that the child is impaired and cannot socially relate within the range of normal behavior. Autism is related to as a neurobiological disorder, and it might very well be. However, we can still relate to the child and family as having the capacity to transform how they are living their lives.

According to the DSM IV, the autistic child "is not capable of having conversation—which is why they are silent or why they perseverate, or why they have rigidified kinds of behaviors." This diagnosis creates the likelihood that parents of autistic children, unlike parents of so-called regular children, will not have normal conversations with their child.

We're working to help the parents see and relate to their child outside of the confines of those diagnostic categories and the stated limitations of what professionals are telling them their child can and can not do.

People say to infants: "Say goodbye to grandma!" They don't know what a "goodbye" is or a "grandma" is, but you're relating to them as a member of your language and conversational community. But autistic children often are not related to as a member of a shared community, of a language community. They are related to as outsiders, which I believe reinforces the alienation of the child in relationship to others. The child quickly learns that he or she is "special." In my experience, how autistic children are related to is about as important as the disability itself. Ways of being in the world called "autistic" are part of the human experience. It is vitally important that we relate to autistic "ways of being" as something we share as human beings.

Q: So Christine, maybe you can think about a recent family that has come to you for help. Can you take us through the first meetings and then can we talk some about what the therapeutic process looks like. And in particular, can you tell us about any moments that were of surprise to the parents or

Christine: . . . to the *therapist*!

I have two very different examples that I think are interesting.

In the first example, Jeremy, a six-year-old boy, had been placed in a class for the developmentally delayed. He was not getting much challenging work in school and overall there was not much emphasis on teaching this child or relating to the child as having the capacity to "be a head taller" than himself.

Jeremy's mother brought him to see us. He was pretty difficult, yelling and screaming a lot. For anyone coming to therapy, whether age four or forty, there's nervousness or anxiety about talking to somebody you don't know about the intimate details of your life. And of course a child knows that he or she is being brought there because they're a problem. So we have to deal with that issue immediately.

Q: This is the intake session?

Christine: Yes. During the intake session Jeremy was anxious. He performed himself with a lot of yelling, turning the lights on and off and knocking chairs over in the therapy office. As he began talking to me, his mother told me some of the history. I tried to have him participate with us, but he wouldn't sit down.

He kept coming up to me and saying, "I'm a big boy. I'm a big boy, right? I'm a big boy, right?" He said that for pretty much forty-five minutes. And his mother, as she has been taught to do by cognitive behavioral methods, was trying to get him to stop repeating himself.

I made other comments to him and asked questions such as, "It's really nice to meet you; I wonder if you're nervous?"

Q: And as you'd ask him questions, he said…?

Christine: He kept saying the same thing, which was fine. I didn't have any need for him to answer my questions, but I did want to relate to him as a member of the community I'm in, that is, as part of a community of people who talk to each other and have conversations. His mother identified the presenting problem being that he could not carry on a conversation and would repeat things, *ad infinitum*.

Q: As you're talking to him as part of this conversation and he's saying, "I'm a big boy, I'm a big boy," what was mom doing?

Christine: She began saying, "I can't believe you're not stopping him from repeating himself. It's driving me crazy."

I told her I was glad she was saying that because in social therapy we don't try to stop anybody from doing anything. It wasn't particularly driving me crazy. Many people tell me that I repeat myself. It's just something that people do. Some people do it more than others. Jeremy, of course, was listening as I said this.

Q: And you're speaking to both of them?

Christine: Yes. And I said to him, "I repeat myself. My friends complain about that, too, the way your mother's complaining about you. And it can be annoying to people, but some people think it's funny and it's not really bothering me at the moment."

I continued getting to know him. At the same time, Jeremy's mother and I continued to talk and he was involved in that process. Sometimes Jeremy sat down. I told him that this was my office and he could not turn the lights on and off or throw things on the floor.

Q: What did he do with that?

Christine: He turned the lights on and off and threw things to see what I was going to do. I stood up and brought him over to sit, which he did. So now, something had happened; something unusual for him. Near the end of the session, he said to me, "You don't think I'm a big boy, do you?

Q: He said that?

Christine: Yes, he said that. After 45 minutes, he stopped repeating. He had something else to say. I said that he was quite right. I could tell that he was very insightful. I did not think he was a big boy. Then there were bloodcurdling screams and uncontrollable sobbing for thirty minutes (we let the session run over).

Q: What did you and his mother do while that was going on?

Christine: We just waited and worked to be with him. His mom tried to be with him. She wanted to comfort him, and that was okay too. I did not have a need to do that. I thought it was important for him to go through this—to have his response to what we were saying to each other. It's painful to come to experience that you're under-developed. I think the conversation highlighted this for him. I told him that I could help him grow and become a bigger boy, because I could see that it was upsetting to him that he wasn't one.

Q: And he heard you?

Christine: Yes. He didn't say anything, but he was listening. It was clear to me that he had listened to the entire session or I don't think he would have been able to say what he did. The work from that point was with his mom.

Q: Did his mom understand that he had been part of the conversation?

Christine: I don't think she understood that initially because she had been living with this child and had a very different experience with him.

In the next session, when I saw his mother alone, we talked about the assumptions and biases that she and we all have with children who have difficulties.

She said she was shocked at his breaking out of his usual behaviors. She asked me why I kept asking him questions when I knew he wasn't able to answer me. I explained that my intent was to perform a conversation with him because in the absence of resorting only to trying to stop him from doing what he was doing, he had no learning environment. He wasn't going to be able to learn anything. I told her that we needed to talk to him conversationally, so he had a shot at *learning what a conversation is*.

She cried and said she realized that she *didn't* have conversations with him. Basically she told him what to do and what not to do, or that she loved him, things like that. But she conducted no conversations with him in any normalized way. She was very taken aback that she had participated in relating to him pathologically, according to the diagnosis he had been given. She learned that her experience of her own child was organized in a very particular way. She was focused on his *limitations*.

Q: Could you say some more about the assumptions we have and the ways we relate to kids who've been diagnosed in this way?

Christine: Okay. You can observe children through your life participation with them. You can decide to see things according to behaviors. And according to a child's current behavior, it may appear that he or she can't do anything else. As social therapists, we work hard not to interpret or become predictive based on a particular set of actions the child is doing.

We use the social therapeutic approach to help adults and children create environments where it's possible to do new things—create new performances. The child experiences herself or himself differently ("Hey, I did something new!"). And adults learn that their children can do all kinds of unexpected things.

Jeremy's mom was very impacted by the first session and decided to go down this road with me. I told her I had no idea whether or not we could help him, but given what the first session looked like, I thought we had a shot. And I thought we were going to discover all kinds of things.

Q: Why was it important for you to say to her that you had no idea if you could help him or not?

Christine: I didn't know if I could (which didn't mean that I couldn't!). But how we were going to determine whether I could help him was by creating environments where we could discover things about who he is and who he's growing up to become.

Children struggle with making choices about how hard it is for them to go beyond what they know how to do, just like adults do. And sometimes along the way children will decide it's too much work, and will let you know: "I'm not going there. I'm not going to do it."

Q: So when you're saying to Jeremy's mom: "I don't know if I can help him," you think you probably can, but that's still to be determined.

Christine: Yes, I don't know what that will look like.

Q: Because, in part, that depends on whether Jeremy's going to decide to go there with you.

Christine: Right. He's going to have to create that with us. He's going to have to make his choices. It's the same with mom and dad. They're going to have to decide how far they're willing to go in their own development. The place we often reach is that the children are in advance of their parents in being able to do developmental work. And in our family therapy groups, we have to deal with that as a grouping of adults and children.

But one thing I wanted to go back to is that Jeremy had all the classic behavioral characteristics of Asperger's Syndrome as defined by DSM IV in 1994.

DSM IV says that these children lack empathy, compassion, and a capacity to put themselves in somebody else's shoes. I was very sick one day during our fifth therapy session together. He had a game he liked to play with me called "The Bears." (It really had nothing to do with bears, but that was his name for it.) I said I didn't think I could play "The Bears" today, and that we had to deal with the fact that I wasn't feeling well.

He kept saying, "No, we're going to play 'The Bears,' right? We're going to play 'The Bears,' right? We're going to play 'The Bears,' right?" And I said, "Well, what about the fact that I'm sick?"

It was a very, very difficult conversation and his mother (who was in the session too) said, "This is what I'm talking about. He doesn't *care* that you're sick!" I said, "Well, I don't know *how* we know that he doesn't care. We know that he's saying he wants to play 'The Bears.' That's all we know." I was very adamant that we should not make interpretations about what we were experiencing with him and make it *mean* something. Because we simply didn't know what it means, and we certainly didn't know that it meant he didn't care.

I asked him if he cared. He said, "No." And then he started crying and saying, "Please play 'The Bears;' please play 'The Bears!'" So I sent mom out, which in this case was a good thing to do because the child often does better. He said to me, "Help me stop crying. I can't stop." I said, "Okay, great, this is how you do it. You start focusing on something else. You move into another activity, and you can sometimes let go of the crying," which he did. I said, "I'll play 'The Bears' the best I can. How's that?" He said, "Okay."

In the course of "The Bears" game, he played my father and constantly ordered me around and tried to stop me from doing what I was doing—which, of course, is his life experience. I started crying, which I often did (that's part of my role in "The Bears"). I protested to him that I didn't want to be sent to my room all the time, that I hadn't done anything anyway, so why was he punishing me? And then (this was a *big* move for him) he said, "I heard you're not feeling well. Why don't I fix you a cup of tea? I think you should rest. I think you're jumping up and down too much. Maybe we should call the doctor."

His entire performance became being extremely sensitive to how I, his son in this case, was doing. It was a very, very lovely moment. It was a breakthrough, since what I had been focusing on therapeutically was building my relationship with him. I felt like he had said to me through his activity, "Yes, I'm in therapy with you. I'm going to recognize that I have an impact on you." And in some sense, that was the beginning of our therapy.

Q: And his mother's reaction when you told her? What did she make of it?

Christine: She didn't know what to make of it. But I think it was the beginning of her being able to see him differently. In a performance you learn all kinds of things about people. People show you things they can't show you in the more stilted ways that we get organized to relate to each other. That's true for everybody, not just Jeremy.

She said she had come to realize that she had essentially written him off. She had no idea that he had the capacity to relate socially. Now he was doing substantially better at home. She was having conversations with him about all kinds of things, so we brought him into group about five weeks later.

Q: Could you tell us more about this group? Who's in it?

Christine: Adults and kids. We make decisions about who needs to be there each week, depending upon what's going on therapeutically. Sometimes it's kids only. Sometimes it's adults only. Other times, we have dads come in with kids. Sometimes we have everybody there.

Christine: So we brought Jeremy and his mother into the group. There are four other families.

Q: Christine, is a therapy group of this kind unusual in the field of family therapy?

Christine: I think it's unusual in that it is not a social skills group—teaching children how to play together—which is what is done more traditionally. It's unusual in that we are not trying to get to the bottom of anything; instead, the activity is focused on creating something together.

I think it's unusual in that it includes both adults and children, with children leading the process. And the kinds of issues that the kids are facing vary dramatically. There are kids who are quite together, doing fine in school, but who have other emotional issues. And there's someone like Jeremy who has a lot of difficulty relating to other people (and basically doesn't).

The day I introduced Jeremy to the group, I had the children come alone. They were totally taken aback. He cried. He had temper tantrums. Nothing he said had anything to do with what we were doing in the group. He talked to himself, out loud. I didn't know to whom he was talking, really—if it was to himself or to anybody. He just talked in a non-relational way, and *very l*oudly.

I said to them that I kind of wanted to let it go and see what he was going to do, and that I thought he was really nervous. Some of the kids tried to get him to stop talking. They said it was annoying them, and that he was not supportive of the group. I asked them why they were asking him to stop and how they know he *could* stop. I asked them whether we ask people to stop doing things without knowing whether they can. They didn't know him.

Q: What do you mean by that, Christine, when you consider whether someone has the capacity to stop doing what he or she is doing?

Christine: Well, people can't do everything. Maybe another child in the group could be quiet. But I knew Jeremy longer than everyone else, and I didn't think he could do that at this time. Another child asked me why I was asking the question. She wanted to know if I was saying that Jeremy couldn't stop talking. I said I didn't know if he could or couldn't, but my experience was that he wasn't stopping.

Then I took a risk. I said that I knew this would be hard for Jeremy to have me say in front of everybody, but that *he wasn't particularly a big boy*, and the group's job was to help him grow. I told the group that I thought we should give him some performance direction on what else he could do.

Q: And what was he doing while you were telling the group this?

Christine: Listening. He was muttering, but listening. He did not scream when I said he wasn't a big boy, as he had previously. One of the leaders of the group, who's nine, said perhaps he could lower the volume. I said I thought that was an excellent direction and Jeremy did. He spoke quietly to himself through the entire group. They had a tissue box that they used as a remote control, which meant, "lower the volume!"

In the fifth group, one of the girls said she hated having him there and wanted him to leave. Basically she was saying he repulsed her. This was a girl who, in some sense, was often in his position. She was one of the least developed kids in the group, and people often had difficulty with her. But now he had usurped her place, and he was the more difficult one. She said she hated his guts.

The other kids responded by saying they didn't hate his guts, but didn't know what to do, either. I said I didn't care whether they liked each other or not. But I did care about their figuring out how they were going to work together because he wasn't going anywhere.

Q: You made that clear?

Christine: I made it very clear that he wasn't going anywhere. Then Jeremy stopped talking to himself. He said, "I get it. I like everybody in here. She hates me [to the girl] and you [Christine] don't care. *(Laughter.)*

I said well, that's close. You're going to have to figure out how to work together whether you like each other or not.

Q: And what did they all do with that?

Christine: They started to figure out how they were going to work together. The boys, in particular, became very supportive of him and worked to include him. In fact, one boy suggested that we play "The Bears," knowing that it was Jeremy's favorite game.

Q: How did they know about "The Bears?"

Christine: One of the ways we introduced Jeremy to the group was that Jeremy and I played "The Bears" together, and we worked on how to include the group in the game. This process was extremely difficult for him. "The Bears" was very scripted, on his part. It went a certain way at a certain time, with almost no variation, except the day I was sick. He cried a lot when the children became involved in "The Bears" because they did different things with the game. I worked very closely with him, as did my co-therapists, to teach him that when you give something to other people—as he had given "The Bears" to the group—that they do different things with it. And that helps you grow.

He has continued to cry through "The Bears," but we continue to play it now and then and he's doing much better. In fact he's now talking to us, and sometimes as part of a very intense, emotional dialogue. And keep in mind that most often, children like Jeremy are related to as if they cannot do that, it's not possible. At times he will start perseverating: "I have something to say! I have something to say! I have something to say!" And sometimes the kids will say, "Hey, you need to wait because so and so is talking. You need to support the other person." And then when the other person's finished, they'll turn to him and say, "Okay, what is it?" And he'll say, "I just want to tell you all that you have a really nice place here, and I like everybody."

So he's learning how to respond emotionally and how to express his caring and respect for people. We're just crazy about him. And we're crazy about this experience that he's having.

Q: It's very beautiful what you're saying. I'm wondering what the repercussions of his development have been in his world.

Christine: Mom has made a decision to change his school and put him in a more challenging environment. Of course, this has been a challenging task for her. A lot of school administrators and teachers, when they meet him and view him through the eyes of people trained in these diagnostic categories, don't want to take him because they feel that he will not be able to function.

His parents finally found a place for Jeremy to go. He also has joined a karate class, which people thought he couldn't do and, I must say I didn't think he would be able to handle. He came back and told me the karate master was mad at him. I said that he had to decide if he wanted to perform being a big boy in that class or not.

All week I was concerned that I had asked him to do something he couldn't do, and that my request was unfair. But it turns out he changed his performance in the karate class and is doing great. So I'm learning that I have my own biases operating, and he's teaching me about them. And he's teaching the group! The other children have learned how to be more inclusive, how to work together, how to work with everybody's differences. They've learned how to deal with their reactions and biases and how to play together cooperatively.

I think the children have learned how to do the social therapy group. They talk group talk, they say things like: "You have to support the group!" and "What does the group want to do?" Someone will say, "I want to do this, does the group want to do that?" They are very aware that what they are doing is building the group. They talk about group leadership—"Who's leading today?"—or commenting, "That's a leadership thing to say." They make good use of their therapist. They ask for help. They have broken out of categorized ways of relating to each other and themselves.

With the parents it's more difficult. As adults, we're just more consolidated into what I call our lack-of- relatedness, our rigidified thinking, and our categorical thinking. It's often very exposing for parents to be in the group because things will come up that are hard to look at. I think in this culture, and probably in others, one of the worst things that you can do is talk about how you're not very good at being a mother or father. I think there are tremendous social constraints on parents being able to talk openly about their struggles as parents.

Q: And they're talking about their struggles as parents in front of the kids?

Christine: We're saying it all in front of the kids. Recently I said to a mother who has some emotional difficulties (in front of the child) that I thought a way that he was in advance of her is that she kept expecting that he (the child) should take care of her. I said that making an emotional demand on him to take care of her when she was having a hard time was a misuse of their relationship. Moreover, he came to the group to get help, but she didn't do that. She went to him for help.

She just reported today (a number of weeks after this conversation) that she was having a very hard time and that her son had said to her, "Do you remember in therapy when Christine said that I don't need to take care of you? What would it look like if we did that right now?" This is a nine-year-old! Mom responded, "Why don't you go out and play, and I'll pick up the phone and call somebody."

Q: And they talked about it in the next group?

Christine: Yes. She said that he made that move with her and that she was able to respond. And that's talked about in front of the kids—in fact not just in f*ront of them*, but also *with* them. And more often than not the kids rise to the occasion of being supportive of their parents.

Q: What makes your work seem to be so vital and important is that you're reaching these kids that no one else has been able to reach, and helping them grow and relate to others.

Christine: Yes. They develop, and develop quickly. It's even quicker than I thought possible.

Q: How are parents are responding to this approach?

Christine: Parents and teachers are interested because they see the changes. Sometimes they write it off as magical. I used to think it was magical myself! Now I have a better understanding of how it's effective.

Q: Are your adult groups as creative as this? I mean, presumably you're not playing "The Bears" with adult groups.

Christine: Yes. They are creative. We're all practicing social therapy. I think adults have their version of "The Bears" game. We all have ways that we talk about ourselves and our histories that are extremely rigidified and limited. We've learned to tell stories and live our lives in ways that are categorical and alienated. In that sense, I think any adult in a social therapy group talking about his or her life is doing "The Bears" game. And the growth process involves letting other people impact on that story, creating different ways of telling stories, even understanding differently what a story is.

I want to share something about working with older people. We have an eighteen-year-old girl who came to us last year, who was diagnosed with Asperger's. She grew up with the diagnosis. She was doing very well while she was in a social context in high school. But then she stopped going to school and was basically in bed sleeping the entire day for a year. Her parents didn't know what to do or how to continue. So she came to therapy with us.

Q: How did she find you?

Christine: Their doctor referred her to us. A lot of doctors refer to us. And one of our therapists, who I am supervising, was working with her. The young woman had all of the characteristics of this diagnostic category. She had also been diagnosed with obsessive-compulsive disorder, which is another part of this whole syndrome. She was very categorical—she liked to talk about certain things only in certain ways. She had very limited, scripted ways of talking.

In many ways we all do these things. But for her, it's just a little bit different. She would ask the therapist, "What's your favorite this? What's your worst this? What do you like best? What do you like least?" etc.

So I told the therapist to participate in that conversation, because I thought that was how to build a relationship with her. And they did that. After about a month or two into the therapy, the therapist made a move and said, "I don't really have a favorite color. I like a lot of different things and I'm mixed about some things. Some things I like: I like a blue dress. But I don't like a blue plate."

The young woman got very, very upset. "No, no, no!!! It *must* be one way or the other." (This is how a lot of these kids tend to relate.) The therapist stood her ground. The young woman said to her, "I'm going to help you figure out what your favorite color is." The therapist said, "That sounds great. Teach me how you do that. How do you do favorite, not favorite, most like, least like? I don't live my life that way. You do. So teach me about that."

What ensued was a very interesting deconstruction of how that young woman thinks about and organizes her life. And off of that five-to-six-week dialogue, they began to have different kinds of conversations about all kinds of things. They talked about being conflicted—about wanting to do something and *not* wanting to, all at the same time. And from there they went to talking about boys, music, and all kinds of things that were much less categorical.

Q: And for the young woman, that was a whole new way of approaching something?

Christine: Yes. Because what would typically happen is that she would have a major temper tantrum if you tried to go outside of how she did things. And so people had stopped trying, because it was so upsetting to her.

I think her parents didn't know how to handle the behavior so they just backed off. A lot of kids with a diagnosis of Asperger's will behave this way.

The frustration level is so high with many of these children—they want to relate and are unable to, and they create havoc.

Q: What was it that led your therapist to say to the client, "Teach me?"

Christine: I think the social therapist has to build with what she's got, while at the same time relate to the person as a head taller than herself. You have to do all of that at the same time.

You want to have her teach it to you as a way of engaging her in a more philosophical conversation that will show the therapist how this young woman understands, as well as to build a relationship. The therapist is investigating why she's come to think this way and why this is so terribly important to her. The therapist allows her to have the experience—that's very important. At the same time the therapist is relating to her as having the capacity to perform a conversation other than the ones she knows how to.

Q: What happened off of this?

Christine: What happened was very interesting. As she began to develop—and this is often the case—her family decided to take her out of therapy.

She was having fewer tantrums and talking with them about what she thought. So they decided to put her in a day treatment program, which we fully supported. She wanted to go somewhere and be able to live her life. And I think the therapy helped them all decide to do that. So she's now in school full time.

The family came to see that she could do something other than what she was doing. She can get out of bed. She can learn. She's expressing her feelings and thoughts in a way that is less hostile, and she has a greater range of ways of relating. And her growth, I think, motivated her family and encouraged them to find something else for her to do other than being alone in the home all day. So the therapy was very brief—two-and-a-half to three months. That was it. And I was just thrilled with it.

Q: I wanted to go back to what you said about the assumption that many professionals have that these kids only have a capacity for some kind of behavioral, cognitive therapy. You had said that Asperger's is seen as a *learning* disorder. By contrast, I hear in everything you've talked about today that the social therapeutic approach relates to the kids' *total* development: cognitive, linguistic, social and emotional. They're learning how to learn; they're philosophizing. And their emotional development is integral to their overall growth.

Christine: Yes. We're doing a unity of learning and development. It's certainly true that we are teaching them social skills. There's no doubt about that. However, how we're going about that I think is very different. We're putting the demand on them that they're going to have to create environments where, with the appropriate help, they can create new ways of performing. They have performances they're doing—some of which are working and, by their own account, some of which are not working. Many of them will say, "I don't have any friends." But we are collectively creating environments—all of us together, children and adults—where they can develop emotionally and socially. And there's no separation for any of it.

It's not a technique. It looks different, depending on who the child is and who the parent is. I think everybody's learning how children and adults can talk together. Usually conversations are segregated: you talk to adults *or* you talk to children. For years, we've been struggling for ways to talk to each other given that some of us are eight and some of us are forty-eight.

Q: You talk about "The Bears" with seriousness and respect. And at the same time, you convey it's a child's game. You don't denigrate it as a child's game. You're not doing silly talk about the child's game. It's a serious consideration of the game.

Christine: Yes. And in the process we are hopefully busting through the children's and the adults' assumptions about what children can understand, who adults are and how they respond, and what children are capable of.

I used to be shocked by the kinds of things children said because they seemed so advanced. But then I had to take a look at how I saw children, and that I romanticized or idealized children in a certain kind of way that doesn't relate to them as workers.

Children work to create their development. They're insightful; they're ridiculous; they have a lot to offer; they have nothing to offer. They're like everybody else. So there's no special treatment in therapy because you're five. As there's no special treatment because you're a mom or a dad. We're working together and you give what you can give, and you give the best you can give. That's the demand.

So the group will often say, "You can do better than that. That's not good enough. You're not going to get away with saying that you're bored. You're going to have to respond to what people in the group are saying." Now these are often *children* saying these things. Or a parent will say: "I can't believe that she (the child) just said that!" And I'll say, "Why not? Why would you not believe she said that? I think you don't know who she is." We're constantly engaging and challenging the expectations and assumptions about how people see who children are. And how they see themselves.

Q: It's almost a cliché the extent to which parents and kids are in a logjam. A child might say to the parent, "You don't understand me. You can't hear me. You don't know who I am." And for their part, adults can get exasperated. That dynamic seems to be a critical part of what is going on in these conversations among kids and adults.

Christine: Yes. I think we're working very hard to create an environment where the adults in the room can see their child and other children in very different and new ways. Not see them simply as *their* child, but see who that child is in the world; see who that child is socially and relationally. See who that child is becoming.

And the same goes for the kids. They're seeing not just *my* mom. The group is saying, "This is your mother, a woman in the world. Do you want to get to know her or do you just want her to do what you want her to do? This is who your dad is. He's not always nice to your mom. That doesn't mean that you get to be not nice to your dad." So parents and kids are learning who each other is in the world. This supports the inherent socialness of who we are. It helps everyone break out of more traditional, confining roles of family life—and of life in general.

Parents will often say, "I feel like I've gotten to know my child." And children will say, "It's okay. This is my mom and dad. And neither one is perfect. They're not even necessarily very good at being parents. But they're here and we're all developing together. We're working. We're not being cute. We're not being mommy. We're not taking care of each other. Everybody's working together." I think that's unusual.

Q: What is your response to, how do you react to, the success of what you're creating here?

Christine: I think that looks a million different ways. I'm beginning to train other people and that's very helpful to me because I'm seeing more clearly what we're doing. For one thing, the work is very emotional. I've seen several children for a number of years. One child I've seen for five years, and a few weeks ago I realized, "Hey, she's going to make it. She's going to be okay!" It was an extraordinary moment. And that's what motivates me.

I want more people to know about these successes. I want more people to challenge the existing methodologies of helping and begin to question what help is, what kinds of social arrangements we need to construct in order to do it with some degree of success. Can we create performatory environments where human beings can develop and not just settle for eradicating negative behavior in and of itself? I believe it can be done, and I want more people to learn how to do it. I saw a new family yesterday. I used to somewhat dread seeing families. But now, I feel excited that we're going to give this to somebody else.

I've worked with young people for a very long time, since I was a young person myself. When I was eighteen I taught in the South Bronx for a couple of years. I've worked with kids who are deaf, learning disabled, gifted, and severely emotionally disturbed. And I think our work in social therapy is a way to help people, young and old, build environments where we can continuously discover how to be both who we are and other than who we are.

And given what's happening with young people today and the epidemic of autism in particular, I think it's vital for us to continue to develop this work. It's in the beginning stages, but small as it is, the work is very significant. And people are seeing that. Teachers are seeing that. The kids are better. The families are happier. People are living more growthful lives.

I'm very dedicated to continuing to create social therapy, and happy to be doing it with more and more people, including therapists from other disciplines who are coming here to train and learn how to do this work with families. These therapists are, in turn, bringing their own sets of skills and creativity to the work, which is also very exciting.

Q: Thank you for sharing this with us.

Christine: Thank you.

REFERENCES

Axline, V. (1947). *Play therapy.* Boston, MA: Houghton Mifflin.

Axline, V. (1950). *Entering the child's world via play experiences. Progressive Education, 27,* 68–75.

Freud, A. (1965). *Normality and pathology in childhood: Assessments of development.* Madison, CT: International Universities Press.

Greenspan, S., & Wieder, S. (2009). *Engaging autism: Using the floortime approach to help children relate, communicate, and think.* Cambridge, MA: Da Capo Lifelong Books.

Holzman, L. (2009). *Vygotsky at work and play.* London: Routledge.

Holzman, L. & Mendez, R. (2003). *Psychological investigations: A clinician's guide to social therapy.* New York, NY: Brunner- Routledge.

Klein, M. (1932). *The Psychoanalysis of Children.* London: Hogarth Press.

Moustakas, C. (1997). *Relationship play therapy.* Northvale, NJ: Jason Aronson, Inc.

Newman, F. & Holzman, L. (1993). *Lev Vygotsky: Revolutionary scientist.* New York, NY: Routledge.

Schaefer, C.E. & Kaduson, H.G. (Eds.) (2007). *Contemporary play therapy: Theory, research, and Practice.* New York, NY: Guilford Press.

Vygotsky, L. (1978). *Mind in Society.* Cambridge, MA: Harvard University Press.

Part III

NEW UNDERSTANDINGS OF PLAY AND PERFORMANCE

Chapter Nine

Play as Deconstruction

Thomas Henricks

Like many official academic organizations, The Association for the Study of Play (TASP) has a stoutly modernist character. Modernism, whose beginnings are often traced to the ideas and events of eighteenth century Europe and sometimes to the Renaissance, is a belief system that emphasizes the ability of human rationality to confront, comprehend, and then reorganize the natural and social worlds (see Docherty, 1993; Rosenau, 1992). At the center of the modernist credo are enterprising, independent individuals, surrounded by the sphere of their own dignity. Such persons are said to have an inherent entitlement to "life, liberty, and the pursuit of happiness"; they are allowed, even encouraged, to live on their own terms. So endowed, they pool those resources to develop scientific and technological marvels, to re-invent and then administer the societies in which they live, and to gain increasingly comprehensive and powerful understandings of themselves. The modernist person does not simply live in the world; she creates or "constructs" it. As a consequence of those acts of making and re-making, she learns both about the world that she has transformed and about herself, as reflected in the "mirror" of her own creations (Marx, 1999).

TASP participates in this tradition. Although it draws its membership from many academic disciplines and welcomes play-related contributions of all types, the organization is strongly influenced by scholars from the fields of early childhood education and human development and by professional play advocates. Those researchers tend to see play as a kind of "magic circle" (Huizinga, 1955, p. 10) cut off from the usual entanglements of life. Inside that circle, people are free—or at least freer than they would be otherwise—to explore the world. Special attention is given to play as a creative activity. The primary source of that creativity is the developing insights and abilities of the individual player. However, play is not merely expressive; it also builds the persons who play. This general viewpoint is summarized well by Lin and Reifel (1999):

> Play is a remarkably important activity for children. Not only is it a means for expanding the self, but it is a major tool of self-preservation. Play is the province of the child. It is a "laboratory" where children can learn new skills and practice old ones in preparation for adult life in society. Play is also a social workshop, an area for trying out roles, both alone and with other children. Play is also an area for expression; it is concerned with the themes and emotions that are experienced in everyday life. By studying children's play, we can understand what they think and how they feel about the world about them. We also have a better understanding of all aspects of their development by studying play. (p. 151)

According to this credo, people—and especially young children—should be given occasions to express themselves on their own terms. Unfortunately, modern society has become so highly organized that there are too few opportunities for children to play informally. What society needs, or so it is said, is more recess in school, free-spirited encounters with nature, and playgrounds designed to encourage active exploration. The author of this chapter agrees with all these themes.

However, this is not the only way to look at play. As Sutton-Smith (1997) argues in *The Ambiguity of Play,* scholars of modern societies tend to emphasize three rather different explanatory systems or "rhetorics" of play: that play promotes development or "progress" (in both humans and animals), that it is an exploration and generator of the individual "self," and that it is a showcase for the "imagination." Against those theoretical directives are understandings of play that arise from its manifestations in pre-modern or traditional societies. Those four rhetorics are: that play is an exploration of the meaning of "power," that it is a participation in community "identity," that it is an exercise in foolishness or "frivolity," and that is a tempting of "fate." Sutton-Smith's point is that there are many play traditions and play scholars would be wise to consult them all before they draw conclusions about what play is or should be.

In that spirit, the current chapter explores a view of play that stands as a strong counter-tradition to modernism: postmodernism. As a wide-ranging intellectual and cultural movement that became important during the second half of the twentieth century, postmodernism defies simple definition. As is frequently noted, postmodernism is less an identifiable school of thought or philosophical position than it is a general approach to contemporary culture and experience (see Harvey, 1990; Bertens, 1995). That looseness of definition exists in part because postmodernist approaches are found in many different disciplines—literature, philosophy, psychology, sociology, anthropology, art and architecture, film studies, ethnic and gender studies, political science, and so forth—and take somewhat different shape in each of those fields. More importantly perhaps, postmodernism tends to be a protest against explicit, uniform definitions; thus it resists attempts to define itself "authoritatively" in one way or another. Indeed, as this author (Henricks, 2001, p. 52) argues, the term *postmodernism* itself is something of a misnomer for the term suggests that the concept is an "ism" (that is, a set of clearly defined beliefs and practices) and that it can be understood to be a separate stage of history that comes "post" or after modernism. Such ideas—of fixed beliefs and distinct historical stages—are antithetical to the postmodern spirit.

However, postmodernism does take shape as a response to some of the human difficulties created by modernism. The spectacular accomplishments of modernism—bureaucracy, the nation-state, independent legislatures and judiciaries, science, capitalism, mass education, and the like—have all been found to create their own sets of problems. Gigantic organizations may well be the constructions of persons, but they ultimately became entities of their own sort bound to their own administrative principles. Capitalism has led to the miseries of the class system and, at least in some views, to a withering of the human spirit. Nation-states have sponsored imperialist schemes and world war. The adoration of scientifically propounded "general laws" or "universal truths" has meant that other, more humanly sensitive forms of knowing are sometimes disregarded. In the context of such difficulties, perhaps modernism is only a belief system of the highly placed that marginalizes the perspectives of less advantaged people. Perhaps the grand overview or "totalizing narrative" that modernism supports is just an administrative scheme that does not describe well the way the contemporary world works or the way people actually deal with that world. Against the modernist trajectory then, many postmodernists revisit and draw inspiration from the themes of the pre-modern world—the centrality of the emotions, the interrelatedness of persons, the joys of being immersed and even out of control in events, the importance of chance, the elevation of the particular over the general, and the view that the goings-on of the world must always be appreciated in the "context" of their presentation (see Spariosu, 1989).

For play scholars, such issues are not simply intellectual curiosities. That is because many postmodernists now claim that play has become a central metaphor for contemporary experience (see Hans, 1981; Rorty, 1986; Spariosu, 1989; Kuchler, 1994; Henricks, 2001). In the postmodern view, contemporary society does not lack for its instances of play. People—of all ages—amuse themselves with their hand-held electronic devices; they "surf" for channels on their televisions and for websites on the internet. Many gamble, "abuse" substances, and engage in risk-taking sexual behavior, most of this in the name of fun. Those who can afford it (and some who cannot) "shop till they drop." Many love fashion, socializing, cooking, and home re-decorating. Vast numbers participate in and watch sports, play video games, and engage in hobbies that defy enumeration. They read mystery novels and romances. Contemporary society is alive with pleasure-driven pursuits, though those pursuits may not be of the type most admired by modernist scholars.

In the postmodern view of play, the theme of chanciness—rather than self-direction takes center stage. Events emerge as the only somewhat predictable interaction of contingent forces. To be sure, there are "rules" and other structural formations that people are obliged to follow, but these are recognized at some level to be little more than artifices that help the activity along. A world depicted in such ways knows only arbitrary beginnings and ends. People find themselves in great swirls of happenings and seek fleeting glimpses of their predicament. And like the participants at a craps table or in an on-line video game, it is often difficult to tell who is controlling the play and who is "in play" in ways they barely understand. Like their modernist counterparts, postmodern players are actively engaged in the circumstances of the magic circle; but the character of that circle—and the relationship of people to it—is somewhat differently conceived.

The presence of these rival traditions makes it pertinent to examine their differences at greater length. Because the readership of this journal is perhaps more familiar with modernist approaches, the author's intention is to show the pertinence of postmodern thinking to a broader understanding of play. To that end, the chapter is divided into three sections. The first section discusses some basic themes of postmodernism as these can be contrasted to modernism. The second section introduces a central concept of postmodernism—deconstruction. Five particular qualities of deconstruction—the presence of absence, the assault on hierarchy, the search for origins, the unfolding of possibility, and the spell of the accidental—are emphasized. The author then contends that many forms of play can be seen as deconstructing activities, in terms of those five themes. The third and final section addresses the ways in which play events—the magic circle—can be seen in the context of (and related to) patterns and activities that stand "outside" that circle. Four visions of this relationship are presented. These are: 1) play as an *alternative world*, 2) play as a *mirror of society*, 3) play as an *anti-structure*, and 4) play as a *blueprint* or "model for" society. These four views of how play disconnects from and then re-connects with external matters are exemplified in the writings of some prominent play theorists. The resulting perspectives are offered here to show how play is not only a constructive activity but also a process of de-construction and re-construction.

BASIC THEMES OF POSTMODERNISM

As discussed above, postmodernism is a very wide-ranging analysis of contemporary culture and of the concerns of people who live in those settings. Different academic disciplines explore different aspects of postmodernism. And individual proponents advocate different strategies for personal and social change. Nevertheless, some general tenets of postmodernism can be noted. These qualities—which should be understood, at least in part, as reactions to or rejections of modernism—are described in this section.

Before beginning that list of tenets, I offer the following proviso. Because postmodernism is a vast cultural movement composed of many scholars and cultural creators, it should not be assumed that all the conclusions presented here apply to all postmodernists. In that light, Rosenau (1992, pp. 14–17) has distinguished two broad types of postmodernists: the *skeptics* and the *affirmatives.* Skeptical postmodernists are those who paint the darkest portraits of the contemporary predicament and who downplay the possibilities for meaningful freedom and action within that setting. Scholars of this sort draw their inspiration from continental philosophy, especially as it stems from Nietzsche and Heidegger (see also Henricks, 2001). Of special importance in this group are French post-structuralists like Baudrillard and Derrida, the latter of whose writing will be addressed in what follows. Because it is the most extreme form of postmodernism—and thereby heightens the contrast to modernism—that approach is given most emphasis.

However, *affirmative* postmodernism is also quite important and indeed, is probably a clearer portrait of the meaning-making activity of most persons. *Affirmatives,* in Rosenau's view, are influenced much more strongly by Anglo-American traditions. They share with other postmodernists the general critique of contemporary society, but they are much more hopeful about the prospects for human agency and for the creation of social solutions that address the dilemmas of a world that is being re-constituted by demographic, economic, political, and cultural forces. That affirmative tradition, which attempts to bridge the failed communication caused by divisions of race, ethnicity, class, age, nationality, and other instances of social location, is also given some consideration below.

The Rejection of Universal Belief Systems

Modernism rests on a belief that people are fundamentally similar and that scholars can reach general conclusions or even discover broad "truths" about the human predicament. That viewpoint applies not only to scientific work but also to work in the humanities, where artistic and literary "geniuses" are thought to provide compelling visions that speak to all people. That one-size-fits-all model is challenged by postmodernists, who argue that such a viewpoint has long been part of an imperialist agenda that disregards the social situations and perspectives of subordinate and marginalized groups (see Bertens, 1992, pp. 92–97). Postmodernists reject what they call the "grand totalizing narratives" of modernists and emphasize instead that belief systems are better understood as stories, ideologies, or "rhetorics" that express and justify the particular circumstances of their proponents.

The Fascination with Uncertainty

Among the glories of modernism is the growth and application of science. Science, at least in its modernist version, is a claim that the world operates according to identifiable sequences of cause and effect and that these processes follow discernible laws. That Newtonian quest for the guiding principles of the universe has been altered by recent scientific thinking, which emphasizes the relativity of any observation and the possibility that randomness and even chaos are fundaments of many processes. Although it tends to find its inspiration in philosophy and literature rather than science, postmodernism also celebrates the relativism, particularism, and uncertainty that characterize the human condition (see Kuchler, 1994; Krieglstein, 1991). In that context, postmodernism can be seen as a claim for the "embeddedness" of people in transient patterns.

The Suspicion of History as Progress

Modernism has long been inspired by a belief that human rationality can produce successively better understandings of the natural and human worlds. That belief in knowledge making as a cumulative enterprise was critical to activity in science and technology, philosophy, and even social and political reform. Such hopeful estimates of civilization's advance have been challenged by a series of humanly made catastrophes during the twentieth century—two world wars, economic depression, totalitarian regimes, nuclear threats, and continuing outbreaks of genocide (see Cantor, 1997, pp. 425–502; Harvey, 1990, pp. 10–38). In many of these, sophisticated technology was used for thoroughly dishonorable ends.

Postmodernism questions not only the idea of worldly improvement but also the idea of history as a coherent record of human occurrence. In the postmodernist view, there are myriads of stories that can be told about the past—and about the present. These stories are always written from the changing vantage point of the present and often are related directly to the economic and political interests of the writer. In other words, historical accounts, like other acts of cultural creation, are at bottom only fables that have been concocted to reassure writers and their audiences.

The Privileging of Culture

Postmodernism is commonly aligned with the academic movement known as cultural studies, an inter-disciplinary effort that explores the implications of the publicly circulated ideas and artifacts that have proliferated in our increasingly commercialized and electronically configured society (see Featherstone, 1991; During, 1999). These public presentations—television shows, ads of every type, magazines, movies, newspapers, websites, consumer products, and so forth—arguably take their places in the universe as new foci of human consciousness and function as models by which people measure the quality of their lives. The expansion of public imagery of this sort has been made possible by a technological and communications revolution. If people once were the principal culture-bearers of societies, now they must share that status with machines of many types and with the symbolically transcribed outputs of those machines. In that light, it is argued that relationships with these mass-produced, technologically supported products and images have altered—and perhaps diminished—older, face-to-face styles of human relating.

The Fragmentary Character of Meaning Systems

Consistently with what has been said above, postmodernists tend to believe that such artifacts and their associated meanings cannot be controlled from any single point. Instead, those meaning systems should be seen as "texts" that are interpreted in relatively personalized ways by the "readers" of those passages. As in a novel or poem, there is no fixed or unitary meaning to texts but rather an abundance of meanings that are generated by the possible relationships among the terms that are found therein. In an age that honors interpretation more than exposition and openness more than closure readers become more important than writers. Indeed, the intentions of writers and other cultural creators matter little at all. Forms quickly escape their producers and acquire a quasi-independent status; people effectively "write" the materials they consume. According to the postmodern credo, all of us dwell in vast fields of symbolic possibility and take from each encounter what self-styled meanings we can. As is sometimes said, writers must die so that readers may live.

Such a viewpoint is extended to all kinds of cultural productions and social events, including dramatic performances, sports events, visits to amusement parks, television programs, and the like. Although such showings and events are "doctored" or "spun" by their producers and distributors to suggest a limited range of meanings, those meanings are by no means closed or definitive (see Ewen, 1999). Quite the opposite, many of the meanings that are superimposed by these creators are only vaguely related to one another or perhaps are entirely contradictory. Thus we watch advertisements with sleek young men and women in luxurious homes or at a resort, laughing, and drinking the alcoholic beverage of their choice. We are not invited to think logically about the elements of that scene (for example, how people so young and unmarked could be sharing such privileges); instead, we are encouraged to savor those images and imagine ourselves amidst those imaginary companions. That is, we color those products and settings with our own preferences in a way that allows us to "fit in." Whatever the meanings we end up supplying to these scenes, it can hardly be denied that artifacts and showings are realities of their own sort and that people interact with the materials presented there.

Affirmative postmodernists focus more on the meaning systems of social groups and communities. Those "discourse communities" (Swales, 1990) are patterns of communication established by their members to permit certain kinds of interaction and to secure socially agreed-upon ends. Those discourse communities, which feature a variety of "texts," tend to have their own histories, conventions that regulate their expression, and powerful groups that sponsor and control them. Part of the affirmative postmodern project is to expose the ways in which those discourses frequently block the opportunities of less powerful categories of people and then to suggest strategies that open-up the expressive possibilities for all.

The De-Centering of the Self

The privileging of culture—albeit as an open-ended rather than tightly closed system—has had consequences for one of social science's most cherished concepts, the self. The modernist self, as developed by James (1952) and Mead (1964), has a firmly developed "me," a set of fairly stable characteristics that the possessor can refer to as a basis of identity and behavior. That general understanding of who we are as persons effectively "transcends" the particular situations we encounter. Said differently, our self-concept is something we carry with us through life, and we use it to decide how we should (or shouldn't) be treated in our relationships with others. Modernist education and therapy can be seen as an attempt to build a solid, comprehensive, powerful, and well-defended self that can help people deal with—or even control—what life throws at them.

In the same way that postmodernists see cultural meanings as being fluid, particular, and ever contextualized, so they apply this approach to the meaning system of the person. Certainly, people are recognized to have subjectivity—that is, privately managed desires, reflections, and decision-making—but they are not thought to possess some integrated and firmly established set of traits. Indeed, some skeptical postmodernists have gone so far as to declare the "death" of the self (see Bertens, 1995, p. 166). Others have claimed that the self is little more than a "position in language" or "effect of discourse" (see Flax 1990). Put differently again, the self is simply a site where the various elements of socio-cultural reality collide.

A less extreme position is that people are effectively social chameleons, who adjust their understandings of themselves as they move from situation to situation. This is the view of Gergen (1995) who says that it is more pertinent to speak now of plural "selves" instead of a uniform "self" or to describe the many "masks" that people wear. Gergen (1991) also uses the imagery of a "saturated self," a condition in which persons are deeply enmeshed in events and draw their energies and directions from the public meanings that abound in those settings. This more socially embedded self is much more aware of the multiple and disparate potentials for being than is her modernist counterpart (1991, p. 69). Such persons are also less likely to stand against the world or to try to change it from the vantage point of their now uncertain principles. Although these qualities of multiplicity, change, and public involvement make it more difficult to achieve an independently functioning self, they can also be the basis for a more expansive and sensitive approach to the world. This is the position of Newman and Holzman (2006), who argue that meaning-making can be re-imagined as an ensemble activity, a gathering together of people to collectively create and manage shared endeavors. The self in this new approach may be de-centered from its individualist basis but it is re-centered by its participation in a community of caring others.

The De-Centering of Society

As noted above, postmodernism is in many ways a response to the grand intellectual and administrative schemes that have been propounded by modernism. Governmental, economic, and media forces are said to have grown beyond human scale. In that light, the bureaucratic impulse—to categorize and analyze persons—has been famously criticized by Foucault (1980), who sees many of society's institutions (such as schools, jails, and mental hospitals) as forcing houses that marginalize, control, and punish persons who are "different." At one level then, postmodernists stand against this social gigantism; at another they claim that these social schemes are ultimately failures.

In particular, such regimes cannot harness the proliferation of cultural forms and meanings that have escaped into the world. In that sense, cultural participation becomes more important than social participation. Indeed, Baudrillard (1983, p. 4) has gone so far as to declare the death of the social and of the discipline which feeds off that "hypothesis" (that is, sociology).

A more restrained view is that the character of the social is being altered. Postmodernists tend to be very distrustful of authority figures who manage social events. Instead, they emphasize the importance of hearing all the "voices" or socially situated perspectives of the persons who find themselves in one another's company. Special attention is given to those who have been socially discredited—including women, poor people, lesbian, gay, bisexual and transgendered people, and people of color. Central to the postmodernist project then is the task of confronting and then overcoming these historic oppositions (rich/poor, male/female, and the like) by showing how these statuses ultimately depend on one another as elements of the same meaning systems. That shift toward "relationality" has also been a theme of feminist social science (see Miller, 1987). One consequence of this general approach has been a tendency to focus on the smaller settings of social life—interpersonal relations, families, school classrooms, communities, and so forth—instead of on the vast macro-level processes that have been described above. In any case, affirmative postmodernism re-invents the idea of "agency" as a collective enterprise that respects the contribution of each member.

The Centrality of Corporate Capitalism

The best-known critique of capitalist economies, Marxism, has focused on forces and relations of production (that is, on technological changes and on the organization of work) and how this affects people's lives. More recent analyses have focused instead on forces and relations of consumption, that is, on the ways in which such processes affect the experiences of the persons using such products (see Jameson, 1984; Jay, 1973; Featherstone, 1991). In advanced industrial societies, an increasing proportion of work concentrates on the generation and dissemination of publicly accessible information and on the provision of personal services. That is, workers in the contemporary period have become technological attendants who create and market specialized applications of culture. Knowledge—and experience more generally—is reconstituted as a commodity. The intended effect of that transaction is to change the personal orientation of recipients, including their idealized visions of society and self.

Postmodernism has been especially attentive to this pattern of culture-as-commodity. In contemporary society, cultural presentations—especially in the profoundly important case of advertising—are essentially rhetorical appeals or sales pitches. The style of these commercial appeals is also adopted increasingly by political, religious, and educational organizations. Arguments produced by such organizations tend to be multi-sensory; claims are vague and image-based. Consumers are allowed—and indeed encouraged—to fit the offered products to their own visions and needs. Assessments of "style" and even "life-style" (as broad, aesthetically based orientations) take the place of more thought-dominated or "principled" assessments. Special attention is given to the idea of "satisfaction," including substantial doses of short-range pleasure. Although such appeals are based ultimately on an ideology of "personal choice," every effort is made by cultural producers to see that these choices are appropriately guided.

The Celebration of Particularity

As postmodernists are suspicious of grand abstractions and claims of universal truth, so it follows scholars of that type should emphasize what remains in a world ridded of such formulations (see Flax, 1990). A society so purged should allow its members to live in the moment, taking what satisfactions they can from intimately regarded persons and objects. If modernism encourages grand administrative schemes, then postmodernism promotes more egalitarian, respectful, even conciliatory modes of relating. If modernism champions the large life, then postmodernism admires the small. As in postmodern art and architecture, particular objects and their surfaces are brought into sharp focus (see Levin, 1980). Those little treasures are thought to be more important than the grand visual arrangements or psychological "principles" that dominate modernist creativity. Said differently, postmodernism shifts the center of artistic concern from intellectual and moral matters (that is, from ideas of truth and justice) to aesthetic matters (addressing one's *feelings* about life). Although postmodern thought is frequently criticized for its "superficiality," that attention to surfaces is held to be a more open and attentive regard for the human condition than modernism's grand schemes.

Conclusions

The current section has indicated some basic themes of contemporary culture that are highlighted in postmodern writing. Especially in the accounts of skeptical postmodernism, contemporary society is reconceived as a firestorm of electronically generated, mass-produced ideas and images that people can discover with the click of a button. Those presentations insinuate many kinds of "meanings." Those meanings are rooted in no unitary logic but instead encourage wide ranges of interpretation. People are encouraged to move from one cultural form to another in a pick-and-choose or "channel-surfing" way. Offerings are selected primarily on the basis of aesthetic criteria, that is, whether they "please" viewers. As with sales pitches of every type, such presentations are to be regarded with some suspicion.

In a world characterized by transience, technologically supplied experience, and the absence of unifying belief systems, it is sometimes argued that the best approach is a "playful" one. People at play recognize that the settings they enter—and the rules they play by—are not entirely "serious." Commitment, therefore, should be light or provisional. Self-interest (and the possibility of subterfuge from others) is to be expected. Satisfactions are anticipated to be the momentary sort. Each person should exploit a situation to the degree they can. They should also realize that they are "in play" as they confront (and are influenced by) social and cultural patterns. This rather dark view of the player—as a cultural or even metaphysical interpreter—is the one that arises from skeptical postmodernism. Postmodern players are those who immerse themselves in video games, romance novels, television, movies, websites, shopping malls, casinos, and the like and maneuver amidst these forms as they can. Partly they are "caught up" in the play forms (Stromberg, 2009); partly they use play to cultivate their desires.

Quite differently, affirmative postmodernism takes seriously the prospect of people's living together in human communities. By those accounts, we are not creatures who derive our fundamental meanings from electronic displays; we learn from our involvement with others. For such reasons, affirmatives provide another view of play. Because cultural meaning arises from the gatherings of persons, play is a kind of "dialogic imagination" (Bakhtin, 1981). That is, social interaction must be seen as the only somewhat predictable interaction of persons and themes. It does not follow firmly established scripts or come to pre-ordained endings. Instead, meaning arises out of encounters that are carnival-like in their qualities. People listen to one another and create what has not been there before. That propulsive process of invention—of both the self and the collectivity that makes the self possible—is given clear expression in Edmiston's (2008) descriptions of the joint meaning-making interactions of himself and his son. In that play, the father does not "lead" the son but rather is a co-player or even co-conspirator in their imaginative forays.

Although these themes will not be developed here, the author's own work (Henricks, 1999, 2006; forthcoming) has emphasized the extent to which expressive life illustrates both "ascending" and "descending" meaning. Ascending meaning refers to the ability of subjectivity to confront and transform the objects and elements of the world according to its own desires and schemes. Modernist views of play tend to emphasize that quality. Individuals draw on their own private resources to manipulate playthings (blocks, words, puzzles, and so forth). This process of private assertion (which also features re-adjustment when matters do not go as the player wishes) reaffirms one's powers of competence and agency (see Piaget, 1962). Skeptical postmodernism describes experiences that are closer to what the author calls "descending" meaning, the immersion of the self in external form. When immersion is done for the sheer pleasure of the activity—as in taking a warm bath, eating a good meal, or enjoying the goings-on at a fair, movie, or concert—the author calls this "communitas." Such activities are play to the extent that the participant exhibits some level of active engagement—choice-making, creative interpretation, innovative performance, and so forth. Compared to this model, affirmative postmodernism exhibits a much stronger role for the individual. However, creativity is not simply a personal affair (as it largely is in modernism) but is instead a collective activity. People join together to establish and sustain meaningful relationships with one another. That process—a mixture of play and communitas—displays open, intimate social bonding and a co-creation of always uncertain meanings. That sense of being in a dance where everyone begins without a commitment to pre-established movements or knowledge of clearly defined ends is at the heart of the postmodern experience.

DECONSTRUCTION

If cultural forms and presentations always exhibit wide ranges of meaning, how can one discover these meanings? In postmodernism, the best-known strategy for accomplishing such ends is called "deconstruction" (see Cullor, 2007; Anderson, 1995; Munslow, 2006). Not a specific type of analysis, deconstruction is instead a set of sensitivities that help one identify the ideas (and especially the background assumptions) that give meaning to social and cultural forms. To deconstruct an act of speech, writing, or other kind of cultural performance is to "un-cover" other formations that make that presentation possible, especially ideas that seem to be excluded but in fact are necessary to make the presentation intelligible. In other words, matters that are hidden or *not said* may be just as important as what is said explicitly. More generally then, deconstruction is an attempt to reveal the cultural context of presentations: what is said directly and what is only implied, what is not said but is essential for understanding, what could have been said but wasn't, what makes any sort of saying possible, and so forth.

The concept of deconstruction is usually attributed to philosopher Jacques Derrida, who uses it in a specialized way to address some problems in continental philosophy. Derrida's work is essentially an extension (and to an extent, rejection) of Husserl's "phenomenological" attempt to discover the structures that frame consciousness (see Derrida, 1978). Husserl believed that people can become aware of—or "bracket"—the conceptual forms they use to perceive the world. Possessed of that new awareness, subjects can confront the objects of consciousness in more direct, less mediated ways. By contrast, Derrida's writing argues that our involvement in conceptual frameworks is much more far-reaching and complicated than this. People are participants in cultural logics or "grammars" that set up the basic oppositions of thought and reveal possible pathways for expression. However, unlike "structuralist" linguists and philosophers, Derrida does not see these conceptual possibilities as being a closed or sharply defined system. Nor does he see any one set of ideas as more important than, dominant over, or "originary" to other ideas. Rather, culture should be understood as a maze of vaguely defined trails or ranges of meaning that are beyond the capabilities of that culture's users to comprehend. Making people become aware of these effulgent (and not uncommonly, contradictory) possibilities is the intention that guides Derrida's writing.

Derrida's best-known concept is *différance,* a term he invented to describe how cultural meanings operate (see Derrida, 1981). For Derrida, the words we use (e.g., "apple," "orange," "piano," and so forth) do not really define or capture conceptually the real-world objects to which they refer. Instead words and marks of that sort (what can be called "signifiers") mostly refer to one another in a purely intra-cultural or "semantic" way. While a person might well celebrate the degree to which symbols effectively channel and direct thought, Derrida tends to take the opposite approach. In his view, such terms really only circulate or *defer* meaning. For example, looking up the meaning of any word in a dictionary leads one to other words; looking up those words leads one to other words and not infrequently back to the very word from which one began. Furthermore, meanings are "culturally" referential in the sense that the definition of any particular term depends on its being compared to things it is *not.* In other words, the conceptual order we live in is essentially a set of oppositions or *differences.* We understand "silence" as being opposite to "noise"; "apples" are thought to be different from other kinds of fruit. Once again, one could make much of the way in which these logical oppositions spell out the possibilities for conception and expression, the project of structural linguistics and structural anthropology. However, Derrida takes the more postmodern line that such oppositions open up—rather than close off—productive lines for thought and feeling to take.

In that context, deconstruction is the process of sorting through the possible meanings suggested by cultural forms. In behavior and expression, all of us present more or less finished forms to others—speech acts, written sentences, artistic representations, and the like—and imagine that we have said or written what we mean and that others will "get" our meaning. However, a deeper analysis of what we have produced quickly reveals that there are many possible interpretations of what has just occurred, that there are contradictions or "accidents" in our constructions, and that there is a vast contextual history or background to what we have said. For someone else to appreciate our finished statements in the ways we intend they must accept all those assumptions, ignore our errors, and so forth. Rarely does such complete agreement between speaker and listener occur, and it occurs even less frequently in the cases of written and visual "texts," where the original producer of the material is absent (or perhaps deceased) and cannot supervise the reader's interpretation. To make matters worse, there is no clear stance (or position in some acknowledged system of thought) where a person can claim that they have gotten the "correct" or "true" meaning. Against the structuralist belief that there are clear perspectives (deeply established psychological frameworks, economic patterns, and the like) that one can use to explain sequences of thought and behavior, Derrida glories in the opposite viewpoint (Cullor, 2007, p. 22). Readers wander in texts without any compelling set of directions for how they should proceed. And postmodern authors may encourage this process by writing in ways that open up the possibilities for interpretation instead of guiding their readers along a clearly marked, linear path.

It should be emphasized that deconstruction—despite its name—is not an attempt to destroy the meaning of texts but rather is a way of looking through—and exposing—their wide-ranging meanings. Those fields of meanings "exist" in a cultural sense, that is, as a field of publicly accessible conceptual possibilities. In the tradition of humanities, it is argued that people's experiences of the world are essentially experiences "of" and "through" symbolic form. When we read a book, see a movie, attend a play, and so forth, we operate within trails of cultural meaning implicated by those "texts." There is always much more going on in those texts than what any of us, singly or even collectively, can grasp. In the process of participating in—and pondering—these events, we un-cover all sorts of things that we would not have discovered on our own, including meanings that the producers of the events did not intend for us to receive.

Play, it is argued here, has a similar spirit. When humans play, they participate in symbolically transcribed forms. Games in particular function as "texts" to the degree that they are culturally recognized formats that make it possible for players to move in certain directions through time. The event to some extent is "produced" by this set of playing rules that detail possible behaviors. Any beginnings and endings—and the various "points" between—are largely artificial; that is, they are generated simply as agreements among players about how the event should unfold. A sense of limitation and eventfulness is also encouraged by designated playing spaces, material implements, and specialized roles for participants.

However, to play a game is not simply to enact the rules in some formal or ritualistic way. Quite the opposite, players are expected to bring a quality of improvisation and even joy to their activity. They are expected to "find out" things about the game, other players, and themselves. People play games to encounter circumstances different from ordinary affairs and to appreciate the forms of psychological and social awareness that attend those circumstances. That process of exploration parallels the activities of deconstruction. To develop this theme further, this section describes five basic issues in deconstruction followed by their parallels in the inquiry that is play.

Deconstruction as the Presence of Absence

Although it is probably fair to say that some postmodern writers are fond of paradoxical or even contra-logical formulations, the idea that absence is a profoundly important aspect of people's understanding of situations seems clear enough. For centuries, modernist scholars have tended to focus on what people actually say and do; they then offer explanations—often in general or categorical terms—for why these particular events occurred as they did. However, it is also important to think about what is *not* being done or is even actively prohibited. The fact that some topic cannot be discussed even though everyone in the room is thinking about it (such as a shameful act someone has committed) or that some important person is not present at a social gathering (perhaps he or she did not choose to attend, was pointedly not invited, or left in a huff) provides a distinctive context and energy to that event. Similarly, people may be thrilled by an invitation to join an exclusive club precisely because specific categories of others have not been invited. Those same people may be pleased to join a church or political party that makes much of its hostility to other groups. Much of this stems from the sheer logic of symbolic opposition. Wealth cannot be appreciated without the idea of poverty, male without female, day without night, and so forth. Arguably, the interpretation of any text—or other meaningful presentation—depends on knowledge that that particular presentation was selected out of a great range of possibilities. To deconstruct a text is to call attention to matters that have been intentionally or unintentionally excluded.

Play as the Presence of Absence

For humans at least, play activities usually are conducted with the awareness that the player *could* be doing other things. Children are told to "go out and play" or to "stop playing with their food". They ask each other if they "want to play." In that context, play is understood by participants to be an enjoyable, even preferred category of activity that has its own boundaries and customs. As this author (Henricks, 2006) has claimed, play scholars also would do well to contrast play with other, somewhat similar kinds of activity—namely, work, ritual, and communitas—as a way of appreciating just how those feelings or difference or specialness are attained. In other words, to comprehend play, one must comprehend what it is *not.*

Arguably, some of the pleasure of entering that special world derives from the fact that the players are avoiding or escaping other responsibilities they may hold. Other parts of that enjoyment may come from the fact that they are "getting" to play while others have to watch or are otherwise not playing. People of all ages know what play is (even if they cannot define it) because they sense that it is different from other kinds of activities. Indeed, even when they become deeply embedded in their play or are otherwise in "flow" (Csikszentmihalyi, 1990), such immersion is understood to be a kind of "forgetting" of external affairs.

In different ways then, players bring "external" or absent matters to the edges of the playground. Sometimes those external matters are kept at the edges to heighten the sense of escape; sometimes they are brought in and pointedly transformed. More curiously yet, players sometimes bring those external themes into the play setting just so they can "negate" or make them "absent" in a new way. Such relationships—between things inside and outside the playground—were themes of Goffman's (1961) writing on play.

In his account of how people create the semi-transparent bubble that is the play "reality," Goffman (1961, pp. 19–34) argues that game players employ three kinds of rules. The first of these he termed "rules of realized resources." Such rules are used to define elements of the external world as elements of play; in that sense, a rock becomes first base, a tree marks an out-of-bounds or "foul" zone, and so forth. In other words, ordinary objects and activities no longer function in their former ways. A second type is what he calls "rules of irrelevance." Just as some objects and activities are brought in and redefined, so other aspects of the broader world are deemed immaterial or unimportant. How much people paid for their baseball mitts, where they bought them, where they learned to play baseball, and so forth all are matters that have no "official" relevance to the game. By processes of inclusion and exclusion then, the play world is configured as a place where matters are defined in a certain way.

Most interesting, in this writer's view, is what Goffman (1961) calls "rules of transformation." Because play events occur in a real world, some of the former rules cannot hold. The outside world—signified by calls from one's mother to come home, temper tantrums or other failures of resolve, losses of money or respect, changes in weather, injuries, and so forth—can quickly break the spell of the game. For that reason, there must be additional procedures for how to deal with these interruptions when they do occur. Through the use of discounting, teasing, cajoling, soothing, and myriad of other devices, players are reconnected to the play reality. All of this is only to acknowledge that players know well there is a world beyond the boundaries of the playground and that skillful players know how to incorporate these absent elements in ways that sustain the character of the event.

Deconstruction as the Assault on Hierarchy

Just as some people and ideas are excluded *from* discourse communities, so differences exist *within* those communities. That is, some voices are given more prominence than others; only some interests are served well. Some of this derives from the sheer logic of opposition described above. As the adage has it: if I am to be white, you must be black; if am to be male, you must be female. In other words, positions of privilege rest on positions of subordination.

In that sense, deconstruction tends to be an inquiry into the foundations of power. Why are some things being said—or are allowed to be said—and not others? Why are some people speaking while others are silent? To some extent, deconstruction tends to be a de-mystification of hierarchy, a revelation that the emperor is either "wearing no clothes" or at least is using expensive clothing to mask his ordinariness. In the hands of the skeptical postmodernists, this inquiry into the underlying assumptions and social supports of privilege leads to an antinomian response to the world. Social and cultural forms are held to be artifices that must be "seen through." For affirmative post modernists, the challenge is not just to impugn hierarchy but to use this knowledge to better include many different voices in conversations and to build a more humane world (see Newman and Holzman, 2006).

Play as the Assault on Hierarchy

In the modernist vision, play is mostly an assertion of individual prerogative, an active transformation of some element of the world and then perhaps a sudden destruction of that which was created. A child spends hours patiently building a sandcastle and then, as if on a whim, tears it apart. Postmodernism, on the other hand, invites analysis of the social and cultural meanings of play, especially as these involve power-relations. Thus Bakhtin's (1981) analyses of carnival are not merely commentaries on the disorderliness—or hectic particularity—of the world. They are also commentaries on the possibilities for conducting normally unpermitted activities—drinking, sexual escapade, masquerade, and the like—and also on opportunities for status reversal. In play people can "take liberties." Sometimes, as in the medieval "feast of fools" (Cox, 1969), they create situations in which the higher status groups do not rule but rather serve them.

This theme of rebellion (by people of every age) has been a theme of Sutton-Smith's writing. Play is, to be sure, a modernist seeking and building of order; but it is also an inquiry into disorder (Sutton-Smith & Kelly-Byrne, 1984). In other words, play—at least in some versions—is a chance to de-stabilize the world. With that end in mind, players frequently assault propriety. They say things they shouldn't; they write on bathroom walls; they go to extremes. Little children in particular produce "folk stories" filled with outrageous behaviors, gigantic bodies (and body parts), and dangerous (and entirely forbidden) adventures. Disorderly behavior of this sort is just as "functional" in its way as orderly behavior (see Henricks, 2009). That is, it reaffirms the ability of people to assert themselves against the authorities of the world. It lets them know what they can (and can't) "get away with."

Deconstruction as the Search for Origins

As suggested above, postmodernists challenge the idea that presentations can be taken at face value, that is, that they have only one "official" meaning. Although public statements (like a written document, speech, or advertising image) do exist as more or less objective happenings in the world, they should not be analyzed simply as expositions, that is, as a creator's declarations about a current state of affairs. Instead those present-time manifestations should be seen in a broader time frame that incorporates ideas of past and future. To take this line of approach is to emphasize the ways in which the world's elements are always in states of becoming; that is, such elements are to be seen as moments in processes rather than as fixed structures. Similar to the way in which a person traces his or her own genealogy through a family tree—an image popular in postmodernism—so meaningful presentations come forward as the legacy of many ancestors. Indeed, there is no clear point at which that ancestry begins. Deconstruction is the hunt for those relatives.

As in the case of family relations, some ancestral traits of appearance and character are expressed in the current generation, some are not expressed but instead carried "recessively," and other, thoroughly illegitimate influences can also be found. "Distinguished" relatives all of us are proud to claim; others we are anxious to forget or deny. Every event, it seems, is the product of its own distinctive combination of past influences, is constructed in a way that showcases publicly only some of those influences, and moves into the future in a similarly calculated way. Postmodernism shows that present-time formations are constructed moments that live between a speculative past and an equally uncertain future.

Play as the Search for Origins

As noted above, deconstruction commonly involves a search for the origins of an activity or expressive product. In that sense, present-time products can be compared to icebergs. For the most part, we see only the shiny surfaces and are left to imagine what vast portions are beneath the water and how it all was formed. Presumably, there are many, many factors that produce objects and events of every sort and our re-construction of those factors is inevitably narrow and self-serving. Deconstructionists look to the origins of things so they can see how they were made, how they may operate in the future, and how people may be able to comprehend and participate in those processes that have—like icebergs perhaps—no fixed beginnings or ends.

Players have a similar spirit. They want to know how and why things in the world occur and what they can do about them. Although it is common to think of players as being forward-looking in their actions—Sutton-Smith's (1997) "play-as-progress" rhetoric that was described above—it should be acknowledged that play is frequently an energetic going backward. That is, play is not uncommonly a sorting through the past—an attempt to revisit past settings, pick up old implements, try out former skills, explore near-forgotten memories, and so forth. In other words, play is routinely a form of "regression."

As this author (Henricks, 2009) has argued, players reclaim the past in at least three different ways. One pattern is the reclamation of the "continuous" past that vanishes into what we call the present. Players routinely return to their experiences from just moments before and reintroduce them in a trial-and-error sort of way. When we play, we feel ourselves to be engaged in processes, to feel continuous with what we have been. In such ways, play cultivates experiences of security and familiarity (see Lieberman, 1977, p. 7). People feel themselves to have "identities" in a world that has a similarly structured character. This overall sensation of familiarity effectively "frames" the activity, and in so doing allows players to notice and address any "novel" elements. Moreover, familiarity gives people the feeling of assurance needed to take on these challenges.

A second type of return is to a past that is more distant or discontinuous. Play of this type is an act of retrieval or remembrance. When people go back to a long-ago past or to disused skills and memories, they experience the various emotions of re-acquaintance. To "play" with these matters, is to bring them back for conscious examination and then to try them out in present-time settings. Such processes are ways of strengthening once-successful strategies and (in the case of failed experiences) of modifying less successful ones. In such ways, play is a re-inspection of the arsenal of personal qualities and accomplishments. When we play, we want to know that some of our tried-and-true procedures from past times are still useful to us. Play of this sort makes us self-conscious about what we can and cannot do.

Most interesting perhaps is a third pattern in which the past somehow imposes itself on current affairs. Although Freud was a student of people's habits and proclivities (the first meaning of the past discussed above) and of our conscious attempts to return to and reuse that past (the second meaning), he was particularly interested in the interruptive function of memories and other psychic formations (see Freud, 1966, pp. 19–86). The Freudian psyche is a like a dark lake whose surface is sometimes broken by the expression of unresolved conflicts and disappointments generated by past events. All of us say things we don't mean, forget things we should remember, misconstrue other people's statements, laugh inappropriately, and so forth. When such things happen, we wonder where "that" came from. For Freud then, play was less a tightly regulated activity than an example of "primary process" thinking, when longstanding (and not always morally worthy) concerns work their way to the surface. Whether people control their uses of the past or not, they play to learn who they have been and to find out whether those identities are still relevant for the lives they have to lead.

Deconstruction as the Unfolding of Possibility

Consistent with its name, cultural studies focuses on culture—rather than on society, the psyche, the body, or the environment—as a field of meaningful relationships. As Derrida (1995) famously claims, "There is nothing outside of the text." (p. 89) Culture is the patterning of symbols, the set of humanly created artifacts that point to publicly accessible conceptions of the world. When people establish culture, they make arbitrary agreements about what words and marks will be used to depict reality and how those symbols will be related to other symbols within systems of abstract ideas. Moreover, they decide how those symbols will be arranged or produced in acts of public communication. One of the most profound examples of culture—language—illustrates this in the sense that language has both a *vocabulary* (that is, a recognized set of symbols) and a *grammar* (a recognized agreement about arrangement). When people communicate, they code and de-code their thoughts using this publicly available system.

Culture is central to human life not only because it allows us to communicate with one another but also because it helps us formulate our perceptions of the world and conduct our private imagining. In that sense, symbols are conduits for reflection. Each culture determines its favored array of words and images (along with their associated meanings) and then dictates appropriate methods for combining these ideas. Grammar—in its broader meaning as a set of rules for selecting and combining symbols—is a network of publicly approved pathways for mental activity.

As noted above, scholars can make much of the orderliness of human expression. That is, they can emphasize both how relatively explicit the connection is between symbols and the abstract ideas to which they refer and how dependent people are on these publicly recognized forms for their communication. Such perspectives are guiding themes of structuralism (see Levi-Strauss, 1967). Postmodernists tend to take the opposite view that the above-described pathways for expression are not that clearly marked and that users frequently fail to follow these formats in any case. After all, the very idea that there are proper rules for thought and communication suggests that there are also improper or discredited opportunities as well. People who stay on the "straight and narrow" path presumably have chosen not to follow other routes. Conversely, people who take those less favored or even forbidden paths typically do this with the knowledge that they should be taking the more publicly approved paths. And of course, there is always the wider maze of pathways that could have been taken but was not. To deconstruct a meaningful expression then is to ponder the placement of that behavior in a much wider context of expressive opportunities. Those opportunities are generated as possible combinations of publicly recognized symbols.

Play as the Unfolding of Possibility

Play may well be a going backward, a gathering up of memories and skills from past events. But it is also a going forward. When people play, they wonder what will happen next. This does not mean, however, that players simply wait for events to unfold; instead, they wish to "make" the future happen. That is, they wish to see how their own interventions in the world produce reactions from that world. People play to learn what they can do to the world and what it can, in return, do to them.

The golfer Ben Hogan is said to have remarked that his chosen sport brings out the "scientist" in a person (see Hogan, 1990). That is, golf—or any other play form—is essentially a wondering what will happen if a person pursues one set of behaviors rather than another. The smallest changes in orientation and execution commonly produce quite different results. In that way, players come to recognize that their decision-making is set within longer chains of events. Looking backward, they ponder why certain things occurred as they did; looking ahead, they imagine the range of consequences that will ensue. As Piaget (1962) emphasized, play is a trying out of strategies. Sometimes events unfold according to our hypotheses of how the world should behave; more frequently—and this is certainly the case with Hogan's sport—things occur in ways that startle, amuse, and disappoint. In that regard Hogan, whom many consider the greatest "striker" of the ball in history, claimed that he only made two or three truly good shots a round. Golf is ultimately a scramble or adjustment. People accommodate themselves to matters they cannot control.

Because players explore sequences of causes and effects, the activity itself often has an interruptive or start-and-stop quality (see Goffman, 1974, pp. 41–43). A certain line of behavior is started and followed until it produces a certain result. Then it is started and stopped again. This is certainly the case in animal play where a limited range of behaviors are practiced but it is also the case in games of most types where players engage in a narrow set of "moves." If those moves always produced the anticipated result, the spirit of the activity would be closer to that of work or ritual, where a perfection of routines (leading to idealized end-points) is the purpose. However, play is interesting—and fun—because the cause-effect relationship is not fully established, and players are continually surprised by what went right and wrong. Sometimes those failures to achieve anticipated results are due to the player's inability to control the elements of play as he or she desires. More commonly, that failure stems from a much more profound inability to recognize all the elements that may be "in play" and how those elements operate.

Against Piaget's view then, Sutton-Smith (2001) has argued that play is essentially an attempt to understand the "variability" of the human condition. People do not play to find out what *will* happen in the next few moments (after all, they could simply wait for this to occur) but rather to find out what *can* happen. That is, people want to acquaint themselves with a broad spectrum of possibilities, to see what "that would be like" and what "they would do" under such circumstances. To that end, they enter unusual environments and take on unusual challenges, sometimes of the most artificial sort. In other words, play has an "if-then" or subjunctive quality. When people play, they imagine chains-of-events or even elaborate scenarios. They endeavor to bring those scenes to life and to install themselves as protagonists in those settings. In Sutton-Smith's view, we do not proceed in this way because we want to get very good at one limited set of strategies (the emphasis of Piaget—and of Hogan) but rather because we seek to develop a wide range of capabilities that may be useful in wide ranges of situations. More generally, Sutton-Smith argues that behavioral flexibility of this sort—and the "curiosity" that motivates such flexibility—is especially useful to certain species in complicated, changing environments. In other words, players play not only to discover how the world “works” in some orderly, routine way but also to find out how it “might work” should circumstances change.

Deconstruction as the Spell of the Accidental

As noted above, structural analyses of culture focus on the relatively firm guidelines provided by symbol systems and on the attempts of people to use this system “intentionally” to communicate the meanings they wish. Postmodernists emphasize that there is always much more meaning in these systems than any of us can manage and that our expressions always say more than we mean (and conversely, mean more than we say). In that sense, postmodern thought reproduces at a cultural level the “over-determination” and non-rationality that Freudians discuss at a psychological level (see Fine, 1962, p. 48). In other words, there is always a great deal “standing behind” or “going on” in symbolic fields of meaning and much of it cannot be controlled “rationally.” Products and presentations are sometimes “condensations” of all those themes. And when we express ourselves, things often pop “up” or “out”.

Postmodern thought is distinguished not only by its debt to Freud but also to Nietzsche (see Tarnas, 1991, p. 395). In Nietzsche’s view, the universe is characterized by an essentially random combination of forces rather than by a singular god’s direction and control. This chanciness leads to many unusual possibilities, which Nietzsche’s romantically conceived hero celebrates and tries to direct in what ways he can. In that light, postmodernism relishes the variety of experience, especially as this is culturally influenced. Because culture forms are not established from any one vantage point, they exist primarily as a vast assortment of conceptual and imagistic elements. People assemble expressions from those elements much in the way people make “poems” on their refrigerators by arranging the magnetized words sold in kits for this purpose. Some of those arrangements startle and delight us. Others make us ponder ideas we would not have come to on our own. In the postmodern view of things, cultural productions come forward as a series of unusual juxtapositions (much like the succession of commercials that is mixed into the breaks of television shows) and people assimilate, transform, or ignore those combinations as they will. Awareness emerges as a series of revelations or discoveries.

Play as the Spell of the Accidental

In a postmodern view, the human condition is somewhat equivalent to the predicament of a tourist in a large metropolis who wishes to catch a cab or make her way across a busy street. That environment is abuzz with mechanical contrivances and electronic displays; people and vehicles speed by from every direction. No one person can discern the logic—or multiple logics—behind all those movements. The best that can be done is to attune oneself to the various rhythms, step forward at the appropriate time, and allow oneself to be carried along in the right direction. All of us live at the intersection of many contingencies; we are "in play" as much as we are players who control our own destinies (see Spariosu, 1989). For such reasons, postmodern writers suggest that personal qualities like cageyness, receptivity, flexibility, and hyper-awareness may be the desired skill set of contemporary people (see Gergen, 1995).

Arguably play, or at least many forms of play, cultivates these qualities. As this author (2006; forthcoming) has claimed, play—as a pattern of activity or interaction—is *contestive*; that is, it features an oppositional relationship between players and their objects. Players resist, manipulate, explore, and respond dialectically to those objects. They do not simply accept or mold themselves to otherness (as in the case of ritual); they "play with it." Because these objects are conceived as elements that challenge, resist, or otherwise "put up a good fight," it is anticipated that things will often *not* go as the player plans. As indicated in the preceding pages, play is very much a marveling at unfulfilled expectations. Some of these discontinuities are accepted with pleasure and even laughter; others make us grit our teeth and try again.

Such improbability is commonly accentuated and made permanent by game rules. Among their other functions, rules are devices that impose artificial restrictions on behavior, make outcomes difficult to predict, and equalize competition. Many games include elements of chance provided by dice, spinners, cards, uneven terrain, irregularly shaped play objects, and so forth. Similarly, to keep one party from being too dominant, players may add to games such features as uneven sides, extra turns, and other forms of "handicapping." Such devices help larger numbers of participants sustain the belief that they can be successful in the enterprise. So fortified, they are more likely to vest themselves emotionally in the event.

To summarize, play shares with deconstructionist inquiry the desire to know all the things that could happen in situations. A hand of cards reveals one set of possibilities. But that one hand (what actually happened) is an almost insignificant sample of what could have happened. To know some of those possibilities, many hands must be dealt and played. A card party displays not only some of these possibilities but also (and much more interestingly) the skill, daring, and emotional reactions of the players to changing circumstances. Even though the various moves of those players are quite limited, no two games are ever the same. Players play to discover the variety of the world and to see how well they can address those possibilities when they occur.

CONCLUSION: CONTEXTUALIZING THE MAGIC CIRCLE

Play is commonly thought to be a microcosm, a little world of its own sort within which specialized events occur. This world tends to be cut away from other portions of society by unusual goals for activity, arcane rules, distinctive costumes, specialized equipment, curiously configured spaces, and so forth. As Huizinga (1955) emphasized, play is also marked by its lack of substantial consequences that transcend the event. That is, play's rationale is the generation of experiences within the event itself; and any accomplishments of participants are usually considered to be important only in that context. This is not to say that "real" play does not become crowded with external, even material incentives (one basis of Huizinga's critique of modern play). However, play tends to be distinguished from other activities by the degree to which featured behaviors are separated from their usual consequences and then re-presented as distinctive (if now safeguarded) challenges for participants.

If play events are distinctive realities, what is the relationship of those events to all the structures, activities, and concerns that characterize or "go on" in the broader world? How are "inside" matters related to things "outside"? This is, after all, the challenge presented by deconstructionist analysis. Present-time formations may seem to be just what they are, but those formations are always set within much wider contexts, and the influence of these contexts pervades the production, event, or showing itself. In what follows then, the author discusses four ways in which the play world may be related to the world of everyday affairs that has been made "absent" by the event. These four patterns are: 1) play as an *alternative world* or relatively independent setting, 2) play as a *mirror* or "model of" society, 3) play as an *anti-structure* or "model against" society, and 4) play as a *blueprint* or "model for" society.

Play as an Alternative World

It can be argued that play is not attached at all to the activities and formations of the wider society or, if it is attached, that this connection is only of the most tenuous nature. Players operate according to the distinctive principles of the "play world." In this author's (2006) view, those principles are the call to participants to transform the circumstances they confront and to do this in consummatory ways—that is, to focus on outcomes and experiences contained within the event. To be sure, the themes of that play may be taken from other areas of life. However, these themes are re-cast in ways that make them suitable play topics.

Perhaps the best example of this approach is Simmel's (1971) essay on "sociability," the play-form of human association (see also Henricks, 2003). For Simmel, a dinner party, gala, or other festive affair is an event of its own type following its distinctive own rules. The purpose of the affair is to cultivate feelings of amusement, happiness, and social support in all who attend. A sense of group unity or group-consciousness should be sustained. To accomplish such ends, people must subordinate their own interests and concerns. That is, they should not talk too much about matters that concern them deeply, such as personal problems they may be having. On the other hand, they should also not dwell excessively on abstract public issues like politics, economics, or religion. Instead, people must strike a balance between these "subjective" and "objective" tendencies. Serious topics, if brought into play, should be treated in a light or fanciful way. No topic should be pursued if anyone in the conversational circle is clearly bored or insulted; and no person should be allowed to separate herself for long from the various circles that comprise the event. The job of the host/hostess is to see that everyone is engaged in a pleasing way, to steer conversations in the right directions, and to repair the standing of anyone who has lost face through an unfortunate exchange.

As noted above, such an event may take themes from the broader society as conversational topics. To that degree, the party *is* connected to external matters. However, these themes are re-constituted for use in the social setting. People are expected to focus on others in a face-to-face way and to honor those connections. They are expected to compliment and court one another, but never too seriously and never to the exclusion of others. An effusive, jaunty, exaggerated style is preferred. In that spirit, people are to circulate from one circle to the next and perform much the same function in each setting. Understood in this way, the sociable gathering can be seen as a "playing at" society, a series of socially supportive gestures that are to be enjoyed in the moments of their offering but otherwise not to be taken too seriously.

To summarize, this view of play emphasizes the extent to which play events are present-time affairs that command the attention of participants. The success of the affair depends in large part on the ability of people to *focus* on one another (and to keep from being distracted by outside affairs). This involvement or embeddedness is seen as a kind of "forgetting" of those external affairs. However, as the deconstructionists remind us, those forgotten matters still hover around the edge of the playground, and when they break into the reality of the event, special procedures (like Goffman's "transformation rules" described above) must be in place to deal with them.

Play as a Mirror of Society

To the degree that play is an alternative world, its emphasis is upon the present-time involvements of players. Rather different are the next two patterns in which players look backward to established social and personal practices.

In the first case, they express and refine those practices; in the second, they seize the opportunity to counter them. This section deals with the former of these possibilities.

When play is a mirror, that activity serves as a "model of" patterns that are already established. These patterns are brought into the playground—either intentionally or unintentionally—and play that follows becomes an exercise or "playing out" those themes. Clearly people cannot "un-do" themselves entirely when they play. All of us have established traits of personality, skill sets, beliefs, and so forth; and play groups exist in societies that have recognized value complexes, patterns of inequality, bases for social identity, styles of socialization, social control procedures, and so forth. Sociological commentators on play activities often emphasize the theme of role play (Mead, 1964). Play in that sense is commonly a rehearsal or "reproduction" of various roles (leaders, followers, friends, antagonists, allies, etc.) that people need to comprehend well if they are to operate effectively in other settings. When we play, we learn how to treat people (and other objects) as these are valued by our societies. We are able to do this because we have "imaginatively inhabited" the perspectives these people hold.

This view of play as an exercise or "playing out" of human capabilities is pertinent to Piaget's (1962) classic account of play. Play for Piaget is "pure assimilation," an exercise of personal strategies over the objects of the world. The ability to manipulate the world *successfully* gives us pleasure, or at least the kind of satisfaction that derives from feelings of consistency and control. For such reasons, Piaget's play tends to have a repetitive quality; people get better and better through practice. When our strategies fail, then we have to invent new ones and begin the process of repetitive manipulation once again.

To the degree that Piaget's theory emphasizes the repetition of already developed skills then this view of play can be seen as an exercising or "mirror" of patterns that already exist. Much as Durkheim (1965) described religious ritual, play of this sort is a reaffirmation, an (often) public declaration that the matters at hand are socially pertinent roles, groupings, values, and skills. Such matters are the "stuff" of play. Like the reflection provided by a mirror however, the presentation of these affairs is never entirely equivalent to their "true" or three-dimensional reality. Instead, in play (as in ritual), matters are ridded of their consequences and other complexities and then confronted as simplified and socially distilled forms. For such reasons, play allows us to see our own "character" (and that of others) in operation, to know the "nature" of friendship, to sense how we respond to abstract challenges, and so forth. In other words, even as we import society's themes into the playground, we "make absent" the usual complexities of such matters.

Play as Anti-Structure

Another way in which players bring external elements into the playground is to include them not as their typical (in the wider society) manifestations but instead as the opposites of those forms. Freudian psychology sometimes analyzes personal commitments as "reaction-formations," that is, as thoughts, habits, and other mental strategies that seek to reverse or dispel the effects of significant events in the life history of the person (see Fine, 1962, p. 68). Because the psychoanalytic viewpoint sees psychic life as an ongoing (and frequently unrecognized) conflict between different kinds of factors and forces—internalized moral commands, bodily desires, forbidden wishes, demands of external situations, and so forth—much attention and energy is spent trying to stay focused in psychically integrated (and socially respectable) ways. Whatever the success of the ego in performing these feats may be (via repression, sublimation, and the like), those drives and desires are not banished completely. Instead, they await their chances for expression.

Viewing play as anti-structure then means seeing that activity as a counterweight or reversal of ongoing psychic, social, and cultural themes. When people play in this way they do not simply wish to escape such patterns; they wish to re-do them and in the process of so doing, to experience the insights and emotions that attend those altered states of being. Such altered patterns may include occasions of status reversal (when the low and high people change places), new activity patterns (such as the replacement of passivity by activity—or vice versa), and new value formations (substituting aggressiveness for consideration, cooperation for competitiveness, and so forth). Arguably, play of this type is a redressing or compensating for the accumulated tensions and anxieties of routine social and psychological formations. By such lights, "stressed out" people may seek moments of protracted lethargy; subordinate individuals make seek to be "queen for a day"; quiet, reflective types may find themselves anew in moments of exaggerated exuberance.

One of the best-known examples of this approach is the anthropologist Geertz's essay on the Balinese cockfight. In Geertz's (1972) view, Balinese society in its more general pattern emphasizes orderliness, decorum, harmony, and courtesy to others. As in many traditional societies, themes related to the "three R's"—ritual, respect, and responsibility—predominate. In Bali, people are expected to comport themselves in carefully controlled and honorable ways. Entirely contradictory to these patterns is the behavior of the Balinese in the cockpit. That occasion is marked by wild, even disastrous gambling as partisans back their favorites. The air is filled with screams and shouts. Everything, it seems, rides on the bloody outcome, when one cock will live and another will die. With the matter so defined, cockfighting is a corrective or antidote to the punctilious decorum of Balinese society. It is a chance for people not only to be other than themselves but to correct the tensions that derive from their normal ways of being.

As in the other instances discussed above, play as anti-structure is another way of dealing with the "absence" of external affairs. That which is banished is brought back, in this case to be negated by playful practice. As the author (Henricks, 1991, pp. 167–181) has argued in another context, if the mirror-of-society perspective is frequently an "idealizing of reality" (a dramatization of existing patterns), then the anti-structure perspective is a "realizing of ideals" (a chance to participate in value formations that are normally denied to participants). When people play in the latter way, they know the thrills of doing what is normally forbidden.

Play as Blueprint

A final view is that play is neither a "model of" nor a "model against" external reality but instead a "model for" realities of that type. In other words, play—in this latter view—is not something people do only to experience the pleasures of affirming or disaffirming routine affairs but something they do to develop patterns they will follow in the future. By such accounts, we do not play because we are driven to do so by the circumstances of regular existence; we do so because we wish to live differently than we do now.

Arguably, the greatest of the play theorists taking this viewpoint is Huizinga. To be sure, Huizinga did not care for "functionalist" explanations of play, that is, attempts to explain play in terms of its consequence or purposes for persons or groups. Play, he claimed, was pleasing or "fun" in its own way, and that sense of aesthetic completion should be considered the principal factor explaining its existence (Huizinga, 1955, p. 3). However, Huizinga was also very concerned to show the pertinence of play for the societies that sponsored such activities. Play is neither a "playing out" of existing ways of being (a mirror) nor a corrective to social blockages and tensions (an anti-structure). Quite the opposite, play is a way of conceiving new possibilities for human relationship. As such—and this is his great if largely unproven thesis—play is one of the engines of history (see Henricks, 2002). When people play, they explore social and cultural arrangements. And some of these invented forms become institutionalized as patterns of knowledge and custom.

For his part, Huizinga was interested in the social and cultural development of societies. However, the view of play as blueprint has been even more prominent in theories of human development. In Sutton-Smith's (1997) "play-as-progress" rhetoric, that activity is seen as the way in which people create new strategies—ideas, physical skills, self-understandings, understandings of otherness, and so forth—for operating in the world. The same process is said to be true for animal play. For both humans and animals, play is commonly thought to be a pattern of "future-building," a way of moving creatures toward adulthood (see Chick, 2001; Burghardt, 1998, pp. 5–6).

Taken together, the four models of play exhibit different ways that humans determine what is to be "inside" and what is to be "outside" events. The first model—of play as an *alternative world*—suggests that players keep the external world at a distance and only incorporate its themes lightly and "playfully." Play of this type focuses on the present and on the particular context that is the event. People play to live intensively in these moments. Play is an escape or forgetting, a movement away from ongoing commitments without much concern for how (or when) one is to return. The second model—of play as a *mirror*—is a more committed incorporation and honoring of established social and personal themes. People play to "reproduce" themselves, to become clearer about who they are now and who they have been. Play of this sort is an act of remembrance, reconnection, or even regression. Tried-and-true procedures are recovered, exercised, and refined.

The third model—play as *anti-structure*—also looks backward but with a different spirit. Play is a chance to counter old identities, deny routine commitments, and upend prevailing social patterns. Those who are routinely controlled by others are given fresh opportunities to supervise those others or at least to control themselves. Customary responsibilities and tensions are mocked or otherwise robbed of their powers. Play is a revolutionary affair, built on the ashes of the current society. Finally, the model of play as *blueprint* alters dramatically the external structures and behaviors that are the "reference" for the event. Play, it seems, is neither about the present nor about the past but about the future. An instrumental ethic pervades the affair. Players cast up new visions of the world—not just so they can inhabit those visions in some enchanted playground—but because they need to carry those visions into the other portions of their lives.

IMPLICATIONS

In all the ways described above, play deconstructs the arrangements of the world. In every case, players explore the meaning of "absence" or otherness. They bring things in and out and know that things brought "in" do not have quite the same meaning as the external equivalents of those things. They know that their little event is "special" because it is set into a wider world that is not configured in the same fashion. Players enjoy the freedom they have to "look about," to sort through the possibilities of things. They understand that matters here are not entirely under their own control; chanciness abounds and people must accommodate themselves to sometimes incomprehensible comings-and-goings. Always, one occurrence leads to another; and participants must decide what role they wish to play in that unfolding. Seen in that context, play is a dabbling in space and time. We play earnestly in sheltered moments of life but we know full well that there are many other activities that have been and will be and that our secluded setting is part of a much bigger world. In that spirit, we take those external themes and "re-construct" a smaller, more intimate world according to the principles of the playground. Whether the understandings produced by this playful interaction remain on the playground or are carried over into the other avenues of life is one of the great questions for play scholarship.

Whether modernist play scholars admire postmodern thinking or not, they must confront the question of how ongoing societal, cultural, and psychological patterns are incorporated into the playground. What external themes seem to be left behind as players enter a play world characterized by its own patterns and principles (the "alternative world" perspective)? What patterns are built into the play setting so that the activity is effectively a working out or refinement of those themes (the "mirror-of-society" perspective)? What external themes are taken up as specific challenges to be countered or resisted by players (the "anti-structure" perspective)? And how do participants take what they have learned in play and apply it to other settings (the "blueprint" perspective)? In every instance, players build their activity from vast arrays of societal possibilities. Some of these themes slide in and out of the play event. Always there is much more of this possibility than any one play moment can realize.

At one level then, postmodernism challenges play scholars to connect play events to wider social and cultural practices and to analyze the patterns of exclusion and inclusion that prevail. However, at another level, it asks researchers to look at the interactive patterns that occur inside those events in unfamiliar ways. The modernist view of play—as a formally regulated, "constructive" affair that leads individuals to frequently pre-imagined ends—has led scholars to focus on the private outcomes of play for the individuals so involved. By contrast, postmodernists view play as a largely unpredictable process that features a kind of dialogic communication between participants. Scholars must demonstrate the extent to which elements of formality and pre-meditation (emphasized in modernism) and informality and responsive attunement (emphasized in postmodernism) apply in any particular play moment. In particular, postmodernist claims about play's co-creation must be substantiated by studies that show the *process by which* groups of players collectively dissemble and then re-assemble meanings. Similarly, any taken-for-granted assumptions about the equality and amiable cooperation of players must be challenged. Issues of power and privilege are also elements—or are at least potential elements—of play. As in any social scientific inquiry, the question is always: who gets to do what to whom before whom in what ways, under what conditions, and for what reasons? Postmodernism invites people not only to scrutinize those processes in fresh ways but also to ponder the "reasons" that people offer for their participation. If play is to be seen as a "text," then the proponents of that metaphor must detail the multiple meanings that surround that activity and display the roles of persons as sponsors, sustainers, and opponents of those meanings.

REFERENCES

Anderson, W. (Ed.) (1995). *The truth about the truth: De-confusing and re-constructing the postmodern world.* New York: Putnam.

Bakhtin, M. (1981). *The dialogic imagination.* Austin, TX: University of Texas Press.

Baudrillard, J. (1983). *Simulations.* New York: Semiotext.

Berghardt, G. (1998). The evolutionary origins of play revisited: Lessons from turtles. In M. Beckoff and J. Byers (Eds.) *Animal play: Evolutionary, comparative, and ecological perspectives* (pp. 1–26). Cambridge: Cambridge University Press.

Bertens, H. (1995). *The idea of the postmodern: A history.* New York: Routledge.

Cantor, N. (1997). *The American century: Varieties of culture in modern times.* New York: Harper Collins.

Chick, G. (2001). What is play for? Sexual selection and the evolution of play. In S. Reifel (Ed.) *Theory in context and out: Play and culture studies 3* (pp. 3–26). Westport, CN: Ablex.

Csikszentmihalyi, C. (1990). *Flow: The psychology of optimal experience.* New York: Harper and Row.

Cox, H. (1969). *The feast of fools.* New York: Harper Colophon.

Cullor, J. (2007). *On deconstruction: Theory and criticism after structuralism.* Ithaca, NY: Cornell University Press.

Derrida, J. (1978). *Writing and difference.* London: Routledge.

Derrida, J. (1981). *Positions.* Chicago: University of Chicago Press.

Derrida, J. (1995). The play of substitution. In W. Anderson (Ed.). *The truth about the truth: De confusing and re-constructing the postmodern world.* Pp. 86–91. New York: Putnam.

Docherty, T. (Ed.). (1993). *Post-modernism: A reader.* New York: Columbia University Press.

During, S. (Ed.) (1999). *The culture studies reader.* New York: Routledge.

Durkheim, E. (1965). *The elementary forms of the religious life.* New York: Free Press.

Edmiston, Brian. (2008). *Forming ethical identities in childhood play.* New York: Routledge.

Ewen, S. (1999). *All-consuming images: The politics of style in contemporary culture.* New York: Basic Books.

Featherstone, M. (1991). *Consumer culture and postmodernism.* London: Sage.

Fine, R. (1962). *Freud: A critical evaluation of his theories.* New York: David McKay.

Flax, J. (1990). *Thinking fragments: Psychoanalysis, feminism, and postmodernism in the contemporary West.* Berkeley: University of California Press.

Foucault, M. (1980). *Power/Knowledge.* C. Gordon (Ed.). New York: Pantheon.

Freud, S. (1966). *A general introduction to psychoanalysis.* New York: Washington Square.

Geertz, C. (1972). Deep play: Notes on the Balinese cockfight. *Daedalus,* 101: 1–28.

Gergen, K. (1991). *The saturated self.* New York: Basic Books.

Gergen, K. (1995). The healthy, happy human wears many masks. In W. Anderson, (Ed.). *The truth about the truth: De-confusing and re-constructing the postmodern world.* (pp. 136–144). New York: Putnam.

Goffman, E. (1961) *Encounters: Two studies in the sociology of interaction.* Indianapolis: Bobbs-Merrill.

Goffman, E. (1974). *Frame analysis: An essay on the organization of experience.* New York: Harper Colophon.

Hans, J. (1981). *The play of the world.* Amherst, MA: University of Massachusetts Press.

Harvey, D. (1990). *The condition of post-modernity.* Cambridge: Cambridge University.

Henricks, T. (1991). *Disputed pleasures: Sport and society in preindustrial England.* New York: Greenwood Press.

Henricks, T. (1999). Play as ascending meaning: Implications of a general model of play. In *Play and culture studies 2: Play contexts revisited,* ed. Stuart Reifel, 257–277.

Henricks, T. (2001). Play and postmodernism. In S. Reifel (Ed.) *Theory in context and out: Play and culture studies 3* (pp. 51–72). Westport, CN: Ablex.

Henricks, T. (2002). Huizinga's contributions to play studies: A reappraisal. In J. Roopnarine (Ed.), *Conceptual, social-cognitive, and contextual issues in the fields of play: Play and culture studies*, 4 (pp. 23–52). Westport, CT: Ablex.

Henricks, T. (2003). Simmel: On sociability as the play-form of human association. In D. Lytle (Ed.), *Play and educational theory and practice: Play and culture studies,* 5 (pp. 19–2).Westport, CT: Praeger.

Henricks, T. (2006). *Play reconsidered: Sociological perspectives on human expression.* Urbana, IL: University of Illinois Press.

Henricks, T. (2009). Play and the rhetorics of time: Progress, regression, and the meaning of the present. In D. Kuschner (Ed.), *From children to red hatters: Diverse images and issues of play: Play and culture studies* 8 (pp. 14–38). New York: University Press.

Henricks, Thomas. (Forthcoming). Play as ascending meaning revisited: Four types of assertive play. In E. Nwokah (Ed.), *Play and culture studies 9.*

Hogan, B. (1990). *Ben Hogan's Five lessons: The modern fundamentals of golf.* New York: Pocket.

Huizinga, J. (1955). *Homo ludens: A study of the play-element in culture.* Boston; Beacon.

James, W. (1952). *Principles of psychology.* Chicago, Il.: Encyclopedia Britannica.

Jameson, F. (1984). Postmodernism or the cultural logic of late capitalism. *New Left Review*, 146: 53–92.

Jay, M. (1973). *The dialectical imagination: A history of the Frankfurt School and the Institute for Social Research, 1923–1950.* Boston: Little, Brown.

Krieglstein, W. (1991). *The dice-playing god: Reflections on life in a post-modern age.* New York: New York University Press.

Kuchler, T. (1994). *Post-modern gaming: Heidegger, Duchamp, Derrida.* New York: Peter Lang.

Levin, K. (1980). Farewell to modernism. *Arts,* 54: 90–92.

Levi-Strauss, C. (1967). *Structural anthropology.* Garden City, NY: Doubleday.

Lieberman, J. (1977). *Playfulness: Its relation to imagination and creativity.* New York: Academic Press.

Lin, S-H. and Reifel, S. (1999). Context and meanings in Taiwanese kindergarten play. In S. Reifel (Ed.), *Play contexts revisited: Play and culture studies,* 2 (pp. 151–176) Greenwich, CT: Ablex.

Marx, K. (1999). Economic and philosophical manuscripts. T. Bottomore (Trans.). In E. Fromm (Ed.), *Marx's concept of man* (pp. 87–196). New York: Continuum.

Mead, G.H. (1964). *On social psychology.* Anselm Strauss (Ed.) Chicago: University of Chicago Press.

Miller, J. (1987). *Toward a new psychology of women*, 2nd ed. Boston, MA: Beacon.

Munslow, A. (2006). *Deconstructing history.* New York: Routledge.

Newman, F. and Holzman, L. (2006). *Unscientific psychology: A cultural-performatory approach to understanding human life,* 2nd ed. New York: iUniverse, Inc.

Piaget. J. (1962). *Play, dreams, and imitation in childhood.* NY: Norton.

Rorty, R. (1986). From logic to language to play: Plenary address to Inter-American Congress. *Proceedings and Addresses of the American Philosophical Association,* 59, 747–753.

Rosenau, P. (1992). *Post-modernism and the social sciences: Insights, inroads, intrusions.* Princeton, NJ: Princeton University Press.

Simmel, G. (1971). Sociability. In D. Levine (Ed.), *On individuality and social forms,* (pp. 127–140). Chicago: University of Chicago Press.

Spariosu, M. (1989). *Dionysus reborn: Play and the aesthetic dimension in modern philosophical and scientific discourse.* Ithaca, NY: Cornell University Press.

Stromberg, P. (2009). *Caught in Play: How entertainment works on you.* Stanford, CA: Stanford University Press.

Sutton-Smith, B. (1997). *The ambiguity of play.* Cambridge, MA: Harvard University Press.

Sutton-Smith, B. (2001). Reframing the variability of players and play. In S. Reifel (Ed.) *Theory in context and out: Play and culture studies 3* (pp. 27–50). Westport, CN: Ablex.

Sutton-Smith, B, and D. Kelly-Byrne. 1984. The phenomenon of bipolarity in play theories. In T. Yawkey and A. Pellegrini (Eds.), *Child's play: Developmental and applied* (pp. 29–47). Mahwah, NJ: Lawrence Erlbaum.

Swales, J. (1990). *Genre analysis: English in academic and research settings.* Cambridge: Cambridge University Press.

Tarnas, R. (1991). *The passion of the Western mind: Understanding the ideas that have shaped our worldview.* New York: Ballantine.

Chapter Ten

Performing Groups as Distributed Creative Systems: A Case Study

Stacy DeZutter

This chapter presents a study of performance creativity as a socially distributed process. I examine the creative work of a student theatre group, ActNow,[1] who develops an improvisational performance of a popular children's book. I argue the necessity of an analytic focus on group-level, rather than individual-level creative processes, using ActNow as an illustration of how collaborative groups can function as distributed creative systems. The study contributes to two related areas of literature: sociocultural research on the creativity of groups and research on theatrical performance.

SOCIOCULTURAL STUDIES OF GROUP CREATIVITY

For most of the twentieth century, research on creativity has focused on the psychological characteristics of creative individuals. In the past two decades, however, this tradition has come under critique, as a growing cadre of researchers has begun to examine the ways in which creativity—even among seemingly isolated creators—is an inherently social enterprise. With the work of scholars such as Amabile (1996) and Csikszentmihalyi (1999), creativity studies has begun to attend to the individual creator within a social context, considering how organizational and societal factors influence the creative process. In recent years, a number of researchers (Farrell, 2003; John-Steiner, 2000; Paulus & Nijstad, 2003; Sawyer 2003a; Sawyer and DeZutter, 2009) have suggested that there are many collaborative creative situations in which individual creativity is less explanatory than group-level processes. These scholars argue for studies of creativity that take a group, rather than an individual, as the unit of analysis.

The shift in creativity studies from a strictly individual focus to one that includes group processes is driven in part by insights from sociocultural psychology. Growing out of the work of Vygotsky (1978, 1987), sociocultural psychology is interested in the ways in which individual cognition and development derive from participation in social and cultural practices. In Vygotsky's theory, language and other mental tools are developed culturally and then become incorporated and used by the individual. The interaction between an individual and society is understood to be continuous and dynamic, and this raises questions about the ability to separate individual cognition from the social processes in which it is embedded. From the sociocultural perspective, to understand human psychology, we must examine group, not just individual, intellectual activity.

In presenting ActNow as an exemplar of group creativity, I follow the lead of other sociocultural scholars who have noted that theatrical improvisation offers a window onto group creative processes that are found in many other domains of activity. Theatrical improvisation is a rich area of study from this perspective, because it allows us to easily observe the social, collaborative act of meaning making that socioculturalists emphasize is present and ongoing in all social groups. Both Sawyer (2003a&b) and Holzman (2009) have discussed the value of studying theatrical improvisation. Holzman has pointed out that improv is a visible example of "the socially completive activity of meaning making" (2009, p. 62) and, similarly, Sawyer (2003 a&b) asserts that improv provides a useful way to examine the creative, collaborative meaning-making processes involved in all human interaction.

Distributed Creativity

As one part of the sociocultural turn in creativity research, Sawyer and I (2009) have proposed bridging studies of creativity with a particular branch of sociocultural research known as *distributed cognition.* While the bulk of sociocultural research has focused on child development, distributed cognition research has examined the social nature of cognition in adult work groups. Arising as a response to the individualist focus of cognitive science, distributed cognition research draws on the insights of Vygotskian theory and therefore "looks for a broader class of cognitive events and does not expect all such events to be encompassed by the skin or skull of an individual" (Hutchins, 2001, p. 2068). Distributed cognition scholars have observed that when a group works together to accomplish a collective task, the group functions as a problem-solving unit. Cognitive processes are distributed across the individuals in the group (as well as artifacts and representations) and intellectual work does not result merely from the accumulation of individual cognitive efforts (Hutchins, 1995, 2001). Therefore, in such situations, an analytic focus on the system as a whole is more appropriate than analysis of individual cognition. Research on distributed cognition seeks to explicate the distinct properties of group-level cognition, so as to better understand the ways in which people in groups are intellectually interdependent with each other and with the tools they use (Rogers, 2006). Key concerns in distributed cognition research include how information is communicated within and processed by a cognitive system, and how the component members of the system coordinate their activity to reach a goal. Typically, distributed cognition research has investigated tasks that are primarily algorithmic or computational, such as ship navigation or flying a plane (Hutchins, 1995; Hutchins & Klausen, 1998). Although this research has documented examples of group creativity in unexpected or emergency situations, the focus of such research has rarely been on activities in which creativity is an objective from the outset.

Sawyer and I (2009) have argued for research on distributed *creative* systems. Such research will address some of the same questions as other distributed cognition studies, including how groups process and communicate information, and how the individuals in the group coordinate their efforts toward their shared goal. At the center of such work, however, will be the question of how a group's generative work gets done—how do many minds function together to produce a shared creative product? The ActNow study serves as an initial foray into the intersections of creativity research and distributed cognition studies by examining how the group functions as a system for creating a performance narrative.

Collaborative Emergence

The focus of the ActNow study is *collaborative emergence*, the key mechanism underlying distributed creativity. In his studies on theatrical improvisation (often called "improv"), Sawyer (2003a&b) articulated the notion of collaborative emergence to describe the process by which creative products emerge through the improvisational interactions of a group. (Sawyer 2003a&b). As an example, consider the following scene created by David Razowsky and Carrie Clifford, an improv comedy duo:

> A man and woman sit side by side in chairs, the woman on the man's left. She puts her hands up to suggest she is holding a steering wheel.
>
> Man: Did you notice I didn't look back while you were turning?
>
> Woman: (slightly teasing) You don't have to, I'm driving.
>
> Man: (matching her jovial attitude, as if to say "Of course. That's what I meant!") That's it! (Pause. The woman "drives" and the man looks around.) I

don't know why we have to look for parking. I mean, we're in an ambulance. We should be able to just park anywhere, if we put the lights on.

Woman: We should be able to, we should be able to. But I feel bad, I mean I don't want to just put the lights on, just to put them on. I mean, cops do that, but I don't do that.

Man: Ok.

Woman: I'll do it, do you want me to do it?

Man: You don't have to do it for me.

Woman: No, I just want—

Man: (casually) But do it for the guy in the back.

(transcribed March 21, 2008 from "Razowsky & Clifford," n.d.)

In this thirty-four second scene, the actors began only with two chairs placed side by side, and created a narrative about paramedics who are looking for a parking space and are comically unconcerned about their passenger. But who exactly created this idea? One way to answer this question would be to attribute to each actor the small pieces of narrative information that each contributed: Clifford contributed the idea of driving, Razowsky contributed the idea of an ambulance, and so on. But this approach overlooks the role of the interaction of the actors' ideas. Razowsky's contribution of the ambulance idea was a response to Clifford's suggestion of driving. If Clifford had begun a different action, reading a menu, for example, the ambulance contribution would not have made sense. Of course, while Clifford's initial action placed some constraint on what Razowsky could logically do next, it did not fully determine his actions. He might, for example, have uttered a line suggesting they were involved in a driving lesson. In fact, his initial line could have been interpreted that way, but instead, Clifford responded to it in a manner that suggested the characters knew each other well, drove together often, and were relative equals. Clifford's interpretation of Razowsky's line made some possibilities more logical than others, and the same is true for each successive turn by each of the actors. Clifford's interpretation also endowed a particular meaning to Razowsky's line, a phenomenon Sawyer (2003a) refers to as *retrospective interpretation*. Often in improv, the full meaning of a line is not determined until subsequent turns, as the actors make particular interpretations and contribute additional narrative information. In the scene above, for example, Clifford's reluctance to use the ambulance lights to acquire a parking space does not gain its full comic impact until Razowsky mentions "the guy in the back."

The creation of this scene cannot be reduced to the creative actions or intentions of individuals. To begin, the performers cannot fully determine the meanings that their own contributions will have within the narrative, because this depends on how their partner responds to those contributions. In addition, the actors are not free to create entirely as they please, but are constrained by each other's prior contributions to the scene. Each successive utterance and action must build in some logical way on what has come previously. Thus, the scene does not result simply from the additive contributions of each actor; it results from their interactions. In collaborative creative efforts like this one, it becomes necessary, therefore, to analyze the creative process at the group level. The group functions as a distributed creative system whose creative accomplishment cannot be explained by examining individual actions or intentions in isolation.

Synchronic and Diachronic Emergence

The ActNow study offers a more complex account of collaborative emergence and considers a somewhat different creative situation from the pure improvisation that Sawyer has typically studied. In pure improv, the aim is to allow a narrative to emerge in-the-moment, and there is no predetermined outcome that constrains what happens on stage, other than that the audience should be able to make sense of the story and should find it engaging. By contrast, the aim of ActNow is to improvisationally tell a story that has already been partially written, because the group is dramatizing a popular children's book. While the actors are unconstrained as to their specific dialogue and actions, the broad contours of the narrative have been determined by the authors of the book, and the aim is to perform that story, rather than anything else. Unlike pure improv, where actors are discouraged from replaying any dramatic material or using characters previously developed, it is acceptable for ActNow to carry forward in each subsequent rehearsal or performance an awareness of what has come before and to reuse particularly successful material from prior improvisations. In working this way, ActNow follows an approach used by many comedy theatres, including Chicago's Second City, where scenes are "re-improvised" across successive rehearsals and/or performances in order to improve the quality of the material while still maintaining a fresh performance (Libera, 2004).

Because ActNow uses this re-improvisation approach, it affords the opportunity to observe how creative work is accomplished through both group interactions in the moment of performance and interactions across time, what Sawyer (2003a) refers to as synchronic and diachronic emergence.[2] The analysis of Razowsky and Clifford's scene, above, describes *synchronic* emergence, the emergence of narrative material through in-the-moment interactions during a single performance. *Diachronic* emergence, on the other hand, refers to emergence across separate, successive creative efforts. If Razowsky and Clifford had re-improvised the ambulance scene, they would have done so with an awareness of their previous performance. Because they are performing improvisationally, they would have the opportunity to make choices about what elements of the scene to revisit and what to reinvent. The scene would have evolved over subsequent performances, as a result of the actors' responses to their previous creations, resulting in diachronic emergence of performance material. With the ActNow study, I document both synchronic and diachronic emergence. Unlike studies of pure improvisation, where it is far less apparent how the group's prior work together (if there was any) contributes to that which is being created in the present, my analysis of ActNow reveals the role of the group's history in its performance creativity. This analysis provides insights that can be applied to other forms of group creativity where the group has a history together prior to a given moment of performance.

STUDYING CREATIVITY IN THEATRICAL PERFORMANCE

The findings from the ActNow study provide insights that can be applied to a wide range of group creative activity, including those outside of theater, and indeed outside the arts. At the same time, the study redresses a gap in a specific area of literature, creativity in theatrical performance. Apart from Sawyer's extensive studies on improv, there has been very little research on theatrical creativity of any form; in the leading creativity journals (*Creativity Research Journal; Journal of Aesthetics, Creativity, and the Arts; Journal of Creative Behavior*), only a handful of studies on theatrical performance has been published (Clements, Dwinell, Torrance, & Kidd, 1994; Goldstein, 2009; Goldstein & Winner; 2009; Kogan, 2002; Nemiro, 1997; Sawyer & DeZutter, 2009; Thomson, Keehn, & Gumpel, 2009). There has been other psychological research on actors, including studies of actors' memorization techniques (Noice & Noice, 1997); studies of actors' personalities (Hannah, Domino, & Hanson, 1994; Hammond & Edelmann, 1991a; Stacey & Goldberg, 1953); and studies of actors' sense of self (Hammond & Edelmann, 1991b; Neuringer & Willis, 1995), but such work is not aimed at elucidating the creative processes involved in performance.

There are several reasons why theatrical creativity has received less research attention than other domains of creative endeavor. For one, there is ambivalence about where the creativity lies—whether the performers themselves are creating anything new, or simply interpreting the creation of a writer. In an oft-cited article, Nemiro (1997) describes actors as "interpretive artists." In her view, the creativity of an actor involves developing an interpretation of a text composed by someone else. This view suggests that writers, who create the text in the first place, would be a more fruitful focus for those interested in understanding creativity. Nemiro's characterization of acting, however, is inconsistent with actors' own view of what they do. Actors view themselves as generative, rather than strictly interpretive artists (DeZutter, 2004). Actors speak about their work in terms of "creating" or "constructing" a character, rather than interpreting one, and they emphasize that their work involves creating each performance anew, improvisationally (DeZutter, 2004). Crease (1997) provides a useful way of understanding the performance creativity of actors by making a distinction between the technology and the artistry of a performance. In a scripted play, each performance may be more or less the same technically; the same words are uttered in the same order, for example. But phenomenologically, each performance is a unique experience for all involved. On this view, actors are creative in that they generate the unique phenomenology of each performance.

Of course, for social scientists, the phenomenology of a performance is a difficult thing to document, and this may be another reason why researchers have stayed away from theatrical creativity. Studying improv, however, offers a way around this problem. Sawyer (2003a) notes that the creative work of an improv ensemble is much easier to study than other types of performance because the foremost concern in these groups is the creation of dialogue and action, which are easily documented. With the present study, I adopt this strategy, examining the creation of a performance text as a proxy for other, more ethereal aspects of performance creativity. I use the findings from this study to suggest a way forward for future work on creativity in other forms theatrical performance.

Given the history of research on creativity, it is perhaps not surprising that all but one of the studies on theatrical performance cited above focus on the actor as an individual creator (the exception is Sawyer & DeZutter, 2009). This focus on individual actors is unfortunate, however, because, again, it is inconsistent with how actors themselves understand their work. Actors recognize that acting is a deeply collaborative art form; performances are created in collaboration with other actors, and with directors, designers, and so on (DeZutter, 2004). Focusing on the creative process of individual actors offers a limited, if not misleading, picture of theatrical creativity. Research such as the present study that examines theatrical creativity as a group-based process provides an important step toward understanding theatre as a form of collaborative creation.

The dirth of research on theatrical creativity may also reflect a historical bias in creativity research toward product over process creativity (Sawyer, 1997). Researchers have tended to focus on creative domains where there is a fixed, tangible product and where the results of creative work can be temporally separated from the process of creating. Performance creativity, where the process of creation and the creative product happen simultaneously, is more difficult to research, because it often does not result in a lasting, tangible product. In recent years, however, researchers have begun to pay more attention to performance domains. For example, in addition to Sawyer's work on improv, a number of researchers have examined jazz music (Becker, 2000; Berliner, 1994; Hodson, 2007; Macdonald & Wilson, 2006; Pressing, 1988, 1998; Sawyer, 1992).[3] The present study contributes to this growing body of performance-focused scholarship.

THE STUDY

The Research Context

ActNow was a theatre company for teen and young adult actors who worked in conjunction with the public library system in a large southern city. The mission of ActNow was to produce drama-based enrichment experiences for children who have limited access to the arts, and the library supported this mission by offering the group the opportunity to bring literature-based performances to children in low-income neighborhoods at no cost. For the present project, the group dramatized *Squids Will Be Squids*, by Jon Scieszka and Lane Smith (1998), a children's book structured as a series of absurd fables that end with "morals" that are ridiculous and nonsensical. The play was performed as a part of the library's Read and Share series, and was followed by a creative dramatics workshop in which the children in the audience worked with the performers to act out their own silly stories in the style of *Squids*. At the time of the study, I was the executive director of ActNow as well as the director of the *Squids* project.

Over the years, the group had done several of these book dramatizations for the library. Initially the approach was to compose a script, cast actors in specific roles, and perform after a period of several weeks' rehearsal. For a variety of reasons, including the disinclination of busy teenagers to memorize a script, the need for flexibility when an actor must miss a rehearsal or when a newcomer wishes to join the group, and the appeal of an improvisational performing style, scripted performances were abandoned in favor of a more improvisational approach. For *Squids*, as with other recent projects, the approach was to develop a basic outline of what was to happen and then improvise through that outline with each performance. This allowed flexibility with regard to casting, since an actor need only know the basic outline in order to take on a new role, which in turn made it easier for the group to accommodate newcomers as well as actors with schedule conflicts. Weekly ninety-minute rehearsals were devoted to exercises for developing improvisation skills as well as to practicing improvising through each of eleven stories from the *Squids* book. We rehearsed *Squids* from December 2001 through May 2002, and began performing in April 2002. At the time of the study, ActNow included thirteen actors aged eleven to seventeen, only three of whom had significant prior improvisation training. *Squids* was performed with a rotating cast, meaning that actors took on different roles with each performance.

Data for the study include video recordings of the final five performances of *Squids* in July and August of 2002, which were transcribed for analysis; field notes taken by me during the rehearsal process; and interviews conducted with six of the actors after the conclusion of the *Squids* project. To understand the evolution of narrative ideas during performance, I conducted an interaction analysis (Jordan & Henderson, 1995) on two of the scenes from *Squids,* across the five recorded performances. This involved creating a detailed index of each narrative idea that appeared in the dialogue and actions of each scene, noting which actor(s) in which roles contributed to each idea, and in what order the ideas appeared. Performances were then compared, attending to differences in what ideas appear, and noting which actors and which characters were responsible for performing ideas that recur. Interviews and field notes were used to construct an account of the rehearsal process. For the interviews, the actor and I watched all five recorded performances, pausing the video tape every few minutes. With each pause, the actor was asked to recount where the ideas in the previous sequence came from, and what they recall about the development of each sequence during rehearsals. (A detailed discussion of the methodology for this study is available in Sawyer and DeZutter, 2009).

Distributed Creativity in Rehearsal

At the first rehearsal, ActNow began work on the play by breaking into small groups of three to five students, who were each assigned to practice improvising one scene from the book and then perform that scene for the full group. For "Rock Paper Scissors," the scene from which the examples in this paper will be drawn, the initial group was Josh, Ryan, Elena, and Zoey. In the Scieszka and Smith (1998) book, the Rock Paper Scissors scene appears as follows.

> Rock, Paper, and Scissors were assigned to be partners for the big end-of-the-year Science project.
> Rock thought up the idea for the project.
> Paper drew all of the charts and graphs and illustrations.

> Scissors did the research and the presentation.
> It wasn't a very good project, and they didn't work very hard on it, so they got a C.
> "You should have done more research," said Rock, hitting Scissors.
> "You should have drawn more illustrations," said Scissors, cutting Paper.
> "You should have thought of a better idea," said Paper, covering Rock.
> Moral: RockPaperScissors say, "Shoot, it wasn't my fault."
> (Scieszka & Smith, 1998, p. 11)

The group reported beginning their work by discussing who would play what role during this first work session. The group chose to add a teacher to the scene so that all four of them would have a role and so this character could help drive the action by assigning and grading the project. Josh volunteered to be the first teacher; Ryan took on the role of Rock, and Elena and Zoey were cast as Paper and Scissors. After this initial discussion, the group started to improvise their way through the scene. Josh, as the Teacher, opened the scene by telling Rock, Paper, and Scissors to think of topics for their science projects. Ryan, as Rock, adopted a self-promoting attitude and proposed to the group that they do their project on rocks. Elena, as Paper, rejected Ryan's project idea and proposed that the topic be butterflies. Zoey, as Scissors, agreed with Paper's proposal.

Elena's counter-proposal of butterflies was intended to create a conflict in the scene. As Miranda explained in an interview, the actors had learned to introduce conflict into improvisational scenes in order to "make the skit longer and more entertaining." But Elena's response to Ryan's topic proposal created a problem not just for the characters, but also for the actors, because in the book Rock rather than Paper was the one to select the topic. Elena's and Zoey's characters would somehow have to be convinced to go along with Rock's idea. This problem was solved by Josh, who reentered the scene as the Teacher and suggested that the students would get a better grade if they selected rocks as their topic, and the girls agreed reluctantly. This idea was later elaborated on by other actors, such that the Teacher developed a fanatical obsession with Rocks. This theme helped explain why Paper and Scissors were uninterested in doing their project—they got outvoted on the project topic.

In the second rehearsal, Rachel played Scissors, and she reused and heightened the character conflict by scooting herself and Miranda (as Paper) away from Rock when the teacher assigned them to a group and then shouting "let's do butterflies" from this position when the question of the project topic arose. In a second run with the same cast, Rachel and Miranda elaborated the "disgust with Rock" idea by clutching each other, inching further away from Rock, and gesturing to the Teacher to let them be in the same group. Josh, as the Teacher, responded to these actions by scooting Ryan, as Rock, toward the girls, and emphasizing that they would all have to work together. From this point forward in rehearsals and performances, Paper and Scissors's proposal of the butterfly topic became part of an emerging theme about peer conflict and the group's unwillingness to work together—which resulted in their not doing their work until the last minute, which in turn explained their low grade.

This description illustrates the two-layered collaborative emergence process through which all of the narrative elements in the show emerged. Collaborative emergence occurred synchronically, within the present iteration of a scene, but also diachronically, across successive iterations. Brian's idea that Rock would suggest rocks as a topic, and Elena's idea to suggest something else, happened in the first rehearsal of the scene, but the actors who ran the scene the next time continued these ideas, and elaborated on them. It's important to note that although Brian's idea about the topic and Elena's idea about the conflict may seem to arise strictly from these individuals, their ideas would not have made it into the narrative as performed unless the other actors had chosen to repeat them in successive re-improvisations. Further, although Elena's "Let's do butterflies" statement eventually led to the emergence of the character conflict theme, this statement did not take on its full meaning at the time it was uttered. The "Let's do butterflies" declaration only became an important moment in the story after the themes of the characters not liking each other and the teacher pushing the topic of rocks were developed. Once these themes were in place, "Let's do butterflies" became the moment where the group's ultimate fate, receiving a low grade on a hastily-executed project, began to unfold. But at the time Elena uttered it, she could not have predicted that the line would serve this function nor could she have caused it to do so, even if she had wanted to, since the evolution, or even the recurrence, of the idea depended on how the other actors responded to it. Elena was deliberately trying to create conflict, but she could not know how this conflict would play out in the rest of the scene, or how other members of the company would embellish it later. The same is true of Ryan's initial utterance, "Let's do rocks." This became a key statement in establishing the character conflict, but Ryan could not have known this when he first spoke the line.

The ActNow rehearsal process demonstrates why an analytic focus on the group is a much more fruitful approach to understanding collaborative forms of creativity than a focus on individuals. It would not make sense to attribute the creation of the character conflict theme to Ryan, who first made a suggestion about their topic; to Elena, whose line first suggested a disagreement; or to Rachel, who first indicated the characters' dislike for each other, because none of them created this theme in its entirety. The role of each individual contribution is collectively determined through retrospective interpretation and the ongoing process in which actors choose which aspects of a previous improvisation to replay. The creation of the performance narrative is not simply the accumulation of individual contributions; it is the product of their interactions, in the moment and over time. Creativity is distributed across the group; individual creative work cannot be meaningfully isolated, because individuals function within the creative system that the group comprises.

Distributed Creativity in Performance

By the time of performance, each scene in *Squids* was relatively stable and extensively elaborated from that which appeared in the book. The Rock Paper Scissors scene typically went like this:

> The actors enter holding signs stating the scene title, which they read to the audience: "Rock, Paper, Scissors." A cast member steps forward as the Teacher, while three other actors sit nearby as students. These three actors play characters named Rock, Paper, and Scissors, and are wearing baseball caps onto which have been glued the items appropriate to their names: a large rock, a piece of notebook paper, and pair of scissors. The Teacher addresses the audience as his class, and announces that the class must work on their science projects today. He assigns Rock, Paper, and Scissors to work together. Paper and Scissors are very happy to learn they will be working together, but disappointed to learn that they must work with Rock. The Teacher tells them to select their topics, and exits. Rock suggests they do their project on rocks, while Paper and Scissors propose butterflies. The three argue over this until the Teacher reenters and asks for their topic. Rock says, "rocks" at the same time that the other two say, "butterflies." The Teacher clearly favors the topic of rocks, which leads to a discussion on the relative merits of rocks versus butterflies. The Teacher asks the audience which they would choose, and suggests that the group is likely to receive a higher grade for doing rocks. He then tells the entire "class" (the audience) to get to work, and exits. The students now divide up the work: Paper reluctantly agrees to draw the charts and graphs and illustrations, Scissors concedes that she will do the research. Rock tries to get off without any additional work since he "thought up the topic," but at the grimaces of the other two, agrees to contribute by putting the project in a nice folder. The group then sits idly for several moments, Scissors noting that she has books on butterflies but not rocks. The Teacher announces that he is coming to grade the projects, and the group quickly assembles a "project" by tossing anything they can find lying about the stage into the folder, including one of the books on butterflies and Rock's rock hat. The Teacher reacts negatively to the ramshackle project, while the group tries to justify it as being "interactive" and noting that the butterfly book contains a picture of a butterfly on a rock. The Teacher gives the students their grade, a C. The students each in turn blame the others, and the skit is brought to an end as the emcee of the show enters and states the moral of the tale.

As the director of the group, I was aware even before analyzing the data that the group had established many stable narrative elements, including the characters that would be in each scene and the basic plot structure for each scene. But what was not apparent until I did a systematic analysis was that the group was telling the story through a series of "bits"[4]—short, cohesive sequences of dialogue and action. Rather than renegotiating how each plot point would be communicated to the audience with each performance, the group was relying on re-usable bits that had emerged in rehearsals or prior performances. Not every bit appeared in every performance, and bits did not always appear in the same order, but in any given performance, about two-thirds of what was performed consisted of bits that had appeared in previous iterations of the scene.

For example, the following bit, "It's Interactive" occurs in four of the performances of the Rock, Paper, Scissors scene, and includes three basic elements: the students hand the Teacher their poorly constructed project; the Teacher has trouble keeping the project from falling apart in his/her hands (indicating that the project is hopelessly disorganized); the students try to put a positive spin on the disorganized project by calling it "interactive."[5]

Teacher (Josh): (nearly dropping the project) Oh, okay, it's kind of falling. Oh, um, //I'm just gonna leave that there

Rock (J'Rhea): //No, no, no

Teacher: //No?

Scissors (Miranda): //No, see it's interactive.

Teacher: Yes?

Scissors: That's the rock part of it.

Teacher: It's interactive, yeah. Very creative. You have some, //a rock,

Scissors: //It's hands on, you know

Teacher: and you //have the word "rock" *(holds up piece of paper with the word "rock" written on it).*

Paper (Rachel): //Look, look *(places scissors hat on top of folder).*

Rock: Yeah.

Paper: And you can draw, //you can draw the rock on the paper and cut it out.

Teacher: //And it's, it won't even help. Trust me, it's ok.

Within the scene, this bit serves to communicate the idea that the students had turned in a very poor-quality project, a fact which they try to cover up by selling the teacher on the idea that it's "interactive." These are useful plot points to include, because they help build the scene toward its ending "moral," in which the student characters are made fun of for not taking responsibility for their work. Thus, this bit does some important work for the actors, serving as a ready-made solution to the problem of establishing that the students were not concerned about working hard for their grade. Rather than reinvent a way to do this in each performance, all the actors need to do is launch this bit, and the rest takes care of itself. As the actors explained in their interviews, this bit also accomplishes another of their goals: it makes the audience laugh. Once this was discovered in an early performance, the bit was replayed. Using proven comic material is less risky and less demanding than looking for new ways to be funny with each performance (See Libera, 2004).

Although there were a few bits that appeared virtually verbatim each time they were performed, most of the bits were performed somewhat differently in each iteration. For example, the "It's interactive" bit, transcribed above from Performance 2, went like this in Performance 4:

> Teacher (Josh): (having trouble grabbing the project) All right, I'll just kind of, ok.
>
> Rock (Sandra): There you go (lifts folder to teacher).
>
> Teacher: There you go, (drops several items from folder) wow, um, hmmm
>
> Rock: Isn't it beautiful?
>
> Teacher: You have a, oh, there's, there's lots of parts to it, which is always a good thing.
>
> Scissors (Miranda): Yeah, it's interactive, it's—
>
> Teacher:—Interactive, I like how you have the scissors hat, that's creative
>
> Scissors: It's, uh-uh.
>
> Rock: Draw the rock on the paper.

And like this in Performance 5:

> Teacher (Josh): This is your project, this, oh and that down there is your project. This is your project?
>
> Paper (Miranda): Um, // that is the main part of our project.
>
> Teacher: *(to audience)* This is their project.
>
> Paper: See, it's interactive, you can actually hold and feel the texture of the rock and yes.
>
> Scissors (Chelsea): This is the main part.

Teacher: Uh-huh. it's ok, you can, uh, thanks, yeah, so in case I didn't know what rocks looked like, I have one.

Paper: Exactly, exactly. This is an example of a rock, yes.

Teacher: Okay, great.

Though each of these three performances contained the same basic ideas, the dialogue unfolded differently each time, with different characters and different actors contributing the various ideas. In Performance 2, Paper suggested drawing the rock on the paper, while in Performance 4 Rock made this suggestion. In the fifth performance, this idea was not brought up at all. Instead, the Teacher and Paper discussed the inclusion of an actual rock as an example of rocks.

Variation in who contributes which ideas within a bit was extremely common, as was variation in who initiates the bits that recur. Of course, there were a few bits that seemed to be linked to just one actor, for example, Josh included a riff on the Teacher's frustration with his low salary, which no other actor used. Also, some bits were necessarily linked to a particular character, such as the bit in which the grade of "C" is assigned to the project. This bit was always initiated by the teacher and performed mostly as a monologue, since it is the teacher's job to grade the students' work. Indeed, actor-linked and character-linked bits were not particularly surprising to discover. It is to be expected that novice improv actors would develop a "bag of tricks," as it is often called, especially when there is no pressure in this setting to avoid doing so. It is also predictable that bits would be tied to particular characters, since certain lines or actions only make sense when coming from particular people within the story. In contrast to these actor- and character-linked bits, however, many of the recurring bits seemed to "float": they were performed by different characters and different actors each time. The presence of floating bits is noteworthy, because it suggests that responsibility for performing many components of the narrative fell to the group in general, not to any one actor or character. Thus, while there was certainly a division of labor that came from particular actors being assigned certain roles, there was also a degree of collective responsibility allocated to the group as a creative system, rather than to any particular individual within that system.[6]

Because the performance was improvisational, the diachronic process that began during rehearsal continued during the performances, with bits evolving each time they were played, and with new bits continuing to emerge. For example, the "Discuss-the grade" bit, which served to communicate that the student characters were not sufficiently aware of how far their project fell short, evolved across the first four performances. The bit began in Performance 1 as an aside between Miranda and Rachel, as Scissors and Paper, regarding the grade they might be assigned. In Performance 2, Josh as the teacher cued Paper (Rachel) and Scissors (Miranda) to replay the bit by asking what grade they thought they should be given, and by Performance 3, the bit appeared in stablized form, performed nearly identically to Performance 2, although this time by Sandra, J'Rhea, Natalie, and Rachel. Performance 4 repeated the elements of the bit from Performance 3, but with one addition: the teacher addressed the question about the grade to the audience as well. This new audience-involvement component recalled an element of the bit that happened in Performance 2. In that performance, the audience spontaneously began shouting out their opinions about the students' grade. In Performance 4, Josh as the teacher re-incorporated audience participation into the bit.

> Teacher (Josh): What do you think you should get on, on this? *(gestures, indicating the project, which has fallen in pieces to the floor)*
>
> Rock (Sandra): An A.
>
> Scissors (Miranda): An A.
>
> Paper (Rachel): An A. Plus.
>
> Teacher: An A? On this?
>
> Rock: Maybe an A minus, I mean I kind of felt bad.
>
> Scissors: Hey, an A.
>
> Teacher: *(to audience, indicating the mess on the floor)* //Ok, what do you think they should get on this?
>
> Rock: Just think we should be realistic here.
>
> Audience member 1: A plus
>
> Audience member 2: A minus
>
> Teacher: *(nods and gestures to the audience members who spoke)* Ok, we'll just "C" in a second. Oh, uh sorry. I'm gonna write it nice and big. You need an A or a B . . .

In the fifth performance, the grading portion of the Rock Paper Scissors scene emerged differently and the Discuss-the-grade bit did not occur at all. In the prior four performances, after examining the project, the Teacher told the students that s/he was ready to assign a grade. But in Performance 5, when Josh as the Teacher comments that the project has a lot of information on butterflies, Ryan responded by introducing a new idea, one that had not appeared in any of the prior four performances.

Teacher (Josh): So, I'm really glad // that I have all this information on butterflies. Even though your topic was—

Paper (Miranda): Yeah. Um.

Rock (Ryan): Can we change it to butterflies?

Teacher: No. What was your topic, everyone look. (takes "Rock" sign from the scene intro, which Ryan had shoved into the folder, and holds it up to the audience) What does it say, what does it say?

Rock: Butterflies.

Audience: Rocks!

Teacher: Rocks, thank you, thank you very much.

Ryan, as Rock, asked to change the topic to butterflies, and Josh responded by asking the audience to read the "Rock" sign so as to remind the students of their topic. Josh's invitation for audience involvement appeared here at about the same point in the scene as the grade discussion in the first four performances, but this time, in response to Ryan's contribution, he asked the audience to read the "Rock" sign, instead of asking the audience about the grade, as in the Discuss-the-grade bit. This was the final performance of *Squids*, but had there been additional performances, "Can we change our topic?/What does the sign say?" might have evolved into a stable bit, giving the group choices for how to handle this point in the story. There were, in fact, other portions of the narrative for which the group had developed multiple bits from which to choose. For example, the actors sometimes used a physical comedy-based bit about the students hiding their work from the teacher as they attempted to finish it quickly, and other times used a dialogic bit in which Scissors attempted to distract the teacher while Rock and Paper hastily assembled the project. Both bits served to emphasize the last-minute nature of the project and provided a comic moment, and so represented two options the group could employ to accomplish the same goals.

DISCUSSION

Bits and Group Creativity

What is the role of bits in ActNow's larger creative process? On the one hand, bits can be viewed as creative products of the group, each bit comprising a small portion of the elaborated version of the Rock Paper Scissors story that the group generated. But this view of bits is complicated somewhat by the fact that the group never arrived, and never intended to arrive, at a final, fully fixed performance text. The ratio of bits to new material remained constant across performances, which suggests that the presence of bits does not represent progress toward a text that ultimately would completely stabilize. Further, the portions of the narrative that were handled by bits versus new material varied across performances, with some bits disappearing in favor of new material and then reappearing in later performances. As mentioned above, for some portions of the performance, the group had multiple bits that could be used interchangeably.

It may be more robust, then, to view bits not only as creative products (or pieces of the creative product) but also as tools to support the creative process, where that process is a matter of improvisationally generating a text for each performance. As I have discussed, bits do useful work for the group, by communicating necessary narrative information or engendering a desired audience reaction. Bits reduce the density of what has to be negotiated in the moment, and also provide a measure of security, since bits are previously tested and therefore less risky than unproven material. Thus, bits can be seen as examples of "tools-and-results," following Holzman's (1997, 2009; Newman & Holzman, 1997) gloss on this concept drawn from Vygotsky (1997). Holzman distinguishes between a "tool-for-result" in which a tool exists prior to its use and "tool-and-result" in which the development of the tool and the use of the tool are inseparable (1997, 2009; Newman & Holzman, 1997). Vygotsky offers the tool-and-result concept as part of a methodological critique of reductionist psychology, but Holzman points out that the construct is also "an apt and rich characterization of the activity of human development itself" (2009, p. 10). What is attractive about the tool-and-result concept, in attempting to characterize bits, is that it does not require the separation of process and product. Bits are at once tools for performance and the performance itself. When bits are understood as tools-and-results, we can observe that ActNow is simultaneously accomplishing its performance aims and developing its capacity for performance.

Future Directions

The example of ActNow reveals why an important next step in the study of creativity is to examine how groups of people function as distributed creative systems. ActNow creates its performance through collaborative emergence, an interactional process in which individual creators do not solely determine the meaning of their own utterances and actions. A focus on individual creativity would not be useful in this case, because the creative efforts of ActNow are not reducible to the creative work of individuals. Creativity is distributed across the group, and therefore a group-level analysis is necessary.

ActNow offers a useful case study in group creativity because its creative product, a performance narrative, is easily observed. The findings from this study can be used to suggest questions for future research on distributed creativity, including research on more elusive creative efforts. For example, ActNow can suggest some possibilities for understanding creativity in scripted theatrical performance. Although scripted performance does not involve the emergence of textual material as was the case with ActNow, it does involve the emergence of other types of performance content. Actors who perform from scripts emphasize that their performance is in fact improvisational because subtextual and emotional content must be generated anew, collaboratively, with each performance (DeZutter, 2004). Collaborative emergence, then, will necessarily be a part of fully-scripted performances just as it is in ActNow's unscripted ones, because even though the words are fixed, other aspects of the performance phenomenology are not. Like ActNow, casts of scripted productions carry with them an awareness of previous rehearsals and performances. Future research might explore this issue, considering what kinds of tools-and-results a performing group develops through rehearsals and successive performances. Does the group develop subtextual bits? Or are there other kinds of social artifacts that the group develops and employs in order to accomplish its performance? Similar questions to these could also be explored with regard to dance and musical performance.

Of course, the implications of the ActNow study are by no means limited to groups working within the arts. The study documents how collaborative emergence results in a distributed creative process, and such emergence will be present in any group whose interactions are to some degree improvisational. The distributed perspective, therefore, will be a useful lens through which to examine any collaborative group. The findings of the ActNow study, particularly the presence of bits, will be especially relevant to groups who work together over time and whose work is in some way performative, in that creative outcomes must be produced "on the spot." Bits are the result of the dual processes of synchronic and diachronic emergence, as ActNow created improvisationally in the moment, and then responded to its past creations in successive re-improvisations. Researchers who want to understand the creative processes of groups who perform together over time may find it useful to examine both synchronic and diachronic processes, and to consider what kinds of social artifacts emerge through these processes.

Sports teams, for example, face a creative situation that is in many ways analogous to that of ActNow. Sports teams accomplish their goals improvisationally, in a highly performative situation. Like ActNow, the aim is not improvisation in and of itself, but to bring about a particular result—in this case, winning the game. Using strategies and plays that have worked before is not only acceptable but also advisable, yet improvisation is always involved, since each new game presents unpredictable challenges. Like ActNow, sports teams work collaboratively; responsibility is distributed across the team, and while there is division of labor, games are won by teams as a unit, not by individuals. The creativity of a sports team, then, will best be understood in terms of its group-level processes, just as is necessary with ActNow. Researchers interested in facilitating such groups' success may wish to examine those processes, including both diachronic and synchronic emergence. What kinds of social artifacts does the group develop and how does it do so? How do these artifacts enhance the group's capacity for performance?

Sports teams are easily compared to ActNow, but there are many other groups who "perform" in some way—although perhaps not publicly as ActNow and sports teams do—for whom the study has similar implications. Study groups, teams of emergency responders, and legal teams are just a few examples of groups who create together across time and who have a performative element to their work. Research examining synchronic and diachronic emergence and the collaborative development of tools-and-results for performance would yield valuable insights for any such group.

The finding of ActNow's bits points to another issue that merits further research attention. Because bits are simultaneously tools and results, they underscore the inseparability of process and product for performing groups; through the creation of bits, ActNow developed its performance process at the same time as it generated its performance. The collaborative creation of a group's creative process, that is, the way in which a group invents the means by which it creates its products, has not yet been a focus of studies on group creativity. This may be a fruitful direction for those interested in understanding or facilitating group creativity, and it may be useful to investigate this with regard to many different types of creative groups, not just those whose work includes a marked-out performance phase. Such research would also contribute to our broader understanding of creativity as a distributed, group-level phenomenon.

REFERENCES

Amabile, T. (1996). *Creativity in context.* Boulder, CO: Westview Press.

Becker, H. (2000). The etiquette of improvisation. *Mind, Culture, and Activity, 7*(3), 171–176.

Berliner, P. (1994). *Thinking in jazz: The infinite art of improvisation.* Chicago: University of Chicago Press.

Clements, R. D., Dwinell, P. L., Torrance, E. P., & Kidd, J. T. (1994). Evaluation of some of the effects of a teen drama program on creativity. *Journal of Creative Behavior, 18*(3), 272–276.

Crease, R. P. (1997). Responsive order: the phenomenology of dramatic and scientific performance. In R. K. Sawyer, (Ed.), *Creativity in performance* (pp. 213–225). Greenwich, CT: Ablex.

Csikszentmihalyi, M. (1999). *Implications of a systems perspective for the study of creativity*. In R. J. Sternberg, (Ed.), *Handbook of creativity* (pp. 313–328). New York: Cambridge University Press.

DeZutter, S. L. (2004, April). *Toward a model of acting expertise: What we can learn from Inside the Actor's Studio*. Paper presented at the annual meeting of the American Educational Research Association, San Diego, CA.

DeZutter, S. & Boote, D. N. (2003, April). *Transactive memory and collaborative emergence in improvisational theatre: An exploration of social and individual processes in a student performing group*. Paper presented at the annual meeting of the American Educational Research Association, Chicago, IL.

Farrell, M. P. (2003). *Collaborative circles: Friendship dynamics and creative work*. Chicago: University of Chicago Press.

Goldstein, T. R. (2009). Psychological perspectives on acting. *Journal of Aesthetics, Creativity and the Arts, 3*(1), 6–9.

Goldstein, T., & Winner, E. (2009). Living in alternative and inner worlds: Early signs of acting talent. *Creativity Research Journal, 21*(1), 117–124.

Hammond, J. & Edelmann, R. J. (1991a). The act of being: personality characteristics of professional actors, amateur actors and non-actors. In G. D. Wilson, (Ed.), *Psychology and the performing arts* (pp. 123–132). Amsterdam: Swets & Zeitlinger.

Hammond, J. & Edelmann, R. J. (1991b). Double identity: The effect of the acting process on the self-perception of professional actors—two case illustrations. In G. D. Wilson, (Ed.), *Psychology and the performing arts* (pp. 25–44). Amsterdam: Swets & Zeitlinger.

Hannah, M. T., Domino, G. & Hanson, R. (1994). Acting and personality change: The measurement of change in self-perceived personality characteristics during the actor's character development process. *Journal of Research in Personality, 28,* 277–284.

Hodson, R. (2007). *Interaction, improvisation, and interplay in* jazz. New York: Routledge.

Holzman, L. (1997). *Schools for growth: Radical alternatives to current educational models*. Mahwah, NJ: Erlbaum.

Holzman, L. (2009). *Vygotsky at work and play*. New York: Routledge.

Hutchins, E. (1995). *Cognition in the wild*. Cambridge: MIT Press.

Hutchins, E. (2001). Distributed cognition. *International encyclopedia of the social and behavioral sciences*. Amsterdam: Elsevier.

Hutchins, E. & Klausen, T. (1996). Distributed cognition in an airline cockpit. In E. Middleton & Y. Engeström, (Eds.), *Communication and cognition at work* (pp. 15–34). New York: Cambridge University Press

John-Steiner, V. (2000). *Creative collaboration*. New York: Oxford.

Jordan, B., & Henderson, A. (1995). Interaction analysis: Foundations and practice. *Journal of the Learning Sciences, 4*(1), 39–103.

Kogan, N. (2002). Careers in performing art: A psychological perspective. *Creativity Research Journal, 14*(1), 1–16. [Abstract only.]

Libera, A. (2004). *The Second City almanac of improvisation.* Evanston, IL: Northwestern University Press.

Macdonald, R. A. R., & Wilson, G. B. (2006). Constructions of jazz: How jazz musicians present their collaborative musical practice. *Musicae Scientiae, 10*(1), 59–83.

Nemiro, J. (1997). Interpretive artists: A qualitative exploration of the creative process of actors. *Creativity Research Journal, 10*(2&3), 229–239.

Neuringer, C. & Willis, R. A. (1995). The cognitive psychodynamics of acting. Character invasion and director influence. *Empirical Studies of the Arts, 13*(1), 47–53.

Newman, F. & Holzman, L. (1997). *The end of knowing: A new developmental way of learning.* New York: Routledge.

Noice, T. & Noice, H. (1997). *The nature of expertise in professional acting: A cognitive view.* Mahwah, NJ: Erlbaum.

Paulus, P. B., & Nijstad, B. A. (2003). *Group creativity: Innovation through collaboration.* New York: Oxford.

Pressing, J. (1988). Improvisation: Methods and models. In J. A. Sloboda (Ed.), *Generative processes in music: The psychology of performance, improvisation, and composition* (pp. 129–178). New York: Oxford University Press.

Pressing, J. (1998). Psychological constraints on improvisational expertise and skill," in B. Nettl & M. Russell (Eds.), *In the course of performance (pp. 47–67).* Chicago: University of Chicago Press.

Razowsky & Clifford. (n.d.) In *MySpace* [fan page]. Retrieved from http://www.myspace.com/razowskyandclifford.

Rogers, Y. (2006) Distributed cognition and communication. In K. Brown, (Ed.), *The encyclopedia of language and linguistics, 2nd Ed.* (pp. 181–202). Oxford, UK: Elsevier.

Sawyer, R. K. (1992). Improvisational creativity: An analysis of jazz performance, *Creativity Research Journal, 5*(3), 253–263.

Sawyer, R. K. (1997) *Creativity in performance.* Greenwich, CT: Ablex.

Sawyer, R. K. (2003a). *Group creativity: Music, theatre, collaboration.* Mahwah, NJ: Erlbaum.

Sawyer, R. K. (2003b). *Improvised dialogues: Emergence and creativity in conversation.* Westport, CT: Greenwood.

Sawyer, R. K. & DeZutter, S. (2009). Distributed creativity: How collective creations emerge from collaboration. *Journal of Aesthetics, Creativity, and the Arts, 3*(2), 81–92.

Scieszka, J., & Smith, L. (1998). *Squids will be squids: Fresh morals, beastly fables.* New York: Penguin Putnam.

Stacey, C. L. & Goldberg, H. D. (1953). A personality study of professional and student actors. *Journal of Applied Psychology, 37*(1), 24–25.

Thomson, P., Keehn, E. B., & Gumpel, T. P. (2009). Generators and interpretors in a performing arts population: Dissociation, trauma, fantasy proneness, and affective states. *Creativity Research Journal, 21*(1), 72–91.

Vygotsky, L. S. (1978). *Mind in society.* Cambridge, MA: Harvard University Press.

Vygotsky, L. S. (1987). *The collected works of L. S. Vygotsky, Vol. 1, Problems of general psychology.* New York: Springer.

Vygotsky, L. S. (1997). *The collected works of L. S. Vygotsky, Vol. 4, The history of the development of higher mental functions.* New York: Springer.

NOTES

1. ActNow and the names of its members are pseudonyms.

2. When Sawyer discusses diachronic creative interactions, he refers to a much larger timescale than I do here. See Sawyer (2003a).

3. Studies of creativity in dance remain rare, perhaps for some of the same reasons I have outlined here.

4. The word "bits" is a commonly used term in theatre to describe such sequences. The presence of bits in *Squids* was first discussed in DeZutter and Boote, 2003.

5. Data transcriptions use the following conventions: marks interruptions (both of oneself or of another speaker) marks the starting point for overlapping speech*(Italics)* describe physical actions or to whom an utterance is directed.

6. In fact, I suspect that many of the actor- or character-linked bits that appeared in my analysis would have become floating bits if performances had continued. I found several examples of actors appropriating ideas from one another in successive performances (for example, see the Discuss-the-grade bit, described next).

Index